PRACTITIONER'S GUIDE TO USING RESEARCH FOR EVIDENCE-BASED PRACTICE

PRACTITIONER'S GUIDE TO USING RESEARCH FOR EVIDENCE-BASED PRACTICE

Allen Rubin, PhD
University of Texas at Austin

John Wiley & Sons, Inc.

Library of Congress Cataloging-in-Publication Data:

Rubin, Allen.
  Practitioner's guide to using research for evidence-based practice / by
Allen Rubin.
        p. ; cm.
  Includes bibliographical references and index.
  ISBN 978-0-470-13665-2 (cloth : paper)
  1. Psychotherapy—Research—Methodology. 2. Psychotherapy—Evaluation—
Methodology. 3. Evidence-based psychiatry. I. Title.
  [DNLM: 1. Psychotherapy. 2. Evaluation Studies. 3. Outcome and Process
Assessment (Health Care) 4. Research Design. WM 420 R8948p 2008]
  RC337.R73 2008
  616.89′140072—dc22   2007013693

Printed in the United States of America.

10 9 8 7 6 5 4 3 2 1

To human service practitioners whose compassion and professionalism spur them to persevere, despite limited support, to seek and critically appraise research evidence so that they can maximize the chances that their efforts will be effective in helping people in need.

Contents ─────────────────────────

Preface ———————————————————————————————

Helping professionals these days are hearing a great deal about evidence-based practice (EBP) and are experiencing increasing pressure to engage in it. In fact, EBP has become part of the definition of ethical practice.

Accompanying the growth in the popularity of EBP in the human services field is a growing concern about how rarely practitioners engage in the EBP process. Various pragmatic factors have been cited regarding this concern, such as time constraints and lack of agency access to bibliographic databases. Another factor is that practitioners typically do not retain the research knowledge that they learned as students. Many practitioners, therefore, are likely to feel unable to implement the EBP process because they feel incapable of appraising accurately the quality of research studies.

There are various reasons why practitioners may not retain the research knowledge that they learned as a student. One is simply the passage of time. Exacerbating that factor is that in their early careers they are unlikely to experience expectations from superiors that they use the research knowledge they gained in school. Another factor is the way that research courses may have been taught. Typically, the emphasis in teaching research has been more on how to do research in the role of researcher than on appraising and using research in the role of a practitioner who is engaged in EBP. Little wonder, then, that so many students who aspire to be service providers—and not researchers—lack enthusiasm for their research courses and soon forget much of what they learned in them.

Consequently, when service providers attempt to heed the call to engage in EBP by finding and appraising research studies, practitioners are likely to experience difficulty in differentiating between those studies that contain reasonable limitations and those that contain fatal flaws. That is, they are likely to feel unable to judge whether a study's limitations merely imply regarding the study with some caution or disregarding it as too egregiously flawed to be worthy of guiding their practice. Lacking confidence in this judgment, it's easy for practitioners to feel discouraged about engaging in EBP.

This book attempts to alleviate that problem. Rather than discussing research from the standpoint of preparing to do research, it provides a practitioner-oriented guide to appraising and using research as part of the

EBP process. Current and future practitioners can use this book as a user-friendly reference to help them engage in all the steps of the EBP process, including that step in which they must differentiate between acceptable methodological research limitations and fatal flaws and accurately judge the degree of caution warranted in considering whether a study's findings merit guiding practice decisions.

By maintaining a constant focus on explaining in a practitioner-friendly manner how to appraise and use research in the context of the EBP process, this book can help readers feel that they are learning about research concepts relevant to their practice—research concepts that can help them improve their implementation of EBP. In turn, the book attempts to empower and motivate readers to engage in that process.

Although most of the book's contents focus on critically appraising research to answer EBP questions, its final chapter simplifies the process of practitioner use of research methods to evaluate their own practice. That's because the final step in the EBP process requires that practitioners employ research techniques to monitor client progress and evaluate whether their client achieved the desired outcome. However, unlike other texts that emphasize rigor in pursuit of causal inferences in single-case designs, the final chapter of this book is based on the premise that the practitioner is just assessing whether clients appear to be benefiting from an intervention whose probabilistic effectiveness has already been supported in the studies examined by the practitioner in the EBP process of searching for and appraising existing evidence. Thus, the emphasis in the final chapter is on feasibility. In light of the much-researched problem of practitioners eschewing the application of single-case designs in their practice, this book's unique emphasis is intended to increase the extent to which practitioners will use single-case design methods to monitor client progress.

In summary, this book aims to provide human services practitioners what they need to know about various research designs and methods so that when engaging in the EBP process they can:

- Determine which interventions, programs, policies, and assessment tools are supported by the best evidence.
- Find and critically appraise qualitative and quantitative research studies in seeking evidence to answer different kinds of EBP questions.
- Differentiate between acceptable limitations and fatal flaws in judging whether studies at various positions on alternative research hierarchies (depending on the EBP question being asked) merit being used with caution in guiding their practice.
- Assess treatment progress with chosen interventions in a feasible manner as part of the final stage of EBP.

ORGANIZATION

The first part of this book contains three chapters that provide a backdrop for the rest of the book. Chapter 1 shows why it's important for readers to learn about research methods from the standpoint of becoming evidence-based practitioners, briefly reviews the history of EBP, defines EBP, discusses the need to develop an EBP outlook and describes what that outlook means, discusses feasibility constraints practitioners face in trying to engage in the EBP process, and offers suggestions for making the various steps in the process more feasible for them.

Chapter 2 describes the steps of the EBP process—including how to formulate an EBP question and how to search for evidence bearing on that question and to do so feasibly. Overviews are provided of subsequent steps—steps that are discussed in more depth in subsequent chapters. As in other chapters, Chapter 2 ends with a focus on feasibility issues.

One of the most controversial and misunderstood aspects of EBP concerns hierarchies for evaluating sources of evidence. Some think that there is only one hierarchy for appraising research and guiding practice. Some believe that unless a study meets all the criteria of the gold standard of randomized clinical trials (RCTs), then it is not worthy of guiding practice. Others are offended by the notion of an EBP research hierarchy and believe it devalues qualitative inquiry and nonexperimental research, such as multivariate correlational studies using cross-sectional, case-control, or longitudinal designs.

Chapter 3 attempts to alleviate this controversy and misunderstanding by discussing the need to conceptualize *multiple* research hierarchies for different types of EBP questions. It explains how and why certain kinds of designs belong at or near the top of one hierarchy yet at or near the bottom of another hierarchy. Thus, the chapter provides examples of EBP research questions for which qualitative studies deserve to be at the top of a research hierarchy for some questions and near the bottom for others and likewise why RCTs belong near the top or bottom of hierarchies depending on the EBP question being asked.

Part II delves into what practitioners need to know so that they can critically appraise studies pertinent to EBP questions about the effectiveness of interventions, programs, or policies. Chapter 4 sets the stage for the remaining four chapters in this section by discussing criteria for inferring effectiveness, including such concepts as internal and external validity, measurement issues, and statistical chance.

Chapter 5 describes the nature and logic of experiments and how to critically appraise them. It does not address the conducting of experiments. Instead, it emphasizes what features to look for in appraising an experiment that might represent minor or fatal flaws despite random assignment. Those features include measurement biases and attrition biases that can lead to erroneous conclusions that an intervention is effective as well as things like diffusion and resentful demoralization that can lead to erroneous conclusions that an intervention is ineffective.

Chapters 6 and 7 describe the nature and logic of quasi-experiments and how to critically appraise them. These chapters do not delve into how to implement them. Instead, they emphasize what features to look for in appraising a quasi-experiment that might represent minor or fatal flaws or that might be important strengths to help offset the lack of random assignment.

Chapter 6 focuses on critically appraising nonequivalent comparison groups designs. It distinguishes between those designs and pre-experimental pilot studies and discusses how the two sometimes are mistakenly equated. It discusses the potential value of pilot studies to practitioners when more conclusive sources of evidence that apply to their EBP question are not available. It also alerts practitioners to the ways in which authors of pre-experimental studies can mislead readers by discussing their findings as if they offer stronger grounds than is warranted for calling the intervention, program, or policy they studied evidence-based. Practitioner-friendly statistical concepts are discussed at a conceptual level, providing readers what they'll need to know to understand the practical implications of—and not get overwhelmed by—multivariate procedures used to control for possible selectivity biases. Chapter 7 extends the discussion of quasi-experiments by focusing on the critical appraisal of time-series designs and single-case designs.

Chapter 8 discusses how to critically appraise systematic reviews and meta-analyses. It includes content on the advantages of both as well as risks in relying exclusively on them. It also addresses how to find them, key things to look for when critically appraising them, and what distinguishes them from other types of reviews. The meta-analytical statistical concept of effect size is discussed in a practitioner-friendly manner.

Part III turns to the critical appraisal of studies for EBP questions that do not emphasize causality and internal validity. Chapter 9 discusses critically appraising nonexperimental quantitative studies, such as surveys, longitudinal studies, and case-control studies. Chapter 10 then discusses critically appraising qualitative studies. Qualitative studies play an important role in EBP when practitioners seek to gain a deeper understanding of the experiences of people whom they want to help and what those experiences mean to those people. Thus, Chapter 10 includes content on what to look for when critically appraising qualitative observation, qualitative interviewing, qualitative sampling, and grounded theory. Different frameworks for appraising qualitative studies are discussed from the standpoints of empowerment standards, social constructivist standards, and contemporary positivist standards.

The final section of this book, Part IV, contains two chapters that address EBP questions pertaining to assessing clients and monitoring their progress. Chapter 11 discusses how to critically appraise and select assessment instruments. It covers in greater depth and in a practitioner-friendly manner the following concepts that also are addressed (in less depth) in earlier chapters: reliability, validity, sensitivity, and cultural sensitivity. It also shows how to locate assessment instruments and—as with other chapters—emphasizes practitioner and client feasibility.

Chapter 12 turns to feasible ways practitioners can implement aspects of single-case design techniques to monitor client progress as part of the final stage of the EBP process. This chapter is distinguished from the way other sources cover this topic by its emphasis on feasibility. Chapter 12 is based on the premise that when practitioners are providing interventions that already have the best evidence, they don't need to pursue elaborate designs that are likely to intimidate them and be unfeasible for them in light of their everyday practice realities. Instead of feeling that they must implement designs that have a high degree of internal validity in isolating the intervention as the cause of the client's improved outcome, they can just monitor progress to check on whether their particular client is achieving a successful outcome or is perhaps among those people who don't benefit from the intervention. This chapter is distinguished from Chapter 7 in that Chapter 7 focuses on appraising published single-case design studies from the standpoint of finding interventions supported by the best evidence. In keeping with its feasibility emphasis, Chapter 12 proposes the B plus (B+) design. It also illustrates some feasible ways in which practitioners can devise their own measures to monitor client progress.

SPECIAL FEATURES

Chapters 4 through 11 end by presenting two synopses of (mainly fictitious) research studies germane to each chapter's purpose. Readers can critically appraise each of these 16 synopses—writing down strengths, reasonable flaws, and fatal flaws and indicating whether and how each could be used to guide decisions about evidence-based practice. Eight appendixes (A through H) at the end of the book provide my brief appraisals of each synopsis to which readers can compare their appraisals. Each of those eight appendixes corresponds to the two synopses in a particular chapter. Appendix A, for example, presents my appraisals of the synopses at the end of Chapter 4, Appendix B corresponds to Chapter 5, and so on.

In addition to the synopses, each chapter also ends with a list of key chapter concepts, some review exercises, and some additional readings pertinent to the chapter contents. Terms that appear in bold in the text are defined in a glossary at the end of the book.

I hope you find this book useful. Any suggestions you have for improving it will be appreciated and can be sent to me at arubin@mail.utexas.edu.

Acknowledgments ——————————————

Thanks go to the following colleagues who reviewed this book: Kevin Corcoran, PhD, JD, of Portland State University; Jeffrey M. Jenson, PhD, of the University of Denver; Edward J. Mullen, DSW, of Columbia University; Aron Shlonsky, PhD, of the University of Toronto; and Haluk Soydan, PhD, of the University of Southern California. Thanks also go to Danielle Parrish, who, as a doctoral student at the University of Texas at Austin, reviewed chapters, made many extremely helpful suggestions, and provided technical assistance in the preparation of some figures. I also appreciate the support of the following people at Wiley: Lisa Gebo (senior editor), Peggy Alexander (vice president, publisher), and Sweta Gupta (editorial assistant).

PART I

OVERVIEW OF EVIDENCE-BASED PRACTICE

Chapter 1 —————————————————

INTRODUCTION TO EVIDENCE-BASED PRACTICE

You've started reading a book about research so you must have some free time. But aren't there other things you could do right now that are less onerous than reading about research? You could dust your office. You could make that overdue visit to your dentist. Or maybe listen to a Barry Manilow CD. Okay, okay, not Barry Manilow! But read about research? What compelled you to do that?

Actually, that's a rhetorical question because I think I know the answer, and I'm just trying to connect with you. Start where the reader (i.e., the client) is at, as it were—sort of like building a therapeutic alliance. My hunch is that you're reading this book because there is significant pressure these days on practitioners to engage in **evidence-based practice (EBP),** which implies (in part) using research findings to guide their practice decisions. If you are like most of the practitioners I know, you probably resent that pressure. But it's a reality you must deal with, and perhaps by reading this book you'll be better prepared to deal with it on your terms. That is, by learning more about how to utilize and appraise EBP research, you'll be better equipped to understand, question, or negotiate with others—like managed care companies—who cite EBP as the

reason they think they know better than you do what you should do in
your practice.

Although the term *evidence-based practice* has become fashionable
only recently, the main ideas behind it are really quite old. As early as
1917, for example, in her classic text on social casework, Mary Richmond
discussed the use of research-generated facts to guide the provision of direct clinical services as well as social reform efforts.

Also quite old is the skepticism implicit in EBP about the notion that
your practice experience and expertise—that is, your practice wisdom—
are a sufficient foundation for effective practice. That skepticism does
not imply that your practice experience and expertise are irrelevant and
unnecessary—just that they *alone* are not enough.

Perhaps you don't share that skepticism. In fact, it's understandable if
you even resent it. Many decades ago, when I first began learning about
clinical practice, I was taught that to be an effective practitioner I had to
believe in my own effectiveness as well as the effectiveness of the interventions I employed. Chances are that you have learned this, too, either
in your training or through your own practice experience. It stands to reason that clients will react differently depending on whether they are
being served by practitioners who are skeptical about the effectiveness of
the interventions they provide versus practitioners who believe in the effectiveness of the interventions and are enthusiastic about them.

But it's hard to maintain optimism about your effectiveness if influential sources—like research-oriented scholars or managed care companies—express skepticism about the services you provide. I first
encountered such skepticism long ago when my professors discussed a
notorious research study by Eysenck (1952), which concluded that psychotherapy was not effective (at least not in those days). Although I later
encountered various critiques of Eysenck's analysis that supported the
effectiveness of psychotherapy, maintaining optimism was not easy in
the face of various subsequent research reviews that shared Eysenck's
conclusions about different forms of human services (Fischer, 1973;
Mullen & Dumpson, 1972). Those reviews in part helped usher in what
was then called an *age of accountability*—a precursor of the current
EBP era.

The main idea behind this so-called *age* was the need to evaluate the effectiveness of all human services. It was believed that doing so would help
the public learn "what bang it was getting for its buck" and in turn lead to
discontinued funding for ineffective programs and continued funding for
effective ones. Thus, this era was also known as the *program evaluation
movement.* It eventually became apparent, however, that many of the en-
suing evaluations lacked credibility due to fatal flaws in their research designs and methods—flaws that often stemmed from biases connected to
the vested interests of program stakeholders. Nevertheless, many scientif-

ically rigorous evaluations were conducted, and many had encouraging results supporting the effectiveness of certain types of interventions.

In addition to studies supporting the effectiveness of particular intervention modalities, perhaps most encouraging to clinicians were studies that found that one of the most important factors influencing service effectiveness is the quality of the practitioner-client relationship. Some studies even concluded that the quality of practitioners' clinical relationship skills has more influence on treatment outcome than the choices practitioners make about what particular interventions to employ. Although that conclusion continues to be debated, as the twenty-first century dawned, mounting scientific evidence showed that practitioner effectiveness is influenced by both the type of intervention employed and relationship factors (Nathan, 2004).

EMERGENCE OF EVIDENCE-BASED PRACTICE

The accumulation of scientifically rigorous studies showing that some interventions appear to be more effective than others helped spawn the EBP movement. In simple terms, the EBP movement encourages and expects practitioners to make practice decisions—especially about the interventions they provide—in light of the best scientific evidence available. In other words, practitioners might be expected to provide interventions whose effectiveness has been most supported by rigorous research and to eschew interventions that lack such support—even if the latter interventions are the ones with which they have the most experience and skills.

In the preceding paragraph, I used the words *in light of* the best scientific evidence, instead of implying that the decisions had to be dictated by that evidence. That distinction is noteworthy because some mistakenly view EBP in an overly simplistic cookbook fashion that seems to disregard practitioner expertise and practitioner understanding of client values and preferences. For example, EBP is commonly misconstrued to be a cost-cutting tool used by third-party payers that uses a rigid decision-tree approach to making intervention choices irrespective of practitioner judgment. Perhaps you have encountered that view of EBP in your own practice when dealing with managed care companies that have rigid rules about what interventions you must employ as well as the maximum number of sessions that will be reimbursed. If so, you might fervently resent the EBP concept, and who could blame you! Many practitioners share that resentment.

Managed care companies that interpret EBP in such overly simplistic terms can pressure you to do things that your professional expertise leads you to believe are not in your clients' best interests. Moreover, in a seeming disregard for the scientific evidence about the importance of relationship factors, managed care companies can foster self-doubt about your own practice effectiveness when you do not mechanically provide the interventions on their list of what they might call "evidence-based practices." Such doubt can hinder your belief in what you are doing and in turn hinder the more generic relationship factors that can influence client progress as much as the interventions you employ.

DEFINING EVIDENCE-BASED PRACTICE

The foregoing, overly simplistic view of EBP probably emanated from the way it was defined originally in medicine in the 1980s (Barber, in press; Rosenthal, 2006). Fortunately, the revised definition of EBP now prominent in the professional medical literature (Sackett, Straus, Richardson, Rosenberg, & Haynes, 2000) as well as the human service professions literature (Rubin & Babbie, 2008) incorporates practitioner judgment and client values and preferences. The more current and widely accepted definition shows that managed care companies or other influential sources are distorting EBP when they define it as merely a list of what intervention to use automatically for what diagnosis, regardless of your professional expertise and special understanding of idiosyncratic client characteristics and circumstances.

The current definition of EBP incorporates two overarching perspectives:

1. EBP is a *process* that includes locating and appraising credible evidence as a part of practice decisions.
2. EBP is a way to designate certain *interventions* as empirically supported under certain conditions.

Although a comprehensive definition of EBP combines these two perspectives, various influential sources define EBP in terms of only one of the two perspectives. For example, as noted previously, some managed care companies or government agencies define EBP solely in terms of the intervention perspective—that is, they will call your practice *evidence based* only if you are providing a specific intervention that appears on their list of interventions whose effectiveness has been supported by a sufficient number of rigorous experimental outcome evaluations to merit their "seal of approval" as an evidence-based intervention. In addition, a recent survey found a great deal of disparity among faculty members as to whether they define EBP solely in terms of the process perspective, solely in terms of the intervention perspective, or (more correctly) in terms of a combination of the two perspectives (Rubin & Parrish, 2007).

Incorporating practitioner expertise and patient values in the revised definition signifies that EBP is more than a static list of interventions that have a "seal of approval" and thus should be provided by clinicians even when clinician knowledge about client idiosyncrasies suggests that an approved intervention appears to be contraindicated. The revised definition also is more consistent with the scientific method, which holds that all knowledge is provisional and subject to refutation. The older, more mechanistic view of EBP solely in terms of a list of approved interventions conflicts with the view that, in science, knowledge is constantly evolving. Indeed, at any moment a new study might appear that debunks current perceptions that a particular intervention has the best empirical support. Rather than feel compelled to adhere to a list of approved interventions that predates such a new study, practitioners should be free to engage in an EBP *process* that enables them to critically appraise and be guided by *emerging* scientific evidence.

A comprehensive definition of EBP—one that is more consistent with definitions that are prominent in the current human service professions literature—is:

> EBP is a process for making practice decisions in which practitioners integrate the best research evidence available with their practice expertise and with client attributes, values, preferences, and circumstances. When those decisions involve selecting an intervention to provide, practitioners will attempt to maximize the likelihood that their clients will receive the most effective intervention possible in light of the following:
>
> - The most rigorous scientific evidence available;
> - Practitioner expertise;
> - Client attributes, values, preferences, and circumstances;
> - Assessing for each case whether the chosen intervention is achieving the desired outcome; and
> - If the intervention is not achieving the desired outcome, repeating the process of choosing and evaluating alternative interventions.

Figure 1.1 shows the original EBP model, illustrating the integration of current best evidence, practitioner expertise, and client values and expectations. Unlike misconceptions of EBP that characterize it as requiring practitioners to mechanically apply interventions that have the best research evidence, Figure 1.1 shows EBP residing in the shaded area, where practice decisions are made based on the intersection of the best evidence, practitioner expertise, and client values and expectations. In discussing this diagram, Shlonsky and Gibbs (2004) observe:

> None of the three core elements can stand alone; they work in concert by using practitioner skills to develop a client-sensitive case plan that utilizes

Figure 1.1   Original EBP Model

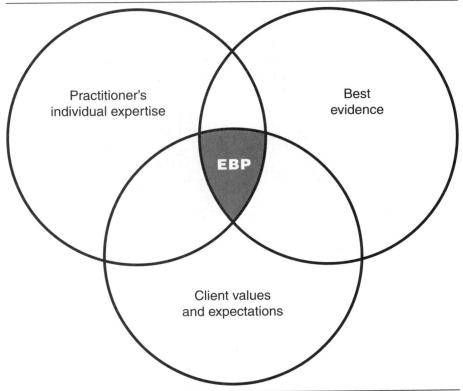

interventions with a history of effectiveness. In the absence of relevant evidence, the other two elements are weighted more heavily, whereas in the presence of overwhelming evidence the best-evidence component might be weighted more heavily. (p. 138)

Figure 1.2 represents a newer, more sophisticated diagram of the EBP model (Haynes, Devereaux, & Guyatt, 2002). In this diagram, practitioner expertise is shown not to exist as a separate entity. Instead, it is based on and combines knowledge of the client's clinical state and circumstances, the client's preferences and actions, and the research evidence applicable to the client. As in the original model, the practitioner skillfully blends all of the elements at the intersection of all the circles, and practice decisions are made in collaboration with the client based on that intersection.

Figure 1.3 illustrates how the diagram in Figure 1.2 is implemented sequentially as a cyclical process with an individual client, not as a one-time application of an "approved" intervention (Mullen, Shlonsky, Bledsoe, &, Bellamy, 2005). The practitioner's knowledge of current best evidence is

Figure 1.2   Newer EBP Model

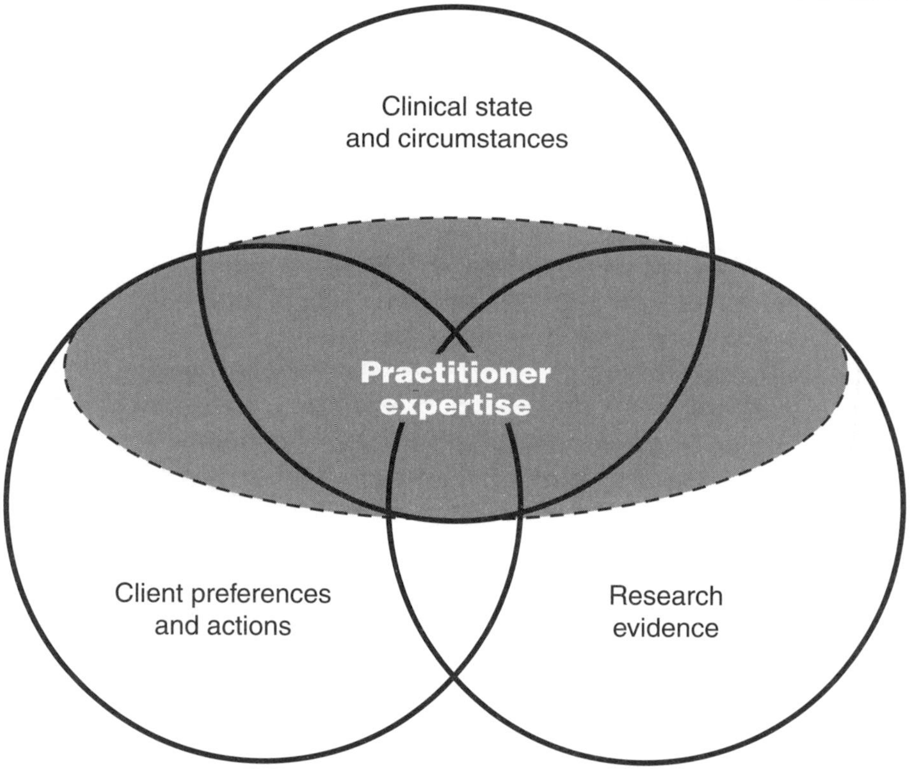

Source: "Physicians' and Patients' Choice in Evidence-Based Practice," by R. Haynes, P. Devereaux, and G. Guyatt, 2002, *British Medical Journal, 324,* p. 1350. Reprinted with permission.

the start of the cycle. Two types of evidence are relevant: (1) evidence about the best (most valid) tools for assessing client problems and needs, and (2) evidence about the most effective services pertaining to those problems and needs. The practitioner then draws on his or her practice expertise in integrating that evidence with information from the other two circles. Moving clockwise, the practitioner decides whether a particular course of action would be appropriate for the particular client, and if not, the cycle begins anew.

The cyclical process of EBP can be conceptualized as involving the following five steps: (1) question formulation, (2) searching for the best evidence to answer the question, (3) critically appraising the evidence, (4) selecting an intervention based on a critical appraisal of the evidence and integrating that appraisal with practitioner expertise and awareness of the client's preferences and clinical state and circumstances, and (5) monitoring client progress. Depending on the outcome observed in the fifth step, the cycle may need to go back to an earlier step to seek an intervention that

Figure 1.3   The Cycle of EBP

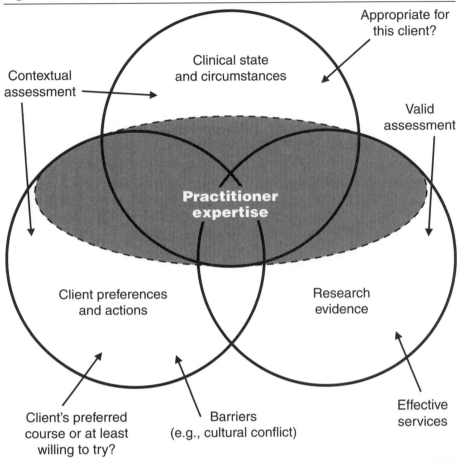

Adapted from "From Concept to Implementation: Challenges Facing Evidence-Based Social Work," by E. J. Mullen and A. Shlonsky, 2004, Setember, Paper presented at Faculty Research and Insights: A Series Featuring CUSSW Faculty Research, New York, NY. Retrieved December 15, 2006, from www.columbia.edu/cu/musher/EBP%20Resources.htm.

might work better for the particular client, perhaps one that has less evidence to support it but which might nevertheless prove to be more effective for the particular client in light of the client's needs, strengths, values, and circumstances. Chapter 2 examines each of these five steps in more detail.

As is implicit in the previous definition and model, EBP decisions are not necessarily limited to questions about the effectiveness of specific interventions. Practitioners might want to seek evidence to answer many other types of practice questions. For example, they might seek evidence about client needs, what measures to use in assessment and diagnosis, when inpatient treatment or discharge is appropriate, understanding cultural influences on clients, determining whether a child should be placed in foster care, and so on.

EVIDENCE-BASED PRACTICE IS NOT RESTRICTED TO CLINICAL DECISIONS

Much of the literature on EBP focuses on the clinical level of practice. However, EBP pertains to decisions made at other levels of practice, as well, such as decisions about community interventions, administrative matters, and policy. Much of the EBP literature focuses on health care policy. An excellent book on that topic, by Muir Gray (2001), is *Evidence-Based Healthcare: How to Make Health Policy and Management Decisions*.

For example, one common area of inquiry regarding evidence-based health care policy pertains to the impact of *managed care*—a term referring to various approaches that try to control the costs of health care. The main idea is for a large organization (such as a health insurance company or a health maintenance organization) to contract with service providers who agree to provide health care at reduced costs. Health care providers are willing to meet the reduced cost demands so that more clients covered under the managed care plan will use their services.

Managed care companies also attempt to reduce costs by agreeing to pay only for the type and amount of services that they consider necessary and effective. Consequently, health care providers may feel pressured to provide briefer and less costly forms of treatment. Trujillo (2004, p. 116), for example, reviewed research on the EBP question: "Do for-profit health plans restrict access to high-cost procedures?" He found no evidence to indicate that patients covered by for-profit managed care plans are less likely to be treated with high-cost procedures than patients covered by nonprofit managed care plans.

Countless hours could be spent trying to list every possible EBP-related question. For now, however, let's focus primarily on EBP decisions about selecting and evaluating interventions in our efforts to maximize treatment effectiveness. Those decisions are most prominent in the EBP literature and in dealing with managed care companies. In later chapters, we examine how to utilize research to answer some of the other types of practice questions.

DEVELOPING AN EVIDENCE-BASED PRACTICE PROCESS OUTLOOK

Becoming an evidence-based practitioner does not begin just by implementing the phases of the EBP process, phases that we examine more thoroughly in Chapter 2. To implement the process successfully, practitioners might have to change the way they have been influenced to think about practice knowledge. For example, relatively inexperienced practitioners typically work in settings where more experienced practitioners and supervisors generally do not value research evidence as a basis for making practice decisions. In their own practice as well as in their influences on newer practitioners, older and more experienced practitioners are likely to resist notions that they should be influenced by such evidence to change the way they intervene (Sanderson, 2002). These practitioners—including many who provide practicum training in professional education—may have been trained and feel proficient in only a small number of treatment approaches—approaches that may not be supported by the best evidence. Not only might they be dogmatically wedded to those approaches, research evidence might have little credibility in influencing them to reconsider what they do. Instead, they might be much more predisposed to value the testimonials of esteemed practitioner colleagues or luminaries renowned for their practice expertise (Bilsker & Goldner, 2004; Chwalisz, 2003; Dulcan, 2005; Sanderson, 2002).

Critical Thinking

Gambrill (1999), for example, contrasts EBP with *authority-based practice*. Rather than rely on testimonials from esteemed practitioner authorities, EBP requires *critical thinking*. Doing so means being vigilant in trying to recognize testimonials and traditions that are based on unfounded beliefs and assumptions—no matter how prestigious the source of such testimonials and no matter how long the traditions have been in vogue in a practice setting. Although it is advisable for practitioners—especially inexperienced ones—to respect the "practice wisdom" of their superiors, if they are critical thinkers engaged in EBP, they will not just blindly accept and blindly conform to what esteemed others tell them about practice and how to intervene—solely on the basis of authority or tradition.

In addition to questioning the logic and evidentiary grounds for what luminaries might promulgate as practice wisdom, critical thinkers engaged in EBP will want to be guided in their practice decisions by the best scientific evidence available. If that evidence supports the wisdom of authorities, then the critical thinkers will be more predisposed to be guided by that wisdom. Otherwise, they will be more skeptical about that wisdom and more likely to be guided by the best evidence. By emphasizing the importance of evidence in guiding practice, practitioners are thus being more scientific and less authority based in their practice.

A couple of critical thinking experiences in my practice career illustrate these points. When I was first trained in family therapy many decades ago, I was instructed to treat all individual mental health problems as symptomatic of dysfunctional family dynamics and to try to help families see the problems as a reflection of sick families, not sick individuals. This instruction came from several esteemed psychiatrists in a prestigious psychiatric training institute and from the readings and films they provided—readings and films depicting the ideas and practice of other notable family therapists. When I asked one prestigious trainer what evidence existed as to the effectiveness of the intervention approaches being espoused, he had none to offer. Instead, he just rubbed his beard and wondered aloud about what personal dynamics might be prompting me to need such certainty.

As a green trainee, his reaction intimidated me, and I said no more. However, shortly after concluding my training, various scientifically rigorous studies emerged showing that taking the approach espoused in my training is actually harmful to people suffering from schizophrenia, as well as to their families. Telling families that schizophrenia is not an individual (and largely biological) illness, but rather a reflection of dysfunctional family dynamics, makes things worse. It makes family members feel culpable for causing their loved one's illness. In addition to the emotional pain induced in family members, this sense of culpability exacerbates the negatively charged emotional intensity expressed in the family. People suffering from schizophrenia have difficulty tolerating this increased negative emotional intensity and are more likely to experience a relapse as a result of it. Thus, the authorities guiding my training were wrong in their generalizations about treating *all* mental health problems as a reflection of sick families.

Much later in my career, after many years of teaching research, I decided to try my hand at practice again by volunteering in my spare time as a therapist at a child guidance center, working with traumatized children. The long-standing tradition at the center was to emphasize nondirective play therapy. Being new to play therapy, I began reading about it and learned that there were directive approaches to it as well. I then asked one of the center's psychologists about her perspective on directive play therapy. She responded as if I had asked for her opinion on the merits of spanking clients. "We never take a directive approach here!" she said with an admonishing tone in her voice and rather snobby facial expression. Once again, I was intimidated. But I kept searching the literature for studies on play therapy and found several studies supporting the superior effectiveness of directive approaches for traumatized children. Although more research in this area is needed, what I found showed me that there was no basis for the psychologist's intimidating reaction to my question. Instead, there was a good scientific basis for the center to question its long-standing tradition, at least in regard to treating traumatized clients.

Evidence-Based Practice as a Client-Centered, Compassionate Means, Not an End unto Itself

My experiences illustrated that being scientific is not an end unto itself in EBP. More importantly, it is a means. That is, proponents of EBP don't urge practitioners to engage in the EBP process just because they want them to be scientific. They want them to be more scientifically oriented and less authority based because they believe that being evidence based is the best way to help clients. In that sense, EBP is seen as both a client-centered and compassionate endeavor.

Imagine, for example, that you have developed some pain from over-doing your exercising. You've stopped exercising for several weeks, but the pain does not subside. So you ask a few of your exercise companions if they know of any health professionals who are good at treating the pain you are experiencing. One friend recommends an acupuncturist who will stick needles in you near various nerve endings. The other recommends a chiropractor who will manipulate your bones and zap you with a laser device. On what grounds will you choose to see either or neither of these professionals? My guess is that before you subject your-self to either treatment you'll inquire as to the scientific evidence about its potential to cure you or perhaps harm you. You'll do so not because you worship science as an end unto itself, but because you want to get better and not be harmed.

Needless to say, you have some self-compassion. What about the com-passion of the two professionals? Suppose you make a preliminary visit to each one to discuss what they do before you decide on a treatment. Suppose you ask them about the research evidence regarding the likelihood that their treatment will help you or harm you. Suppose one pooh-poohs the need for research studies and instead says he is too busy to pay atten-tion to such studies—too busy providing a treatment that he has been trained in and that he believes in. Suppose the other responds in a manner showing that she has taken the time to keep up on all the latest studies. I suspect that because the latter professional took the time and effort to be evidence based you would perceive her to be more compassionate.

But human service interventions, such as alternative forms of psy-chotherapy, don't involve poking people with needles, manipulating their bones, or zapping them with lasers. At least not yet! If you are familiar with such controversial treatments as touch field therapy or rebirthing therapy, you might wonder what's next. You might also have read about a child's death that resulted from rebirthing therapy (Crowder & Lowe, 2000). But human service interventions can be harmful without causing physical dam-age. For example, the studies I alluded to in discussing my family therapy training found that certain intervention approaches for schizophrenia had unintended harmful effects. Instead of increasing the amount of time be-tween relapses of schizophrenia, they decreased it (Anderson, Reiss, & Hogarty, 1986; Simon, McNeil, Franklin, & Cooperman, 1991).

Moreover, providing an ineffective intervention to people who are suffering—even if that intervention does not make matters worse—is harmful if we miss the opportunity to have alleviated their suffering with an available intervention that has been scientifically shown to be more effective.

Evidence-Based Practice and Professional Ethics

Thus, developing an EBP outlook is not just about science; it is about being more client centered, more compassionate, and even more ethical. Why ethical? Because, as you probably already have observed in your profession's code of ethics, ethical practice involves keeping up on the scientific evidence as part of trying to provide your clients with the most effective treatment possible. For example, the "Code of ethics" of the National Association of Social Workers (1999) specifically requires social workers to include evidence-based knowledge in guiding their practice. It further states that practitioners have an ethical obligation to "fully utilize evaluation and research evidence in their professional practice" (5.02).

EASIER SAID THAN DONE

Being scientific and evidence based is a lot easier said than done. In Chapter 2, we examine various feasibility constraints practitioners face in trying to engage in the EBP process. For now, let's just note two problems. One problem is that searching for and finding the best scientific evidence to guide practice decisions can be difficult and time consuming. Another problem is that even when you find the best evidence, it may not easily guide your practice decisions. Perhaps, for example, equally strong studies reach conflicting conclusions. In the vast literature evaluating the effectiveness of exposure therapy versus eye movement desensitization and reprocessing (EMDR) therapy in treating posttraumatic stress disorder (PTSD), for example, there are approximately equal numbers of rigorous clinical outcome experiments favoring the effectiveness of exposure therapy over EMDR and favoring EMDR over exposure therapy (Rubin, 2003).

Some searches will fail to find any rigorous studies that clearly supply strong evidence supporting the effectiveness of a particular intervention approach. Perhaps, instead, you find many seriously flawed studies, each of which supports the effectiveness of a different intervention approach. Some searches might just find what interventions are ineffective. (At least those searches might help guide you in deciding what *not* to do.)

Some searches might find the best scientific evidence supports an intervention approach that doesn't fit some aspect of your practice situation. Although exposure therapy and EMDR both have strong evidence for their effectiveness in treating PTSD, for example, some clients refuse to participate in them because they fear that the treatment process will be too painful in requiring them to recall and discuss the details of the trauma or perhaps visit places in vivo that resemble the site of the trauma. (Clinicians often succeed in helping clients surmount their fears of these therapies, but this is not always the case.)

Likewise, some interventions with the best evidence might never have been evaluated with a population of clients like yours, and your clients might have attributes that in some important ways are not like the attributes of those clients who participated in the evaluations. Suppose, for example, you reside in Alaska and want to start a program to treat Native Alaskan girls who have been victims of physical or sexual abuse and who suffer from PTSD. If you search the literature for effective treatments for PTSD, you are likely to find the best evidence supports the effectiveness of interventions such as exposure therapy, EMDR, or cognitive restructuring. I say the "best" evidence because those interventions are likely to have been supported by the most scientifically rigorous outcome evaluations. However, in a search that I recently completed in preparing for a talk on EBP that I presented in Anchorage, Alaska, I found no rigorous evaluations of the foregoing evaluations in which Native Alaskans participated.

I did, however, find numerous articles discussing the high prevalence of comorbidity with substance abuse among physically or sexually abused Native Alaskan girls. That illustrates another difficulty. Most of the evaluations offering the best evidence regarding the effectiveness of these treatments have excluded participants whose PTSD was comorbid with substance abuse. Thus, you would face a double whammy in trying to develop your treatment program based on the best evaluations. You would have serious doubts as to whether the findings of those studies can be generalized to Native Alaskan girls or girls with comorbidity. Even if the ethnicity issue didn't matter, the comorbidity issue might matter a great deal.

Even if you can't find the best sorts of evidence supporting the effectiveness of an intervention with clients just like yours, you still can operate from an EBP framework. One option would be to look for less rigorous evaluations that have involved clients like yours and which—while not offering the best evidence from a scientific standpoint—are not fatally flawed and thus offer some credible evidence supporting a particular intervention. If that option doesn't pan out, an alternative would be to use your practice judgment in deciding whether an intervention supported by the best evidence with clients unlike yours seems to be worth proposing to your client. If you monitor client progress (or lack thereof) during your client's treatment, you can change course if the intervention is not achieving the desired result. In the next chapter, as we examine the steps in the EBP process, you will continue to see the importance of your practice expertise and idiosyncratic client circumstances and preferences in that process.

KEY CHAPTER CONCEPTS

- Although the term *evidence-based practice* is new, its underlying ideas are quite old.
- One of the most important factors influencing service effectiveness is the quality of the practitioner-client relationship.

- EBP is a process for making practice decisions in which practitioners integrate the best research evidence available with their practice expertise and with client attributes, values, preferences, and circumstances.
- Some misconstrue EBP in an overly simplistic cookbook fashion that seems to disregard practitioner expertise and practitioner understanding of client values and preferences.
- EBP is more than a static list of approved interventions that should be provided by practitioners even when practitioner knowledge about client idiosyncrasies suggests that an approved intervention appears to be contraindicated.
- Unlike authority-based practice that relies on testimonials from esteemed practitioner authorities, EBP requires critical thinking.
- Critical thinking involves the ability to spot unfounded beliefs and assumptions and to inquire about the logic and evidence supporting them.
- Developing an EBP outlook is not just about science; it is about being more client centered, more compassionate, and more ethical.

Review Exercises

1. *Before reading Chapter 1, had you encountered colleagues using the term* evidence-based practice? *If yes, how did they characterize it? Did they portray it in a manner that is consistent with the way it is defined in Chapter 1? If not, what would you tell them to improve their perception of, and perhaps their attitude about, evidence-based practice?*

2. *Try to recall a situation in your education, in-service training, or interactions with colleagues when someone espoused a particular intervention or practice idea based on authority or tradition. How did you react? Why did you react that way? To what extent was your reaction based on critical thinking? In light of what you have read in Chapter 1, how would you react now in a similar situation. Why would you react that way?*

3. *Think of a client you have worked with. Using the shaded area in Figure 1.1, identify elements of each of the three circles that would fit the shaded area with respect to that client, your expertise, and any evidence you are aware of regarding an intervention that fits that client.*

ADDITIONAL READINGS

Brownson, R. C., Baker, E. A., Leet, T. L., & Gillespie, K. N. (2003). *Evidence-based public health.* New York: Oxford University Press.

Drake, R. E., Merrens, M. R., & Lynde, D. W. (Eds.). (2005). *Evidence-based mental health practice: A textbook.* New York: Norton.

Gambrill, E. (2005). *Critical thinking in clinical practice* (2nd ed.). Hoboken, NJ: Wiley.

Gibbs, L. E. (2003). *Evidence-based practice for the helping professions.* Pacific Grove, CA: Brooks/Cole.

Jackson, C. A. (1998). *Evidence-based decision-making for community health programs.* Santa Monica, CA: Rand.

Muir Gray, J. A. (2001). *Evidence-based healthcare: How to make health policy and management decisions* (2nd ed.). New York: Churchill-Livingstone.

Norcross, J. C., Beutler, L. E., & Levant, R. F. (Eds.). (2006). *Evidence-based practices in mental health: Debate and dialogue on the fundamental questions.* Washington, DC: American Psychological Association.

O'Hare, T. (2005). *Evidence-based practices for social workers: An interdisciplinary approach.* Chicago: Lyceum Books.

Roberts, A. R., & Yeager, K. R. (Eds.). (2004). *Evidence-based practice manual: Research and outcome measures in health and human services.* New York: Oxford University Press.

Strauss, S. E., Richardson, W. S., Glasziou, P., & Haynes, R. B. (2005). *Evidence-based medicine: How to practice and teach EBM* (3rd ed.). New York: Elsevier.

Williams, J. B. W., & Ell, K. W. (1998). *Advances in mental health research: Implications for practice.* Washington, DC: NASW Press.

Chapter 2 ———————————

STEPS IN THE EBP PROCESS

As discussed in Chapter 1, various authors have recommended a number of steps in the evidence-based practice (EBP) process. Although not all authors agree on the exact number of steps and how to label them, they generally agree that the number is around five or six. More importantly, there is wide agreement as to what is to be done overall, regardless of the number of steps used to order them. In this chapter, five main steps in the EBP process are discussed in more detail. The chapter ends with a discussion of various daunting feasibility constraints that you are likely to encounter in trying to implement these EBP steps in the real world of practice.

STEP 1: QUESTION FORMULATION

Before you start searching for evidence, you need to know what question you are trying to answer. Your question typically will pertain to a practice decision you must make. In Chapter 3, we discuss some common types of EBP questions that a practitioner might ask. One of the most common questions pertains to ascertaining which interventions, programs, or policies have the best evidence supporting their effectiveness.

Suppose, for example, that you are planning to establish a residential treatment facility for physically or sexually abused girls who have emotional or behavioral problems, and you need to decide what treatment modalities to employ. Your EBP question might inquire as to which treatment modalities have the best evidence supporting their effectiveness with girls who share the projected characteristics of your clients. Alternatively, you might have reason in advance to suspect that one or more particular modalities will be most effective based on what you have read or heard about it from a theoretical standpoint. For example, colleagues involved in a similar program elsewhere might rave about the great success they've experienced using eye movement desensitization and reprocessing (EMDR). Colleagues in another program might claim to have had little success with EMDR and much more success with exposure therapy. Perhaps you've read clinical books on both modalities, and both look equally promising to you from a clinical standpoint. Consequently, instead of asking a broader question about the effectiveness of the gamut of possible treatment modalities, you might narrow your search to the question of whether EMDR or exposure therapy is more effective with the types of clients you plan to treat.

STEP 2: EVIDENCE SEARCH

There are various ways to search for evidence related to your practice question. You could, for example, conduct an exhaustive literature search in a scholarly fashion. Unless you are currently a student, however, your busy practice demands probably don't leave enough time for that. Moreover, you probably lack access to some of the resources that students and academicians have, such as a university library (not to mention significant time to spend there) or a subscription to expensive professional literature databases. Fortunately, if you have access to a more popular search engine such as Google or Yahoo, you might find some of the evidence you need there. For example, if you enter the search term *exposure therapy* or *EMDR*, Google or Yahoo will list a large number of links to web sites on those treatment modalities.

Most of the sites, however, will not enable you to read the original research studies yourself. Instead, they'll present summaries of the research and perhaps offer EBP guidelines. Later in this book, you'll learn what attributes to look for in those reviews to give you a sense of the quality of the review.

You should be cautious and exercise some healthy skepticism when encountering these sites. Some sites might have a vested interest in promoting or debunking the particular treatment modality you are investigating. Table

2.1 lists five of the first nine links that came up when I entered the search term *EMDR* in Yahoo. Notice that the first three entries are web sites for organizations that promote EMDR. The fourth site is an Internet book-seller offering testimonials on the wonders of EMDR to promote a book about it. The fifth site is skeptical about EMDR and seeks to debunk it.

Some Useful Web Sites

You should look for web sites that provide objective reviews. Two highly regarded sources of rigorous, objective reviews can be found at the web sites of the Cochrane Collaboration and the Campbell Collaboration. Both of these sibling collaborations recruit groups of experts to conduct each review. The reviews provided by the Cochrane Collaboration focus on health care interventions and can be accessed at www.cochrane.org. In addition to its reviews, that site provides links to critical appraisals of the reviews, bibliographies of studies, and other

Table 2.1   Web Site Excerpts

EMDR Institute, Inc EMDR, a complex psychological methodology, accelerates the treatment of a wide range of pathologies and self-esteem issues related to upsetting past events and present life conditions. ... American Psychiatric Association Practice Guidelines. • EMDR was given the highest level of ... Traumatic Stress. Washington, DC. • EMDR was placed in the "A" category ...www.emdr.com

Eye Movement Desensitization and Reprocessing (EMDR)1 integrates elements of many effective psychotherapies in structured protocols that are designed to maximize treatment effects. ... and body-centered therapies2. EMDR is an information processing therapy and uses ...www.emdr.com/briefdes.htm

International EMDRIA Association Welcome to EMDRIA's new website! EMDRIA is a professional association where practitioners and researchers seek the highest standards for the clinical use of EMDR ... assuring that therapists are knowledgeable and skilled in the methodology of EMDR ...

Barnes & Noble...... EMDR: The Breakthrough "Eye Movement" Therapy for Overcoming Anxiety, Stress, and Trauma--...... I read this book after having been treated using EMDR. This therapy strategy did wonders for me in ... statements to the effect that EMDR helps provide balance between the two ...

Eye Movement Desensitization and Reprocessing (**EMDR**) over 400 skeptical definitions and essays on occult, paranormal, supernatural and pseudoscientific ideas and practices with references to the best skeptical literature . . . **EMDR** is a therapeutic technique in which the patient moves his or her eyes back and forth, hither . . . literature.°) It is claimed that **EMDR** can "help" with "phobias, generalized anxiety . . .

Note: Search performed using Yahoo on August, 1, 2006.

information, including information to help readers appraise the quality of their review system.

The Campbell Collaboration reviews focus on social welfare, education, and criminal justice. You can access its web site at www .campbellcollaboration.org.

Another other highly regarded source is the American Psychological Association's web site (www.apa.org/divisions/div12/rev_est/) on empirically supported treatments.

Government sites can be another good option. One such site, for example, is the National Center for Post-Traumatic Stress (www.ncptsd.va.gov /publications/cq/v5/n4/keane.html).

Rather than rely exclusively on reviews, which as I have noted can be risky, you can review individual studies yourself. One way to do that is by going to the National Institutes of Health government web site (www. nlm.nih.gov) to get free access to a professional literature database called MedLine, which is provided by the National Library of Medicine.

Another option is provided by Google and is called Google Scholar. You can access it through Google by entering *Google Scholar* as your search term.

Search Terms

Whether you use Medline, Google Scholar, or some other professional literature database, the process for electronically retrieving individual studies is essentially the same. Typically, you begin by entering a search term connected to your practice question. For example, questions about what interventions are most effective in treating physically or sexually abused girls with posttraumatic stress disorder (PTSD)—or about the comparative effectiveness of exposure therapy versus EMDR—might entail entering search terms like *PTSD, exposure therapy, EMDR, sexual abuse, child abuse,* and so on.

Your search term at some sites can be rather long. For example, at Google Scholar I conducted a search using the term: *treatment outcome with sexually abused Native Alaskan girls with PTSD.* (Actually, I didn't need to use the word "with" in the search term, but I have kept it here to make the term more readable to you.) Alternatively, some databases will give you the option of coupling shorter search terms by using the connecting word and to more narrowly target the number of studies that will come up. For example, if you just enter the search term *PTSD,* you'll get an overwhelming list of bibliographic references covering all aspects of PTSD. However, if your search terms include both *PTSD* and *treatment outcome,* the list will be shorter and will be limited to references dealing with treatment outcome in PTSD. If you want to reduce further the number of irrelevant references that you'll need to wade through, you can expand your search term using the word *and* twice. For example, if your search term contains *PTSD and treatment outcome and sexually abused girls*, you'll get a much shorter list.

You can also limit the types of research designs that will come up. For example, you can enter the search term *PTSD and treatment outcome and randomized experiments and sexually abused girls*. If you narrow your search term too much, however, you might not get enough useful references. For example, if your search term is *PTSD and treatment outcome and randomized experiments and sexually abused girls and Native Alaskans*, you'll probably find no references that meet all your specifications. (I tried this and found none, although some tangential references did come up.)

If your search term is so narrow that you get too few (or perhaps no) useful references, you should restart your search with a broader term—one less *and,* perhaps. Another way to broaden your search is by using the connecting word *or.* For example, if you are searching for studies on the treatment of trauma symptoms among children exposed to domestic violence, and your search term is *treatment outcome and children and domestic violence,* you might get more references to children who *witness* domestic violence and not get some useful ones on children who are themselves abused by a perpetrating family member. To broaden your search to pick up more of the latter type of useful references, you could use the search term: *treatment outcome and children and domestic violence or child abuse.*

The box titled "An Internet Search Using Google Scholar and PsycINFO" illustrates how you might have to play around with a variety of search terms to find what you need and feel confident that you haven't missed something relevant and valuable. There is no one simple way to conduct your search, so you might ask, "Is it really worth the time and effort?" Well, what if you were the client in great distress and hoping that the practitioner treating you cared enough to make every effort to provide you with the treatment that had the best chance of success? What would your answer be?

AN INTERNET SEARCH USING GOOGLE SCHOLAR AND PSYCINFO

A while back, in preparing to give a lecture on the EBP process, I decided to conduct an Internet search pertaining to a child I once treated. I conducted this search before gaining more expertise on using Internet bibliographic databases, so my experience might resemble what you encounter when you start using these resources. My EBP question was as follows:

> What interventions have the best empirical support for treating the trauma symptoms of a 6-year-old African American boy who witnessed domestic violence?

I conducted this search in several phases. Not wanting to miss any kinds of studies bearing on my question, I began by using Google Scholar and entered my entire EBP question as the search term. (Actually, Google Scholar provides an advanced search option that would have allowed me to just enter certain words like *interventions* and *trauma* and *domestic violence*. The screen for that option is displayed in Figure 2.1.)

Ten links came up, but only four of them seemed like they might be even remotely relevant to my EBP question. One turned out to be an article on assessment and intervention with parents to stabilize children who have witnessed violence. It did not report a specific evaluation of a particular intervention. Another reviewed in very broad terms mental health treatments for children who are refugees. A third reported a study of the perspectives of battered mothers on the impact of domestic violence on urban preschool children, but did not evaluate an intervention for the children. The fourth was a book chapter that argued that the gender of the perpetrator and the victim are related to aggression during childhood.

So far, not so good! So I tried the search term: *effective interventions with traumatized children* (again using Google Scholar, I really didn't need to include the word *with* in my search term). I found hundreds of abstracts, but only eight addressed treatment effects. Not fully satisfied

Figure 2.1   Screen for Advanced Search Option in Google Scholar

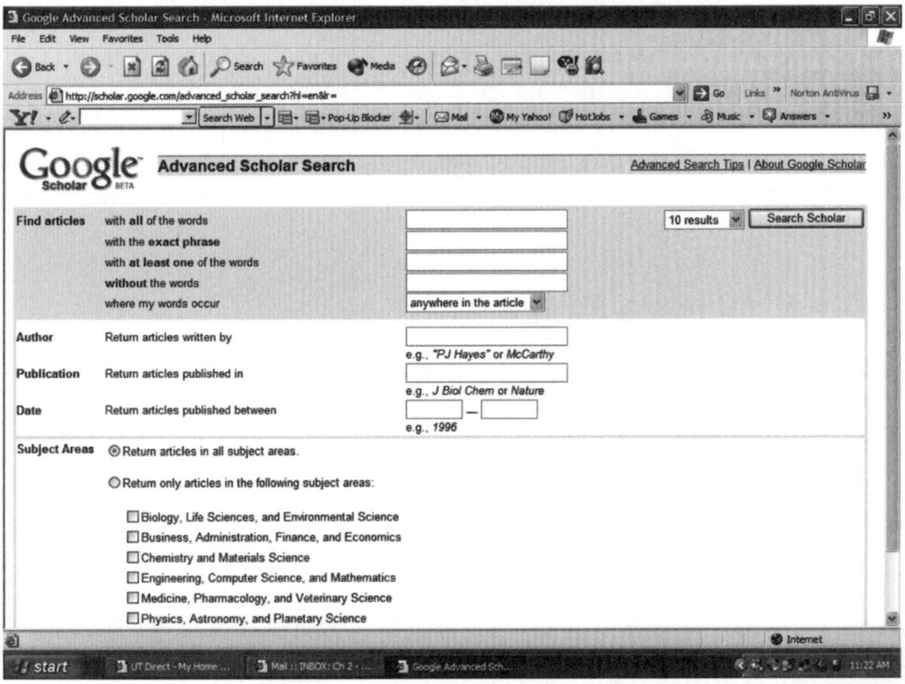

with the results of that search, I tried again with a different search term: *effective interventions with children who witness domestic violence.* Still Using Google Scholar, again I found hundreds of abstracts, most of which did not address treatment effects, and only two that were not already found in the previous search.

Next, I went to the PsycINFO professional literature database to which I have access through the university where I work. Many local libraries are now making PsycINFO and other related databases available at no cost to the public. These databases can be accessed remotely from your office or home free of charge.

PsycINFO provides a drop-down menu in between the search terms that includes and/or/not. It also includes a methodology search filter where you can select the types of studies you're looking for, such as an empirical study, treatment outcome study, and so on. You might want to enter the methodology search filter that best fits your research question first, and then work your way down to other types of research designs depending on what you find or don't find. (Chapter 3 discusses what types of research designs tend to go best with different types of EBP questions.)

Wanting to start with a very broad search before attempting to narrow it down, I used the keywords: *treatment* and *traumatized children.* Alternatively, I could have used filters to narrow things down regarding research designs or my client's characteristics. When you conduct a search, it might be best to try it both ways. Then you can get a sense of what kinds of evidence you'll find using either approach. In my broad search on PsycINFO, however, I found only four references that seemed to be relevant to my EBP question.

Consequently, I returned to Google Scholar to see what would happen if in addition to the main search term, *effective interventions with children who witness domestic violence,* I added the term *experimental design* in the next box. In other words, I searched for links to sources that had all of the words *effective interventions with children who witness domestic violence* anywhere in the reference *and* with the exact phrase *experimental design* anywhere in the reference. This time, 153 references appeared. Thus, by adding the filter term *experimental design,* I came up with a more manageable list of articles. The vast majority of them, however, were still not adequately relevant to my EBP question. For example, the irrelevant ones addressed things like the prevention of violence among adult perpetrators, the treatment of battered women, dating violence among older children, and so on. Moreover, by stipulating that I was only interested in studies employing experimental designs, I was filtering out studies using other designs that might have been more relevant to my EBP question and the particular client characteristics in it.

Finally, I repeated the last step, but this time entering the words *battered women* in the box labeled *without the words.* (See Figure 2.1 for a display of the window for the advanced search option in Google Scholar.) Doing so, however, cut the number of references to only 19, and none of them addressed empirical support for the effectiveness of interventions germane to my client.

So, what lessons can be drawn from my various searches? One is that there is no pat answer—no panacea—for simplifying your Internet database search for studies relevant to your EBP question. Even if you use the *and* conjunction with filter terms, you might have to wade through many irrelevant references to find the ones that are pertinent to your EBP question. Moreover, by narrowing your search that way, you might miss some studies that are pertinent. Instead of expecting to find what you need easily with one set of search terms, you'll probably have to play around with a variety of terms to be sure you aren't missing something relevant and valuable. Also, you'll probably have to wade through many irrelevant references to be sure to find the real gems.

When working with similar clients, you may not need to repeat this process each time. What you find the first time might apply again and again. However, keep in mind that evidence might change over time. Therefore, if several months or more elapse after your search, you might want to repeat it to see if any new studies have emerged supporting different interventions. Moreover, some newer studies might be more applicable to your client's unique characteristics or your unique practice situation.

A Time-Saving Tip

When conducting your own search, you don't have to read every study that you find. You can examine their titles and abstracts to ascertain which ones are worth reading. For example, several years ago, when I conducted a review of the effectiveness of EMDR versus exposure therapy in treating PTSD, I encountered an abstract depicting a study that concluded that EMDR helps "bereaved individuals experience what they believe is actual spiritual contact with the deceased" (Botkin, 2000, p. 181). I could tell from the title of the study that it was not relevant to my review regarding PTSD. (But given its bizarre claim, I read it anyway!)

You can decide which studies to read based on the relevance of the study to your practice question as well as any mention in the abstract of attributes that might tip you off about the quality of the study. For example, if one abstract tells you that the study offers a practitioner's anecdotal account of providing exposure therapy to one client, and another abstract depicts a large, multi-site experiment evaluating the effectiveness of exposure therapy with many clients, you might be more predisposed to read the latter study. Much of this book is devoted to giving you the information and understanding you'll need to appraise the quality of the various studies you'll find. This brings us to the next step in the EBP process, critically appraising studies and reviews.

STEP 3: CRITICALLY APPRAISING STUDIES AND REVIEWS

As I've already intimated, the individual studies and reviews that you'll find in your search might vary greatly in regard to their objectivity and rigor. Some studies and reviews, for example, will be conducted and reported by individuals or groups with vested interests. But reviews and studies can be flawed even when no vested interests are involved. Some objective investigators do the best they can with limited resources to overcome some practical obstacles that keep them from implementing their study in a more ideal manner. A while back, for example, I conducted an experiment evaluating the effectiveness of EMDR in a child guidance center (Rubin et al., 2001). I had no funding for the study and conducted it simply because—as a professor—I am expected to do research and I was quite curious about whether EMDR was really as effective with children as its proponents were touting it to be. The administrative and clinical leaders in the center projected that in a year's time over 100 clients would participate in my study. They were wrong. It took three years for them to refer 39 clients to my study.

Some flaws are egregious and fatal. That is, they destroy the credibility of the study's findings. To illustrate a fatally flawed fictional study, suppose Joe Schmo invents a new therapy for treating anxiety disorders. He calls it psychmotherapy. If it is effective, he will be rich and famous. To evaluate its effectiveness, he uses his own clinical judgment to rate client anxiety levels—on a scale from 0 to 100—before and after he provides psychmotherapy to 10 of his clients. His average before rating is 95, indicating extremely high anxiety. His average after rating is 10, indicating extremely low anxiety. He concludes that psychmotherapy is the most effective intervention available for treating anxiety disorders—a miracle cure so to speak. You probably can easily recognize the egregious bias and utter lack of trustworthiness evident in Joe Schmo's study.

Other flaws are more acceptable. For example, suppose instead of using the foregoing evaluation approach, Joe Schmo proceeds as follows. He collaborates with a colleague who works in his mental health clinic and who specializes in cognitive-behavioral treatment for anxiety disorders. Joe provides psychmotherapy to the first 10 new clients referred to him for treatment of anxiety disorders. His colleague provides cognitive-behavioral treatment to the first 10 new clients referred to him with anxiety disorders. To measure outcome, a graduate student who does not know what the study is about is hired to interview each client briefly before and after treatment and ask him (or her) to rate his average daily anxiety level (from 0 to 100) during the previous 7 days. Regardless of the findings, we can see that this study is more credible than the previous one. It has flaws, but its flaws are neither egregious nor fatal. Maybe, for example, there are some differences in the types of clients referred to the two therapists, making one group more likely to improve than the other. Maybe all the clients in both groups exaggerated the improvements in their anxiety levels because they wanted to believe the treatment helped them or wanted the study's findings to please their therapist.

While these flaws may not be fatal, they are important. If you can find studies less flawed than this one, you'd probably want to put more stock in their findings. But if this study is the best one you can find, you might want to be guided by its findings. That is, it would offer somewhat credible—albeit quite tentative—evidence about the comparative effectiveness of the two treatment approaches. Lacking any better evidence, you might want—for the time being—to employ the seemingly more effective approach until better evidence supporting a different approach emerges or until you see for yourself that it is not helping your particular client(s).

Unlike these fictional examples, it is not always so easy to differentiate between reasonable "limitations and fatal flaws; that is, to judge whether the problems are serious enough to jeopardize the results or should simply be interpreted with a modicum of caution" (Mullen & Streiner, 2004, p. 118). What you learn in the rest of this book, however, will help you make that differentiation and thus help you judge the degree of caution warranted in considering whether the conclusions of an individual study or a review of studies merit guiding your practice decisions.

STEP 4: SELECTING AND IMPLEMENTING THE INTERVENTION

As discussed earlier in this chapter, a common misinterpretation of EBP is that you should automatically select and implement the intervention that is supported by the best research evidence, regardless of your practice expertise, your knowledge of idiosyncratic client circumstances and preferences, and your own practice context. No matter how scientifically rigorous a study might be and no matter how dramatic its findings might be in supporting a particular intervention, there always will be some clients for whom the intervention is ineffective or inapplicable.

Moreover, we often don't know why some clients don't benefit from our most effective interventions. Suppose an innovative dropout prevention program is initiated in one high school, and 100 high-risk students participate in it. Suppose a comparable high school provides routine counseling services to a similar group of 100 high-risk students. Finally, suppose only 20 (20%) of the recipients of the innovative program drop out, as compared to 40 (40%) of the recipients of routine counseling. By cutting the dropout rate in half, the innovative program would be deemed very effective. Yet, it failed to prevent 20 dropouts.

Importance of Practice Context

When an intervention is considered to be more effective (or more evidence based) than alternative interventions, it simply means that it has the best evidence indicating that it has the best *likelihood* of being effective. That is a far cry from implying that it will be effective with every case or even most cases or in all practice situations. Furthermore, we may know of important differences between our clients or practice context and the clients or contexts that comprised the studies supplying the best evidence. Perhaps we are serving clients from ethnic groups that did not participate in the best studies. Perhaps our clients are younger or older than the studied clients. Perhaps we are managing an agency in which our practitioners have less experience and training in the supported intervention than was the case in the best studies. Consequently, they may not be as effective in providing the intervention. Maybe their inexperience, or perhaps their heavier caseloads, will make them completely ineffective providers of that intervention. An autobiographical story from my experience illustrates the importance of practice context in the section titled "The Importance of Practice Context." That section also illustrates the applicability of EBP to administrative policy decisions.

In light of the influence of practice context, deciding which intervention to implement involves a judgment call based in part on the best evidence; in part on your practice expertise; in part on your practice context; and in part on the idiosyncratic characteristics, values, and preferences of your clients. While you should not underestimate the importance of your judgment and expertise in making the decision, neither should you interpret this flexibility as carte blanche to allow your practice predilections to overrule the evidence. The fact that you are well trained in and enjoy providing an intervention that solid research has shown to be ineffective or much less effective than some alternative is not a sufficient rationale to eschew alternative interventions on the basis of your expertise. Likewise, you should not let your practice predilections influence your appraisal regarding which studies offer the best evidence.

You should base that appraisal on what you learn from reading subsequent chapters in this book. Just as you would not want to be treated by a physician who mechanically prescribes treatments for you without first learning about your idiosyncratic health factors (an allergy to the most effective medication, for example), neither would you want to be treated by a physician who

does a thorough diagnosis and takes a thorough health history and then provides a treatment solely based on his or her comfort level and experience in
providing that treatment, ignorant of or dismissing research on its effectiveness solely on the basis of his or her own predilections.

THE IMPORTANCE OF PRACTICE CONTEXT: A POLICY EXAMPLE

Several decades ago, assertive case management came to be seen as a
panacea for helping severely mentally ill patients dumped from state hospitals into communities in the midst of the deinstitutionalization movement. Studies supporting the effectiveness of assertive case management
typically were carried out in states and communities that provided an
adequate community-based service system for these patients. Likewise,
ample funding enabled the case managers to have relatively low caseloads,
sometimes less than 10 (Rubin, 1992). One study assigned only two cases
at a time to their case managers and provided them with discretionary
funds that they could use to purchase resources for their two clients
(Bush, Langford, Rosen, & Gott, 1990). These were high-quality studies,
and their results certainly supported the effectiveness of assertive case
management when provided under the relatively ideal study conditions.

I had recently moved from New York to Texas at the time that those
studies were emerging. My teaching and research in those days focused
on the plight of the deinstitutionalized mentally ill. Included in my focus
was the promise of, as well as issues in, case management. My work
brought me into contact with various case managers and mental health
administrators in Texas. They pointed out some huge discrepancies between the conditions in Texas compared to the conditions under which
case management was found to be effective in other (northern) states.
Compared to other states, and especially to those states where the studies were conducted, public funding in Texas for mental health services
was quite meager. Case managers in Texas were less able to link their
clients to needed community services due to the shortage of such services. Moreover, the Texas case managers lamented their caseloads,
which they reported to be well in excess of 100 at that time. One case
manager claimed to have a caseload of about 250! To these case managers, the studies supporting the effectiveness of assertive case management elsewhere were actually causing harm in Texas. That is, those
studies were being exploited by state politicians and bureaucrats as a way
to justify cutting costlier direct services with the rationale that they are
not needed because of the effectiveness of (supposedly cheaper) case
management services.

How Many Studies Are Needed?

One of the thornier issues in making your intervention decision concerns the number of strong studies needed to determine which intervention has the best evidence. For example, will 10 relatively weak, but not fatally flawed, studies with positive results supporting Intervention A outweigh one very strong study with positive results supporting Intervention B? Will one strong study suggesting that Intervention C has moderate effects outweigh one or two relatively weak studies suggesting that Intervention D has powerful effects? Although we lack an irrefutable answer to these questions, many EBP experts would argue that a study that is very strong from a scientific standpoint, such as one that has only a few trivial flaws, should outweigh a large number of weaker studies containing serious (albeit perhaps not fatal) flaws. If you find that Intervention A is supported by one or two very strong studies and you find no studies that are equally strong from a scientific standpoint in supporting any alternative interventions, then your findings would provide ample grounds for considering Intervention A to have the best evidence.

However, determining that Intervention A has the best evidence is not the end of the story. Future studies might refute the current ones or might show newer interventions to be more effective than Intervention A. Although Intervention A might have the best evidence for the time being, you should remember that EBP is an ongoing process. If you continue to provide Intervention A for the next 10 or more years, your decision to do so should involve occasionally repeating the EBP process and continuing to find it to have the best supportive evidence.

Client Informed Consent

There may be reasons why Intervention A—despite having the best evidence—is not the best choice for your client. As discussed, your client's idiosyncratic characteristics or your practice context might contraindicate Intervention A and thus influence you to select an alternative intervention with the next best evidence base. And even if you conclude that Intervention A is the best choice for your client, you should inform the client about the evidence and involve the client in the decision. I am not suggesting that you overwhelm clients with lengthy, detailed descriptions of the evidence. You might just tell them that based on the research so far, Intervention A appears to have the best chance of helping them. Be sure to inform them of any undesirable side effects or discomfort they might experience with that intervention. With this information, the client might not consent to the treatment, in which case you'll need to consider an alternative intervention with the next best evidence base. A side benefit of engaging the client in making an informed decision is that doing so might improve the client's commitment to the treatment process, which in turn might enhance the prospects for a successful treatment outcome.

STEP 5: MONITOR CLIENT PROGRESS

Before you begin to provide the chosen intervention, you and the client should identify some measurable treatment goals that can be monitored to see if the intervention is really helping the client. This phase is important for several reasons. One reason, as noted previously, is even our most effective interventions don't help everybody. Your client may be one of the folks who doesn't benefit from it. Another reason is that even if your client could benefit from the intervention, perhaps there is something about the way you are providing it—or something about your practice context—that is making it less effective than it was in the research studies. Also, by monitoring client progress, you'll be better equipped to determine whether you need to continue or alter the intervention in light of goal attainment or lack thereof. Monitoring client progress additionally might enable you to share with clients on an ongoing basis charted graphs of their treatment progress. This sharing might further enhance client commitment to treatment. It also provides more chances for clients to inform you of things that they might have experienced at certain points outside of treatment that coincide with blips up or down on the graphs. Learning these things might enhance your ability to help the client. Chapter 12 of this book is devoted to this phase of the EBP process.

FEASIBILITY CONSTRAINTS

In your real world of everyday practice, you may encounter some practical obstacles limiting your ability to implement the EBP process in an ideal fashion. Your caseload demands may leave little time to search for evidence, appraise it, and then obtain the needed skills to provide the intervention you'd like to provide.

If you lack the time and access to bibliographic databases needed to conduct a thorough search for and appraisal of evidence, you might need to cut some corners. Instead of searching for and critically appraising individual studies, for example, you might choose to rely on books, reviews, and practice guidelines developed by EBP experts who have reviewed the literature, identified interventions supported by the best evidence, and described the nature of that evidence. Table 2.2 lists some web sites that can be useful in accessing such materials. As I mentioned earlier, however, authors of some sources might have a vested interest in promoting or debunking a particular treatment modality, and you should be cautious when relying exclusively on those sources. You should rely mainly on resources known for their objectivity; some of which I identified when discussing Step 2 of the EBP process. Chapter 8 of this book discusses what to look for in appraising whether a particular review has sufficient credibility to merit guiding practice.

Table 2.2   Internet Sites for Reviews and Practice Guidelines

Organization	Internet Site
American Psychological Association (empirically supported treatments)	http://www.apa.org/divisions/div12/rev_est/
BMG Clinical Evidence	http://www.clinicalevidence.com/ceweb/conditions/index.jsp
California Evidence-Based Clearinghouse for Child Welfare	http://www.cachildwelfareclearinghouse.org/
Campbell Collaboration	http://www.campbellcollaboration.org/index.html
Cochrane Collaboration	http://www.cochrane.org
Center for Substance Abuse Prevention	http://modelprograms.samhsa.gov/template.cfm?page=default
Crisis Intervention, Comorbidity Assessment, Domestic Violence Intervention, and Suicide Prevention Network	http://www.crisisinterventionnetwork.com
Department of Health and Human Services: Agency for Healthcare Research and Quality Evidence-Based Practice	http://www.ahcpr.gov/clinic/epcix.htm
The Evidence-Based Program Database	http://www.alted-mh.org/ebpd/
Evidence Network (United Kingdom)	http://www.evidencenetwork.org/home.asp
Expert Consensus Guidelines Series	www.psychguides.com
National Center for Posttraumatic Stress Disorder	www.ncptsd.va.gov/publications/cq/v5/n4/keane.html
National Guidelines Clearinghouse (Department of Health and Human Services)	www.guidelines.gov
Office of Juvenile Justice and Delinquency Prevention Model Programs Guide	http://www.dsgonline.com/mpg2.5/mpg_index.htm
Oregon Evidence-Based Practice Center	http://www.ohsu.edu/epc/
Substance Abuse and Mental Health Services Administration National Registry of Evidence-Based Programs and Practices	http://www.nrepp.samhsa.gov/find.asp

Before you can provide the interventions that have the best support-ive evidence, you might have to learn more about them. You can start by obtaining readings on how to implement the intervention. Some in-terventions have treatment manuals that provide very specific step-by-step guidance. After reading about the intervention, you might realize that you need to attend a continuing education workshop or profes-sional conference providing training in it. Perhaps you can arrange to take an elective course on it at a nearby professional school. Once you feel ready to start implementing the intervention, you should try to arrange for consultation or supervision from a colleague who has greater expertise and experience in providing that intervention. You might even be able to join or organize a support group of colleagues who are using the intervention, who meet regularly to discuss their ex-periences with it, and who can give you feedback about how you are implementing it.

The time and costs to learn and provide some interventions, however, might be out of your reach. For some of the most effective interventions, the evidence supporting them is based on evaluations involving clinicians who—as part of the research study and before they delivered the interven-tions to the research participants—received extremely extensive and costly training and repeated practice under supervision and monitoring. Franklin and Hopson (2007) point out that this training process "is too slow, cumber-some, inflexible, and time intensive for many community-based organiza-tions" (p. 8). As an example, they cite Brief Strategic Family Therapy, which "has considerable research support for Hispanic families who need help with an adolescent with a drug abuse problem . . . but costs $4,000 per ther-apist to participate in the training" (p. 10).

If you implement such interventions having received less training than the clinicians in the study received, you might be less effective than they were. Not all desired interventions require such extensive training and supervision. With those that do, however, you have several options. One is to find a practitioner or agency that is well prepared to provide the in-tervention and refer the client there. If that option is not feasible, an al-ternative would be to learn how to provide the intervention yourself as best you can, and then make sure you implement Step 5 of the EBP pro-cess carefully—in which you monitor client progress. Be prepared to alter the treatment plan if the client is not making the desired progress and you do not appear to be as effective as you had hoped to be. At that point, you might switch to an intervention that has been supported by some credible evidence and in which you are more skilled and experi-enced. Of course, a third option would be to have provided the latter in-tervention in the first place, particularly if you are unable to learn enough about the new intervention to reach a comfort level in providing it. Implementing Step 5 will still be important even with interventions with which you are more comfortable. Your comfort level does not guarantee effectiveness.

One more longer range option bears mentioning. You can try to educate policymakers who fund community programs about the long-range cost savings of the most effective interventions that have steeper up-front costs. Franklin and Hopson point out:

> Researchers have shown, however, that adopting some costly evidence-based practices ultimately saves money because they can prevent the even more costly consequences of going without treatment. Multisystemic therapy, for example, may save money for communities by preventing incarceration and residential treatment for adolescents who use drugs (Schoenwald, Ward, Henggeler, Pickrel, & Patel, 1996). Other researchers demonstrate that the benefits of evidence-based practices outweigh the costs in cost-benefit analyses (Chisholm, Sanderson, Ayuso-Mateos, & Saxena, 2004).

Despite the feasibility obstacles that you might encounter in the EBP process, it is hard to justify not doing the best you can to implement it, even if that involves some of the shortcuts discussed earlier. After all, the alternative would be to practice in utter disregard of the evidence, which would not be ethical or compassionate. Thus, I hope this chapter has whet your appetite for EBP and for reading the rest of this book to learn more about how to utilize research in the EBP process.

KEY CHAPTER CONCEPTS

- The first step in the EBP process is to formulate a question about a practice decision. If the question pertains to the selection of an intervention, it can be open-ended or it can inquire as to the comparative effectiveness of one or more interventions that are specified in the question.
- The second step in the EBP process is to search for evidence. This can involve going to web sites that offer reviews as well as searching literature databases.
- When searching literature databases, using connectors such as *and* or *or* in your search terms can limit or broaden the range of resulting references.
- When conducting your own search, you don't have to read every study that you find. You can examine their titles and abstracts to ascertain which ones are worth reading.
- The third step in the EBP process involves critically appraising the evidence. A key aim in this phase is to distinguish studies

(continued)

that have fatal flaws from those whose flaws are less serious and more acceptable.

- A study that is very strong from a scientific standpoint, such as one that has only a few trivial flaws, should outweigh a large number of weaker studies containing serious (albeit perhaps not fatal) flaws.
- The fourth step in the EBP process involves selecting and implementing the intervention. Rather than just automatically selecting and implementing the intervention with the best evidence, you need to consider the importance of the practice context. Also, you should inform the client about the evidence and involve the client in the decision of which intervention to use.
- The fifth step in the EBP process involves monitoring client progress. Even the most effective interventions don't help everybody. Moreover, even if your client could benefit from the intervention, perhaps there is something about the way you are providing it—or something about your practice context—that is making it less effective than it was in the research studies.
- In the real world of everyday practice, you may encounter some practical obstacles limiting your ability to implement the EBP process in an ideal fashion. Common obstacles include a lack of time, training, and access to Internet databases. You should always do the best you can, even if that involves taking some shortcuts. Not doing so, and thus practicing in disregard of the evidence, is not ethical or compassionate.

Review Exercises

1. *Formulate an EBP question to guide an intervention decision in a practice situation with which you are familiar. Using the Internet, search for studies providing evidence to inform that decision. In your search, see how the use of different search terms and different connectors (and versus or) affect the range and types of studies that display. Just by examining titles, and perhaps reading some abstracts from some of the studies that seem most relevant to your question, determine whether some of the studies are reviews of studies. Briefly describe the different kinds of results you get using different search terms.*
2. *After examining some of the studies that you find in your review in Exercise 1, discuss how the practice context, including*

> *idiosyncratic client characteristics, might make one of the studies you find inapplicable to your practice decision even if that study might provide the best evidence from a research standpoint.*
>
> 3. *Go to the following web site:* www.lib.umich.edu/socwork /rescue/ebsw.html. *Explore some of its links to additional sites relevant to EBP. Briefly describe one or two things you find that seem likely to be helpful to you in implementing the EBP process.*

ADDITIONAL READINGS

Corcoran, J. (2003). *Clinical applications of evidence-based family interventions.* New York: Oxford University Press.

Foa, E. B., Keane, T. M., & Friedman, M. J. (2000). *Effective treatments for PTSD.* New York: Guilford Press.

Reddy, L. A., Files-Hall, T. M., & Shaefer, C. E. (Eds.). (2005). *Empirically based play interventions for children.* Washington, DC: American Psychological Association.

Roberts, A. R., & Yeager, K. R. (Eds.). (2004). *Evidence-based practice manual: Research and outcome measures in health and human services.* New York: Oxford University Press.

Chapter 3 ————————————————————

RESEARCH HIERARCHIES

Now that you understand the importance and nature of the evidence-based practice (EBP) process, it's time to examine in more detail at how to critically appraise the quality of the evidence you'll encounter when engaged in that process. We take a look at that in this chapter and in several chapters that follow. As we do that, you should keep in mind that our aim is not to learn how to find the perfect study. No such study exists. Every study has some limitations. Instead, we examine how to distinguish between evidence that, despite its relatively minor limitations, merits guiding our practice versus more seriously flawed evidence that should be viewed more cautiously.

Chapter 2 alluded to differentiating between studies with reasonable limitations versus studies with fatal flaws. If you appraise many studies, however, you'll soon realize that things aren't black and white. That is, the universe of practice-relevant studies contains not only exemplary studies and fatally flawed ones; there are many shades of gray. You'll want to exercise some degree of caution in being guided by any evidence you find, and the various types of evidence you find will reside along a continuum with regard to how much caution is warranted. Moreover, it will not always be easy to conclude that one intervention has the best evidence. You might encounter some ties for the best. Also, as I discussed in Chapter 2, your practice expertise and client attributes and preferences often will influence your course of action—sometimes even swaying you toward a course based on evidence that is less than best.

MORE THAN ONE TYPE OF HIERARCHY FOR MORE THAN ONE TYPE OF EBP QUESTION

If you've read much of the literature about EBP, or have discussed it with many colleagues, you already know that EBP is controversial. Some of the controversy is quite understandable, particularly when it is based on disputes about how realistic the EBP process is for busy practitioners who work in settings that lack resources or support for the process. Other sources of controversy, however, tend to be based on misconceptions about EBP. One of the most prominent misconceptions is that EBP is a mechanical, cookbook approach that leaves no room for practitioner expertise or client differences. Chapter 2 explained why that view is wrong.

Another prominent misconception is that EBP implies an overly restrictive hierarchy of evidence—one that only values evidence produced by tightly controlled quantitative studies employing experimental designs. In those designs, clients are assigned randomly to different treatment conditions. In one treatment condition, some clients receive the intervention being tested and other clients are assigned to a no-treatment or routine treatment control condition. Treatment effectiveness is supported if the intervention group's outcome is significantly better than the no-treatment or routine treatment's outcome.

It is understandable that many critics of EBP perceive it as valuing evidence only if it is produced by experimental studies. That's because tightly controlled experiments actually do reside at the top of one of the research hierarchies implicit in EBP. That is, when our EBP question asks about whether a particular intervention really is effective in causing a particular outcome, the most conclusive way to rule out alternative plausible explanations of outcome is through tightly controlled experiments.

When thinking about research hierarchies in EBP, however, we should distinguish the term *research hierarchy* from the term *evidentiary hierarchy*. Both types of hierarchies imply a pecking order in which certain types of studies are ranked as more valuable or less valuable than others. In an evidentiary hierarchy, the relative value of the various types of studies depends on the rigor and logic of the research design and the consequent validity and conclusiveness of the inferences—or evidence—that it is likely to produce.

In contrast, the pecking order of different types of studies in a research hierarchy may or may not be connected to the validity or conclusiveness of the evidence associated with a particular type of study. When the order does depend on the likely validity or conclusiveness of the evidence, the research hierarchy can also be considered to be an evidentiary hierarchy. However, when the pecking order depends on the relevance or applicability of the type of research to the type of EBP question being asked, the research hierarchy would *not* be considered an evidentiary hierarchy. In other words, different research hierarchies are needed for different types of EBP questions because the degree to which a particular research design attribute is a strength or a weakness varies depending on the EBP question being asked and because some EBP questions render some designs irrelevant or infeasible.

Experiments get a lot of attention in the EBP literature because so much of that literature pertains to questions about the effectiveness of interventions, programs, or policies. However, not all EBP questions imply the need to make causal inferences about effectiveness. Some other types of questions are more descriptive or exploratory in nature and thus imply research hierarchies in which experiments have a lower status because they are less applicable.

For example, suppose you administer a shelter for homeless people and want to find out why so many homeless people refuse to use shelter services. Your hope is that this information will guide your efforts to increase their use of your shelter. Although experiments are geared to providing the most conclusive evidence about what causes people to do (or not to do) things, it is difficult to imagine how researchers could conduct experiments with homeless folks that would answer your question about the reasons why they refuse to use shelters. Even if it were feasible to conduct some type of experiment, the researchers would first need information about the reasons for non-use before they could conceive of the nature of the experiment.

Instead of searching for or reading about experiments, a better way to try to answer your question would be to read about qualitative studies that employ in-depth, open-ended interviews of homeless people that include questions about shelter utilization. Equally valuable might be qualitative studies in which researchers themselves live on the streets among the homeless for a while as a way to observe and experience the plight of being homeless, what it's like to sleep in a shelter, and the meanings shelters have to homeless people. Thus, although the latter types of studies might offer less conclusive evidence about cause and effect, they would reside above experiments on a research hierarchy for your EBP question.

Even when we seek to make causal inferences about interventions, EBP does not imply a black-and-white evidentiary standard in which evidence has no value unless it is based on experiments. Again, there are various shades of gray, and thus various levels on a hierarchy of evidence regarding the effects of interventions, as you will see throughout this book.

QUALITATIVE AND QUANTITATIVE STUDIES

In contrast to quantitative studies like experiments, the homelessness example falls under the rubric of *qualitative inquiry*. Qualitative studies tend to employ flexible designs and subjective methods—often with small samples of research participants—in seeking to generate tentative new insights, deep understandings, and theoretically rich observations. In contrast, quantitative studies put more emphasis on producing precise and objective statistical findings that can be generalized to populations or on designs with logical arrangements that are geared to testing hypotheses about whether predicted causes really produce predicted effects. Some studies combine qualitative and quantitative methods, and thus are called *mixed-method studies.*

Some scholars who favor qualitative inquiry misperceive EBP as devaluing qualitative research. Again, that misperception is understandable in light of the predominant attention given to causal questions about intervention effectiveness in the EBP literature, and the preeminence of experiments as the "gold standard" for sorting out whether an intervention or some other explanation is really the cause of a particular outcome. That misperception is also understandable because when the EBP literature does use the term *evidentiary hierarchy* or *research hierarchy* it is almost always in connection with EBP questions concerned with verifying whether it is really an intervention—and not something else—that is the most plausible cause of a particular outcome. Although the leading texts and articles on the EBP process clearly acknowledge the value of qualitative studies, when they use the term *hierarchy* it seems always to be in connection with causal questions for which experiments provide the best evidence.

A little later in this chapter, we examine why experiments reside so high on the evidentiary hierarchy for answering questions about intervention effectiveness. Right now, however, I'd like to reiterate my proposition that more than one research hierarchy is implicit in the EBP process. For some questions—like the earlier one about homelessness, for example—I'd put qualitative studies at the top of a research hierarchy and experiments at the bottom.

Countless specific kinds of EBP questions would be applicable to a hierarchy where qualitative studies might reside at the top. I'll just mention two more examples: Are patient-care staff members in nursing homes or state hospitals insensitive, neglectful, or abusive—and if so, in what ways? To answer this question, a qualitative inquiry might involve posing as a resident in such a facility.

A second example might be: How do parents of mentally ill children perceive the way they (the parents) are treated by mental health professionals involved with their child? For example, do they feel blamed for causing or exacerbating the illness (and thus feel more guilt)? Open-ended and in-depth qualitative interviews might be the best way to answer this question. (Administering a questionnaire in a quantitative survey with a large sample of such parents might also help.) I cannot imagine devising an experiment for such a question, and therefore again would envision experiments at the bottom of a hierarchy in which qualitative interviewing (or quantitative surveys) would be at or near the top.

TYPES OF EBP QUESTIONS

You might be wondering why the foregoing two questions can be called EBP questions. What distinguishes an EBP question from other sorts of research questions dealing with the human services? An EBP question is formulated by a practitioner and pertains to knowledge needed to guide practice. Other research questions might have implications for guiding practice, but when they are formulated by the researcher, and not by a practitioner, we do not call them EBP questions. For example, suppose a researcher conducts a study to answer the question: What factors best predict the duration of a foster-care placement? Suppose further that the researcher is not a practitioner and conducts the study because it has the promise of guiding child welfare practice decisions. Even though the question has clear EBP implications, I would not call it an EBP question. But if a practitioner asks the same question to guide practice decisions, then it would be an EBP question. For example, the practitioner might be a child welfare administrator or caseworker who wants to minimize the odds of unsuccessful (and therefore short-lived) placements that might subject children to further abuse or that might exacerbate attachment problems.

Much of our focus on EBP questions so far has dealt with practice decisions concerned with choosing interventions supported by the best evidence regarding their effectiveness. But, as in the foster-care placement example, there are other sorts of practice questions. For example, asking, "How insensitive, neglectful, or abusive are patient-care staff members in nursing homes or state hospitals?" can be an EBP question if your practice involves decisions in administering a nursing home or state hospital, working as a patient advocate or case manager, or influencing state policies.

Likewise, asking, "How do parents of mentally ill children perceive the way they (the parents) are treated by mental health professionals involved with their child?" can be an EBP question if your practice involves working with support groups for such parents, supervising clinicians who work with such parents, or planning or administering mental health programs. As a clinician working with such parents, the answers to this question might not tell you which intervention has the best evidence, but they will give you information that might improve your empathy and therapeutic alliance with such parents. Those answers might in turn provide some tentative clinical guidance in selecting from among interventions that have not yet had sufficient testing. For example, they might predispose you to eschew an intervention that implies blaming parents for their child's disorder and to select a psychoeducational intervention that involves supporting and forming a therapeutic alliance with parents. (As you may know, the latter type of intervention currently is supported by solid evidence, but had you been practicing in the days when the evidence about it was less conclusive, the answers to this question might have steered you toward it anyway.)

Four common types of EBP questions that a practitioner might ask are:

1. What intervention, program, or policy has the best effects?
2. What factors best predict desirable or undesirable outcomes?
3. What's it like to have had my client's experiences?
4. What assessment tool should be used?

If research hierarchies were to be developed for each of these types of questions, experimental designs would rank high on the first, but would either be infeasible or of little value for the others. Qualitative studies would rank low on the first, but high on the third. Let's now look at the types of research studies that would rank high and low for each type of question. In doing so, let's save the question about effectiveness for last. We'll examine the other three types of questions in the order that they appear here.

What Factors Best Predict Desirable or Undesirable Outcomes?

Later in this chapter, we'll see that correlational studies rank relatively low on a research hierarchy for questions about effectiveness. We'll see that although they can have value in guiding practice decisions about the selection of an intervention with the best chances of effectiveness, other designs rank higher. Experimental outcome studies, for example, rank much higher. But for questions about circumstances or attributes that best predict prognosis or risk, correlational studies are the most useful. With these studies, multivariate statistical procedures can be employed to identify factors that best predict things we'd like to avoid or see happen.

Suppose you work in a Big Brother/Big Sister agency, for example, and are concerned about the high rate of mentor-youth matches that get terminated prematurely. A helpful study might analyze case record data in a large sample of Big Brother/Big Sister agencies and assess the correlations between duration of mentor-youth match and the following mentor characteristics: age, ethnicity, socioeconomic status, family obligations, residential mobility, reasons for volunteering, benefits expected from volunteering, amount and type of volunteer orientation received, and so on. Knowing which factors have the highest correlations, after statistically controlling for other factors, can guide your decisions about how to improve the duration of matches. For example, suppose you find that when all other factors are controlled, the longest matches are those in which the youth and mentor are of the same ethnicity. The implication would be obvious regarding your practice decisions about where and how to concentrate your volunteer recruitment efforts and how best to match youths and mentors.

Returning to the foster-care example discussed earlier, suppose you are a child welfare administrator or caseworker and want to minimize the odds of unsuccessful foster-care placements. One type of correlational study that you might find to be particularly useful would employ the **case-control design.** A study using this design to identify the factors that best predict whether foster-care placements will be successful or unsuccessful might proceed as follows:

> First, it would define what case record information distinguishes successful from unsuccessful placements.

> Next, it would obtain a large and representative sample of foster-care placements depicted in case records.

> It would then divide those cases into two groups: those in which the foster-care placement was successful and those in which it was unsuccessful.

> All of the placement characteristics would be entered into a multivariate statistical analysis, seeking to identify which characteristics differed the most between the successful and unsuccessful placements (when all other factors are controlled) and thus best predicted success or failure.

If your previous research courses extolled the wonders of experiments, at this point you might exclaim, "Hold on a minute! Why rank correlational studies above experiments here?" It's a good question, and I'll answer it with three others: Can you imagine the staff members of any child welfare agency permitting children to be assigned randomly to different types of foster placements? What would they say about the ethics and pragmatics of such an idea? What might they think of someone for even asking?

Correlational studies are not the only ones that can be useful in identifying factors that predict desirable or undesirable outcomes. Qualitative studies can be useful, too. For example, let's return to the question of why so many homeless people refuse to use shelter services. Studies that employ in-depth, open-ended interviews of homeless people—or in which researchers themselves live on the streets among the homeless and experience what it's like to sleep in a shelter—can provide valuable insights as to what practitioners can do in designing a shelter program that might alleviate the resistance homeless people might have to utilizing the shelter.

What's It Like to Have Had My Client's Experiences?

In Chapter 1, we saw that some studies suggest that one of the most important factors influencing service effectiveness is the quality of the practitioner-client relationship, and that factor might have more influence on treatment outcome than the choices practitioners make about what particular interventions to employ. We also know that one of the most important aspects of a practitioner's relationship skills is empathy. It seems reasonable to suppose that the better the practitioner's understanding of what it's like to have had the client's experiences—what it's like to have walked in the client's shoes so to speak—the more empathy the practitioner is likely to convey in relating to the client.

When we seek to describe and understand people's experiences—particularly when we want to develop a deep empathic understanding of what it's like to walk in their shoes or to learn about their experiences from their point of view—qualitative studies reside at the top of the research hierarchy. Gambrill (2006) illustrates the superiority of qualitative studies for this EBP purpose, via a study by Bourgois, Lettiere, and Quesada (2003). Their research question was: "What kinds of risks (if any) do street addicts take?" (p. 297). Bourgois immersed "himself in the shooting galleries and homeless encampments of a network of heroin addicts living in the bushes of a public park in downtown San Francisco" (p. 260). Virtually all of the addicts reported that when they are surveyed with questionnaires, they distort their risky behavior. Often they underreport it so that it takes less time to complete the questionnaire. Also, they may deceive themselves about the risks they take because they don't want to think about the risks. Consequently, quantitative methods like surveys would rank lower on a hierarchy for this type of EBP question.

What Assessment Tool Should Be Used?

Practitioners often must select an assessment tool in their practice. Many times it is for the purpose of diagnosing clients or assessing their chances of achieving a goal or their level of risk regarding an undesirable outcome. Other purposes might be to survey community residents as to their service needs, to survey agency clients regarding their satisfaction with services, or to monitor client progress during treatment.

Common questions to ask in selecting the best assessment instrument are:

- Is the instrument *reliable?* An instrument is reliable to the extent that it yields consistent information. If you ask an 8-year-old boy if his parent is overly protective of him, he may answer yes one week and no the next—not because his parent changed, but because he has no idea what the term "overly protective" means and therefore is just giving a haphazard answer because he feels he has to give some answer. If you get different answers from the same client to the same question at roughly the same point in time, it probably means there is something wrong with the question. Likewise, if an instrument's total score indicates severe depression on October 7 and mild depression on October 14, chances are the instrument as a whole is unreliable.

- Is the instrument *valid?* An instrument is valid if it really measures what it is intended to measure. If youth who smoke marijuana every day consistently deny doing so on a particular instrument, then the instrument is not a valid measure of marijuana use. (Note that the instrument would be reliable because the answers, though untrue, would be consistent. Reliability is a necessary, but it is not a sufficient condition for validity.)

- Is the instrument *sensitive* to relatively small, but important changes? If you are monitoring client changes every week during a 10-week treatment period, an instrument that asks about the frequency of behaviors during the past 6 months won't be sensitive to the changes you hope to detect. Likewise, if you are treating a girl with extremely low self-esteem, meaningful improvement can occur without her achieving high self-esteem. An instrument that can only distinguish between youth with high, medium, and low self-esteem might not be sufficiently sensitive to detect changes as your client moves from extremely low self-esteem to a better level of low self-esteem.

- Is the instrument *feasible?* If you are monitoring a child's progress from week to week regarding behavioral and emotional problems, a 100-item checklist probably will be too lengthy. Parents and teachers may not want to take the time to complete it every week, and if you are asking the child to complete it during office visits, there go your 45 minutes. If your clients can't read, then a written self-report scale won't work.

- Is the instrument *culturally sensitive?* The issue of an instrument's cultural sensitivity overlaps with the issue of feasibility. If your written self-report scale is in English, but your clients are recent immigrants who don't speak English, the scale will be culturally insensitive and unfeasible for you to use. But cultural insensitivity can be a problem even if your scale is translated into another language. Something might go awry in the translation. Even if the translation is fine, certain phrases may mean different things in different cultures. Ask me if I feel blue, and I'll know you are asking if I'm in a sad mood. Translate that question into Spanish and then ask a non-English-speaking person who just crossed the border from Mexico, "Esta azule?" and you almost certainly will get a very strange look. Cultural sensitivity also overlaps with reliability and validity. If the client doesn't understand your language, you might get a different answer every time you ask the same question. If clients think you are asking whether they are blue (skin color, perhaps), they'll almost certainly say no even if they are in a very sad mood and willing to admit it.

Many studies can be found that assess the reliability and validity of various assessment tools. Some also assess sensitivity. Although there are fewer studies that measure cultural sensitivity, the number is growing in response to the current increased emphasis on cultural competence and diversity in the human services professions. Most of the studies that assess reliability, validity, and cultural sensitivity use correlational designs. For reliability, they might administer a scale twice in a short period to a large sample of people and assess test-retest reliability in terms of whether the two sets of scale scores are highly correlated. Or they might administer the scale once and see if subscale scores on subsets of similar items correlate to each other. For validity, they might administer the scale to two groups of people known to be markedly different regarding the concept being measured and then see if the average scores of the two groups differ significantly. For sensitivity, they might use a pretest-posttest design with no control group and administer the scale before and after treatment to see if the scale can detect small improvements. Although experiments and quasi-experiments are rarely the basis for assessing a scale's validity or sensitivity, it is not unheard of for an experiment or a quasi-experiment to provide new or additional evidence about those features of a scale. That is, if a treatment group's average scores improve significantly more than the control group's, that provides evidence that the scale is measuring what the treatment intends to affect and that the scale is sensitive enough to detect improvements.

We return to these issues and cover them in greater depth in Chapter 11. That entire chapter is devoted to critically appraising and selecting assessment instruments.

What Intervention, Program, or Policy Has the Best Effects?

As I've already noted, tightly controlled **experimental designs** are the gold standard when we are seeking evidence about whether a particular intervention—and not some alternative explanation—is the real cause of a particular outcome. Suppose, for example, we are employing an innovative new therapy for treating survivors of a very recent traumatic event such as a natural disaster or a crime. Our aim would be to alleviate their acute trauma symptoms or to prevent the development of posttraumatic stress dissorder (PTSD).

If all we know is that their symptoms improve after our treatment, we cannot rule out plausible alternative explanations for that improvement. Maybe our treatment had little or nothing to do with it. Instead, perhaps most of the improvement can be attributed to the support they received from relatives or other service providers. Perhaps the mere passage of time helped. We can determine whether we can rule out the plausibility of such alternative explanations by randomly assigning survivors to an experimental group that receives our innovative new therapy versus a control group that receives routine treatment as usual. If our treatment group has a significantly better outcome on average than the control group, we can rule out contemporaneous events or the passage of time as plausible explanations, since both groups had an equal opportunity to have been affected by such extraneous factors.

Suppose we did not randomly assign survivors to the two groups. Suppose instead we treated those survivors who were exhibiting the worst trauma symptoms in the immediate aftermath of the traumatic event and compared their outcomes to the outcomes of the survivors whom we did not treat. Even if the ones we treated had significantly better outcomes, our evidence would be more flawed than with random assignment. That's because the difference in outcome might have had more to do with differences between the two groups to begin with. Maybe our treatment group improved more simply because their immediate reaction to the trauma was so much more extreme that even without treatment their symptoms would have improved more than the less extreme symptoms of the other group.

As another alternative to random assignment, suppose we simply compared the outcomes of the survivors we treated to the outcomes of the ones who declined our services. If the ones we treated had on average better outcomes, that result very plausibly could be due to the fact that the ones who declined our treatment had less motivation or fewer support resources than those who wanted to and were able to utilize our treatment.

In each of the previous two examples, the issue is whether the two groups being compared were really comparable. To the extent that doubt exists as to their comparability, the research design is said to have a *selectivity bias*. Consequently, when evaluations of outcome compare different treatment groups that have not been assigned randomly, they are called **quasi-experiments.** Quasi-experiments have the features of experimental designs, but without the random assignment.

Not all quasi-experimental designs are equally vulnerable to selectivity biases. A design that compares treatment recipients to treatment decliners, for example, would be much more vulnerable to a selectivity bias than a design that provides the new treatment versus the routine treatment depending solely on whether the new treatment therapists have caseload openings at the time of referral of new clients. (The latter type of quasi-experimental design is called an *overflow design.*)

So far we have developed a pecking order of four types of designs for answering EBP questions about effectiveness. Experiments are at the top, followed by quasi-experiments with relatively low vulnerabilities to selectivity biases. Next come quasi-experiments whose selectivity bias vulnerability represents a severe and perhaps fatal flaw. At the bottom are designs that assess client change without using any control or comparison group whatsoever.

But our hierarchy is not yet complete. Various other types of studies are used to assess effectiveness. One alternative is called **single-case designs.** You may have seen similar labels, such as *single-subject designs, single-system experiments,* and so on. All these terms mean the same thing: a design in which a single client or group is assessed repeatedly at regular intervals before and after treatment commences. With enough repeated measurements in each phase, it can be possible to infer which explanation for any improvement in trauma symptoms is more plausible: treatment effects versus contemporaneous events or the passage of time. We examine this logic further later in this book. For now, it is enough to understand that when well executed, these designs can offer some useful, albeit tentative, evidence about whether an intervention really is the cause of a particular outcome. Therefore, these designs merit a sort of medium status on the evidentiary hierarchy for answering EBP questions about effectiveness.

Next on the hierarchy come **correlational studies.** Instead of manipulating logical arrangements to assess intervention effectiveness, correlational studies attempt to rely on statistical associations that can yield preliminary, but not conclusive, evidence about intervention effects. For example, suppose we want to learn what, if any, types of interventions may be effective in preventing risky sexual behavior among high school students. Suppose we know that in some places the students receive sex education programs that emphasize abstinence only, while in other places the emphasis is on safe-sex practices. Suppose we also know that some settings provide faith-based programs, others provide secular programs, and still others provide no sex education. We could conduct a large-scale survey with many students in many different schools and towns, asking them about the type of sex education they have received and about the extent to which they engage in safe and unsafe sex. If we find that students who received the safe-sex approach to sex education are much less likely to engage in unsafe sex than the students who received the abstinence-only approach, that would provide preliminary evidence as to the superior effectiveness of the safe-sex approach.

Correlational studies typically also analyze data on a variety of other experiences and background characteristics and then use multivariate statistical procedures to see if differences in the variable of interest hold up when those other experiences and characteristics are held constant. In the sex education example, we might find that the real explanation for the differences in unsafe-sex practices is the students' socioeconomic status or religion. Perhaps students who come from more affluent families are both more likely to have received the safe-sex approach as well as less likely to engage in unsafe sex. In that case, if we hold socioeconomic status constant, we might find no difference in unsafe-sex practices among students at a particular socioeconomic level regardless of what type of sex education they received.

Suppose we had found that students who received the abstinence-only sex education approach, or a faith-based approach, were much less likely to engage in unsafe sex. Had we held religion constant in our analysis, we might have found that students of a certain religion or those who are more religious are both more likely to have received the abstinence-only or faith-based approach as well as less likely to engage in unsafe sex. By holding religion or religiosity constant, we might have found no difference in unsafe-sex practices among students who did and did not receive the abstinence-only or a faith-based approach.

Although correlational studies are lower on the hierarchy than experiments and quasi-experiments (some might place them on a par with or slightly above or slightly below single-case experiments), they derive value from studying larger samples of people under real-world conditions. Their main drawback is that correlation, alone, does not imply causality. As illustrated in the sex education example, some extraneous variable—other than the intervention variable of interest—might explain away a correlation between type of intervention and a desired outcome. All other methodological things—such as quality of measurement—being equal, studies that control statistically for many extraneous variables that seem particularly likely to provide alternative explanations for correlations between type of intervention and outcome provide better evidence about possible intervention effects than studies that control for few or no such variables.

However, no matter how many extraneous variables are controlled, there is always the chance of missing the one that really mattered. Another limitation of correlational studies is the issue of time order. Suppose we find in a survey that the more contact youths have had with a volunteer mentor from a Big Brother/Big Sister program, the fewer antisocial behaviors they have engaged in. Conceivably, the differences in antisocial behaviors might explain differences in contact with mentors, instead of the other way around. That is, perhaps the less antisocial youths are to begin with, the more likely they are to spend time with a mentor and the more motivated the mentor will be to spend time with them.

Thus, our ability to draw causal inferences about intervention effects depends not just on correlation, but also on time order and on eliminating alternative plausible explanations for differences in outcome. When experiments randomly assign an adequate number of participants to different treatment conditions, we can assume that the groups will be comparable in terms of plausible alternative explanations. Random assignment also lets us assume that the groups are comparable in terms of pretreatment differences in outcome variables. Moreover, most experiments administer pretests to handle possible pretreatment differences. This explains why experiments using random assignment rank higher on the hierarchy for assessing intervention effectiveness than do correlational studies.

At the bottom of the hierarchy are the following types of studies:

- Anecdotal case reports
- Pretest-posttest studies without control groups
- Qualitative descriptions of client experiences during or after treatment
- Surveys of clients asking what they think helped them
- Surveys of practitioners asking what they think is effective

Residing at the bottom of the hierarchy does not mean that these studies have no evidentiary value regarding the effectiveness of interventions. Each of these types of studies can have significant value. Although none of them meet the three criteria for inferring causality (i.e., establishing correlation and time order while eliminating plausible alternative explanations), they each offer some useful preliminary evidence that can guide practice decisions when higher levels of evidence are not available for a particular type of problem or practice context. Moreover, each can generate hypotheses about interventions that can then be tested in studies providing more control for alternative explanations.

Table 3.1 lists the various types of studies and their levels on the evidentiary hierarchy for answering EBP questions about effectiveness and prevention. Notice that I have not yet discussed the types of studies residing in the top two levels of that table. You might also notice that Level 3 contains the single term *randomized experiment*. What distinguishes that level from the top two levels is the issue of *replication*. We can have more confidence about the results of an experiment if its results are replicated in other experiments conducted by other investigators at other sites. Thus, a single randomized experiment is below multi-site replications of randomized experiments on the hierarchy. This hierarchy assumes that each type of study is well designed. If not well designed, then a particular study would merit a lower level on the hierarchy. For example, a randomized

Table 3.1 Evidentiary Hierarchy for Evidence-Based Practice Questions about Effectiveness

Level	Type of Study
1	Systematic reviews and meta-analyses
2	Multi-site replications of randomized experiments
3	Randomized experiment
4	Quasi-experiments
5	Single-case experiments
6	Correlational studies
7	Other:
	–Anecdotal case reports
	–Pretest/posttest studies without control groups
	–Qualitative descriptions of client experiences during or after treatment
	–Surveys of clients about what they think helped them
	–Surveys of practitioners about what they think is effective

Note: Best evidence at Level 1.

experiment with egregiously biased measurement would not deserve to be at Level 3 and perhaps would be so fatally flawed as to merit dropping to the lowest level. The same applies to a quasi-experiment with a severe vulnerability to a selectivity bias.

Typically, however, replications of experiments produce inconsistent results (as do replications of studies using other designs). Moreover, replications of studies that evaluate different interventions relevant to the same EBP question can accumulate and produce a bewildering array of disparate findings as to which intervention approach is the most effective. The studies at the top level of the hierarchy—systematic reviews and meta-analyses—attempt to synthesize and develop conclusions from the diverse studies and their disparate findings. Thyer (2004) describes systematic reviews (SR) as follows:

> In an SR, independent and unbiased researchers carefully search for every published and unpublished report available that deals with a particular answerable question. These reports are then critically analyzed, and—whether positive or negative, whether consistent or inconsistent— all results are assessed, as are factors such as sample size and representativeness, whether the outcome measures were valid, whether the interventions were based on replicable protocols or treatment manuals, what the magnitude of observed effects were, and so forth. (p. 173)

Although systematic reviews typically will include and critically analyze every study they find, not just randomized experiments, they give more weight to randomized experiments than to less controlled studies in developing their conclusions.

A more statistically oriented type of systematic review is called *meta-analysis*. Meta-analyses usually include only randomized experiments. The main focus of meta-analyses is to aggregate the statistical findings of different studies that assess the effectiveness of a particular intervention. A prime aim of meta-analysis is to calculate the average strength of an intervention's effect in light of the effect strength reported in each individual study. Meta-analyses also can assess the statistical significance of the aggregated results. When meta-analyses include studies that vary in terms of methodological rigor, they also can assess whether the aggregated findings differ according to the quality of the methodology.

Some meta-analyses will compare different interventions that address the same problem. For example, a meta-analysis might calculate the average strength of treatment effect across experiments that evaluate the effectiveness of exposure therapy in treating PTSD, then do the same for the effectiveness of eye movement desensitization and reprocessing (EMDR) in treating PTSD, and then compare the two results as a basis for considering which treatment has a stronger impact on PTSD.

You can find some excellent sources for unbiased systematic reviews and meta-analyses in Table 2.2 in Chapter 2. Later in this book, we examine how to critically appraise systematic reviews and meta-analyses. Critically appraising them is important because not all of them are unbiased or of equal quality. It is important to remember that to merit a high level on the evidentiary hierarchy, an experiment, systematic review, or meta-analysis needs to be conducted in an unbiased manner. In that connection, what we said earlier about Table 3.1 is very important, and thus merits repeating here:

> This hierarchy assumes that each type of study is well designed. If not well designed, then a particular study would merit a lower level on the hierarchy. For example, a randomized experiment with egregiously biased measurement would not deserve to be at Level 3 and perhaps would be so fatally flawed as to merit dropping to the lowest level. The same applies to a quasi-experiment with a severe vulnerability to a selectivity bias.

Philosophical Objections to the Foregoing Hierarchy: Fashionable Nonsense

Several decades ago, it started to become fashionable among some academics to raise philosophical objections to the traditional scientific method and the pursuit of logic and objectivity in trying to depict social reality. Among other things, they dismissed the value of using experimental design logic and unbiased, validated measures as ways to assess the effects of interventions.

Although various writings have debunked their arguments as "fashionable nonsense" (Sokal & Bricmont, 1998), some writers continue to espouse those arguments. You might encounter some of their arguments—arguments that depict the foregoing hierarchy as obsolete and perhaps even sexist and ethnocentric. Using such terms as postmodernism and social constructivism to label their philosophy, they argue that social reality is unknowable and that objectivity is impossible and not worth pursuing. They correctly point out something that virtually every social scientist and human service practitioner knows: Each individual has his or her own subjective take on social reality. From that well-known fact, they leap to the conclusion that because we have multiple subjective realities, that's all we have, and that because each of us differs to some degree in our perception of social reality, an objective social reality, therefore, does not exist.

They correctly note that we can never be completely objective and value free, but then again leap to the conclusion that it's not worth even trying to protect our research as best we can from our biases. Some further argue that if a research study aims to produce findings that support noble aims, then it does not matter how biased its design or data collection methods might be. Because it is impossible to be totally objective and value free, they reason, a biased research study that aims to achieve results that might help empower the disempowered is justified by its noble aims. Along these lines, they argue that an emphasis on objectivity and logic in research is just a way for the powers that be to keep down those who are less fortunate.

Critics have depicted their philosophy as relativistic because it espouses the view that because truth is in the eyes of the beholder it is therefore unknowable and that all ways of knowing are therefore equally valid. Critics have portrayed their philosophy in terms of an all-or-nothing, black-and-white thinking problem. In other words, it does not follow that just because perfect objectivity is an unattainable ideal we should therefore not even try to minimize the extent to which our biases influence our findings. Imagine what would happen if we applied that type of thinking to morality. Because none of us is a perfect saint, why even try to be moral? I lied to my friend about being sick instead of attending his boring wine-tasting party. I think I'll rob his house! I heckled Barry Manilow when he started singing "I Write the Songs" a cappella earlier at this charity cocktail party; I think I'll rip out his tongue before he leaves!

Critics also point to an internal contradiction in relativism. If relativists believe it is impossible to assess social reality objectively and that anyone's subjective take on external reality is just as valid as everyone else's, then how can they proclaim their view of social reality to be the correct one? In other words, relativists argue that all views about social reality are equally valid, but that my view that it is knowable is not as good as their view that it is unknowable. Say what?!

Finally, critics point out that in the long run the notion that there is no objective truth actually works against the aim of empowering the disenfranchised. If no take on social reality is better than any other, then on what grounds can advocates of social change criticize the views of the power elite? It follows that, despite its noble aims, relativism ultimately leads to totalitarianism. Sokal and Bricmont (1998) put it this way:

> If all discourses are merely "stories" or "narrations," and none is more objective or truthful than another, then one must concede that the worst sexist or racist prejudices and the most reactionary socioeconomic theories are "equally valid," at least as descriptions or analyses of the real world (assuming that one admits the existence of a real world). Clearly, relativism is an extremely weak foundation on which to build a criticism of the existing social order. (p. 209)

Let's apply this philosophical issue to a couple of important concerns in human services practice. First, let's consider its implications for interventions regarding domestic violence. Although the relativistic argument is enticing when expressed in terms of concern for the disempowered, what does it imply for perpetrators and victims of domestic violence? Shall we not question the alleged perpetrator who denies the abuse or justifies it? Shall we just shrug and conclude that since objective social reality is unknowable, there is no point in attempting to conduct an objective investigation? How much would that empower the alleged victim?

I once attended a presentation at an academic conference by a leading proponent of relativism in practice research. Based on her relativistic philosophy, the proponent depicted as obsolete the use of experiments and objective measurements to evaluate the effectiveness of human service interventions. In the Q&A time that followed, I asked her what she would recommend as an alternative way to evaluate intervention effectiveness. Her answer was simply to ask practitioners what they think and that that would be sufficient. So much for concerns such as the practitioner's biases and possible selective perceptions, possible biases in what clients say or do when being asked or observed, controlling for the possible impact of extraneous events or the mere passage of time on client improvement, and so on.

Those who believe in a relativistic philosophy don't buy any of what you have read or are yet to read in this book. And if you encounter some of their writings, I hope you will not be intimidated if they use obscure terminology and a perplexing way of expressing their argument. Just because an argument is incomprehensible doesn't make it profound or mean that you aren't worthy of understanding a clearer expression of it. On the other hand, if you are a firm believer in relativism, you might want to stop reading this book because its take on reality is different from yours. No, on second thought, keep reading. Its take is as good as yours.

KEY CHAPTER CONCEPTS

- A prominent misconception is that EBP implies an overly restrictive hierarchy of evidence—one that only values evidence produced by tightly controlled quantitative studies employing experimental designs.
- EBP does not imply a black-and-white evidentiary standard in which evidence has no value unless it is based on experiments.
- An EBP question is formulated by a practitioner and pertains to knowledge needed to guide practice.
- Not all EBP questions imply the need to make causal inferences about intervention effects.
- Four common types of EBP questions that a practitioner might ask are: What intervention, program, or policy has the best effects? What factors best predict desirable or undesirable outcomes? What's it like to have had my client's experiences? What assessment tool should be used?
- Different research hierarchies are needed for different types of EBP questions.
- Qualitative studies tend to employ flexible designs and subjective methods—often with small samples of research participants—in seeking to generate tentative new insights, deep understandings, and theoretically rich observations.
- Quantitative studies put more emphasis on producing precise and objective statistical findings that can be generalized to populations or on designs with logical arrangements that are geared to testing hypotheses about whether predicted causes really produce predicted effects.
- Although some scholars who favor qualitative inquiry misperceive EBP as devaluing qualitative research, countless specific kinds of EBP questions would be applicable to a hierarchy where qualitative studies might reside at the top.
- Correlational and qualitative studies can be useful in identifying factors that predict desirable or undesirable outcomes.
- Qualitative studies would reside at the top of a research hierarchy for EBP questions that ask: "What's it like to have had my client's experiences?"
- Various kinds of studies can be used to answer the question: "What assessment tool should be used?"
- When seeking evidence about whether a particular intervention—and not some alternative explanation—is the real cause of

a particular outcome, experiments are at the top of the hierarchy of research designs, followed by quasi-experiments with relatively low vulnerabilities to selectivity biases.

- Because of the importance of replication, systematic reviews and meta-analyses—which attempt to synthesize and develop conclusions from the diverse studies and their disparate findings—reside above experiments on the evidentiary hierarchy for EBP questions about effectiveness.
- Some postmodern philosophies dismiss the value of using experimental design logic and unbiased, validated measures as ways to assess the effects of interventions. They argue that social reality is unknowable and that objectivity is impossible and not worth pursuing. Critics have portrayed such philosophies as an example of an all-or-nothing thinking problem that is logically incoherent.

Review Exercises

1. *Suppose Intervention A appears to be the most effective way to engage Cuban American parents in the family component of a substance abuse treatment program for adolescents in Miami. You administer a similar program for first-generation Mexican American teens in Laredo, Texas, and wonder whether Intervention A might be the most effective way to engage their parents in your family component. Formulate four EBP questions pertaining to your concern, each of which implies a different type of research hierarchy.*

2. *A husband and wife come to you for marital therapy. The wife complains that the husband is abusive to her and their children. The husband disagrees. He argues that his behavior is just a normal and acceptable reaction to his wife's provocations. The wife adamantly denies that she provokes his behavior and insists that it is abusive. Thus, each has a different view of social reality. As their therapist, you have your own view of their social reality. Explain why each of you can have your own separate takes on social reality without that necessarily implying that there is no such thing as an objective social reality that is worth attempting to assess in an objective fashion. Explain why rejecting the view of an objective social reality in this example would be illogical and potentially harmful.*

ADDITIONAL READINGS

Norcross, J. C., Beutler, L. E., & Levant, R. F. (Eds.). (2006). *Evidence-based practices in mental health: Debate and dialogue on the fundamental questions.* Washington, DC: American Psychological Association.

Sokal, A., & Bricmont, J. (1998). *Fashionable nonsense: Postmodern intellectuals abuse of science.* New York: Picador USA.

PART II

CRITICALLY APPRAISING STUDIES FOR EBP QUESTIONS ABOUT INTERVENTION EFFECTIVENESS

Chapter 4 ————————————————

CRITERIA FOR
INFERRING EFFECTIVENESS

When critically appraising a study that purports to test the effectiveness of an intervention, program, or policy, the following four questions are key:

1. **Internal validity:** From a logical standpoint, was the intervention, program, or policy the most plausible cause of the observed outcome, or is some alternative explanation also quite plausible?

2. **Measurement validity** and **bias:** Was outcome measured in a valid and unbiased manner?

3. **Statistical conclusion validity:** What is the probability that the apparent effectiveness, or lack thereof, can be attributed to statistical chance?

4. **External validity:** Do the study participants, intervention procedures, and results seem applicable to your practice context?

This chapter is organized according to these four questions and types of validity.

INTERNAL VALIDITY

A study of the effectiveness of an intervention (or a program or policy) has **internal validity** to the extent that its design arrangements enable us to ascertain logically whether the observed outcome really reflects the effectiveness (or lack thereof) of our intervention versus some alternative explanation. As mentioned in Chapter 3, three criteria are required to conclude logically that an intervention is really the cause of a particular outcome. Those three criteria are:

1. **Time order:** The provision of the intervention must precede or coincide with the change in the outcome being measured.
2. **Correlation:** Changes in the outcome measure must be associated with changes in the intervention condition.
3. **Plausible alternative explanations** for the correlation must be ruled out.

To illustrate the meaning of internal validity and these three criteria, let's suppose we are evaluating the effectiveness of eye movement desensitization and reprocessing (EMDR) in alleviating trauma symptoms among survivors of hurricane Katrina, which devastated New Orleans and the nearby Gulf Coast of the United States in 2005. Suppose a year following that horrific disaster we interview a large sample of survivors, ask them if they had received EMDR after surviving Katrina, and then also ask them some questions that will enable us to rate the current severity of their trauma symptoms. Suppose the EMDR recipients evince fewer and less severe symptoms than the nonrecipients. That information would establish correlation, but would fail to address the other two criteria for inferring causality. Regarding time order, for example, perhaps the EMDR recipients had fewer trauma symptoms in the aftermath of Katrina to begin with. Maybe that explains why they were able to utilize EMDR. It is not uncommon in human services practice for the more poorly functioning people to be less motivated or less able to access, engage in, and complete treatment programs than their less poorly functioning counterparts.

Threats to Internal Validity

Suppose that, instead of waiting a year to commence our study, we tested recipients of EMDR before and after they received it. Suppose we found that their symptoms improved after receiving EMDR. That would handle time order, but would fail to address any of the various plausible alternative explanations for that finding. Those alternative explanations are called **threats to internal validity.** Three such threats pertinent to our fictional EMDR/Katrina scenario are:

1. **History** (or contemporaneous events),
2. **Passage of time** (or **maturation**), and
3. **Statistical regression to the mean.**

History refers to the possibility that other events may have coincided with the provision of the intervention and may be the real cause of the observed outcome. Maybe the EMDR recipients were receiving some other services at the same time, and if so, maybe one or more of those other services was the real cause of the improvement. It's also plausible that family members came to their aid, providing material and emotional support that impacted their symptoms. If so, then the family impact could have been the real cause of their improvement. Or maybe it was the *combined* impact of the family and the other services.

Perhaps the mere *passage of time* helped. Although some survivors who developed severe or chronic posttraumatic stress disorder (PTSD) in the aftermath of Katrina might not experience any alleviation of symptoms during the 1-year study period just due to the passage of time, it is reasonable to suppose that survivors whose immediate trauma symptoms in the aftermath of Katrina were only acute and not meriting a full-blown PTSD diagnosis would experience a diminution in those symptoms over time even without any treatment for the symptoms.

Maturation probably would be inapplicable in this study. However, suppose we are testing the long-range effects of a drug abuse intervention with young adults. As the young adults become more emotionally mature, that alone might explain why many of them quit messing with drugs. Likewise, suppose we are testing the long-range effects of a safe-sex education program with 60-something-year-old politicians whose entourage always contains ambitious interns who admire them. As the politicians get older, many of them will not want as much sex or have less capacity for it, and that alone might explain an overall diminution of unsafe-sex incidents.

That brings us to the more complicated concept of *statistical regression to the mean.* Notice that in our hypothetical scenario I did not mention any distinguishing characteristics of the survivors who received EMDR. What if I had said that due to our shortage of EMDR-certified therapists, we chose to triage and thus treat only those survivors who—at pretest—received the worst scores on our measure of symptoms? Some of them—perhaps a lot of them—might not have scored as poorly had we assessed them the day before or a day later.

To understand this concept, try to compare your mood right now to your mood on a recent day when some good things or some stressful things happened to you. Chances are, your mood right now is considerably better or worse than on that notable previous day. If you completed a scale right now measuring your mood and completed the same scale on that other day, your scores would probably differ a lot. If we measured your mood with that scale every day for a few weeks, you'd probably have a typical score on most days, an atypically elevated score on a couple days, and an atypically low score on a couple of other days. Your mean (average) score would be close to the scores you get on your typical days, and your elevated or low scores would *regress to the mean* (return to their more typical level) on most days.

Imagine a day when the following things happened: You got very little sleep the night before. Your kids were ornery that morning, and you had difficulty getting them to school on time. Running late yourself, you got a speeding ticket on your way to work. Consequently, you arrived too late for an important staff meeting. Just before lunch you got a call from your real estate agent. Someone outbid you for the lovely house you so badly wanted to buy. Lunch was with colleagues, one who usually feels the need to compete with you and to make snide remarks that demean you in front of others. That colleague was particularly aggravating during lunch that day. On returning from lunch, your spouse (or partner) called and chastised you on hearing of your speeding ticket. Then it's off to see your new therapist, who you hope will help you with the anxiety symptoms you've been experiencing in recent months. At the start of the therapy session, your therapist has you complete a brief scale measuring your anxiety symptoms. Your score that day will serve as a baseline to be compared to your posttreatment score 10 weeks later. Completing the scale in the immediate aftermath of your lousy sleep and stressful day, you answer the items in ways that depict a worse level of anxiety than you would on a more typical day.

Suppose your therapist is a real schnook (perhaps highly recommended by your snide colleague!). You complete the treatment anyway, despite eventually realizing its worthlessness. After your final session, your therapist has you complete the anxiety symptom scale again. Life has been pretty routine for you during the previous 2 weeks, devoid of stressful events like the ones that occurred just before your first therapy session. Consequently, your answers to the scale items are more indicative of your typical level of anxiety, and it is the same level as it was on typical days before you started treatment with your schnook of a therapist. Before you leave, your therapist shows you the improvement in your scores and praises you for your improvement (implicitly praising himself, as well!). You are impressed! But then you read this chapter and realize that the improvement probably had nothing to do with the therapy. The more plausible alternative explanation is regression to the mean! You then make a photocopy of this page, mail it to your schnook therapist, and ask for a refund. (Just kidding about the refund!)

Now that you (hopefully) understand the concept of *statistical regression to the mean,* let's apply it to our fictional EMDR/Katrina scenario. Recall that due to our shortage of EMDR-certified therapists, we chose to triage and thus treat only those survivors who—at pretest—received the worst scores on our measure of symptoms. Because an extremely poor score was our eligibility criterion for EMDR treatment, there is a good chance that some of the scores were atypical, coming from individuals who were just having an unusually bad day when they were tested. Consequently, even without any treatment, odds are that their scores would improve when they were tested on a later date.

Suppose, for example, that all 100 pretest scores were 80, depicting an extremely elevated level of symptoms. The mean (average) pretest score then would be 80. (We'll keep the math simple.) Suppose, however, that 30 of the pretest scores came from people having an atypically bad day, and that had we assessed them on a more typical day, all their scores would have been 40. That would mean that instead of having 100 pretest scores of 80, we would have had 30 scores of 40 and 70 scores of 80. Thirty times 40 equals 1,200. Add that to 70 times 80 equals 5,600, and you get a total of 6,800. Divide the 6,800 by 100 (which is the total number of pretest scores), and you get a mean pretest score of 68 instead of 80.

But because we used extreme scores as our eligibility criterion, we really did get 30 atypically elevated scores (along with the 70 equally elevated scores that were not atypical). Thus, our pretest mean really was 80. Due to the 30 atypically elevated scores that will probably regress to their mean of 40, even with an utterly ineffectual treatment, the overall mean posttest score is approximately 68, reflecting a *misleading* degree of improvement from 80.

Selectivity Bias

Whenever a study is conducted in a way that compares two groups that are not really comparable, that study is vulnerable to a **selectivity bias,** which is another threat to internal validity. Suppose that in addition to pretesting and posttesting our 100 recipients of EMDR, we also pretested and posttested 100 Katrina survivors who requested EMDR treatment but whose pretest scores were less extreme and who therefore did not meet our triage-related eligibility criterion for the EMDR treatment. Statistical regression to the mean would still be a threat to the internal validity of our study. That's because our treatment group would be likely to contain a greater proportion of atypically extreme pretest scores than would our nontreatment group.

If one group has a greater likelihood to regress to its mean than the other group, then the two groups are not really comparable. But a greater likelihood for statistical regression is only one of many ways that groups can be incomparable. Perhaps one group is more motivated to change than the other, such as when we compare people who volunteer for treatment with counterparts who refuse the treatment. Comparing treatment completers with treatment dropouts would be another example. Perhaps the two groups differ in regard to their proportion of minorities, average level of functioning or disturbance, economic or social support resources, and so on.

Random Assignment

As mentioned in Chapter 3, the best way to avoid a selectivity bias is by randomly assigning clients to the different treatment conditions being compared. **Random assignment** does not mean *haphazard* assignment. It is a controlled process in which every study participant has the same chance of being assigned to either treatment condition. We could, for example, toss a coin for each participant. Heads they are assigned to Treatment A; tails to Treatment B. Or we could use a table of random numbers commonly found in basic research methods or statistics texts. Such a table would contain a very lengthy list of numbers that lack any order. Part of it might look something like this:

82

31

47

60

25

00

93

17

54

78

.

.

.

etc.

If 100 clients were participating in our experiment, and we wanted to randomly assign 50 of them to each treatment condition, first we would give them each a separate case number from 0 to 99. Then we would use a table of random numbers to pick the 50 that would go to one of the treatment conditions. If the first 10 numbers we encountered in that table were the ones listed here, then the clients that had those case numbers would be assigned to that treatment condition. We would continue to go down the lengthy list to pick 40 more numbers, skipping any numbers that had already been assigned. The remaining 50 cases, with case numbers that we had not yet encountered in the list, would then be assigned to the other treatment condition.

Suppose we had used random assignment in our fictional EMDR/Katrina study. What are the odds that all 30 of the extreme scorers would have been assigned to the EMDR treatment group? Had we flipped a coin to assign them, with heads meaning EMDR assignment, the odds that all 30 would get heads would be much less than one in a million! Imagine, for example, flipping a coin 30 times and getting 30 heads or 30 tails. Even getting 20 heads and 10 tails (or vice versa) would happen only rarely. The vast majority of the time you would get a more proportionate split. And the chances of getting a proportionate split increase with a larger sample of flips. For example, if you flip a coin 1,000 times, the chances of getting 60% heads are infinitesimally smaller than if you flip the coin 10 times. Thus, by using random assignment with a sufficiently large number of study participants, the risk of a selectivity bias is not plausible.

With a very small number of participants divided into two groups— say, about 20 (10 per group)—there is a plausible risk of getting randomly assigned groups that might not really be comparable. However, the risk would not result from a bias; instead, it would be due to a nonbiased fluke stemming from having a small sample. Nevertheless, the risk would still represent a threat to the internal validity of the study, especially if the researchers do not provide persuasive data showing no meaningful pretreatment differences between the groups.

In addition to controlling for selectivity biases and statistical regression, random assignment of participants to different groups also controls for the threat of history and the threat of passage of time (or maturation). Because the participants in each group are assigned randomly, with a sufficiently large sample of participants it is not plausible to suppose that that the contemporaneous events experienced by one group will be much more benign or harmful than the contemporaneous events experienced by the other group. Also, since each group experiences the same amount of elapsed time, the threat of passage of time can be ruled out as an alternative explanation for group differences in outcome.

History, passage of time, statistical regression, and selectivity bias are not the only types of threats to internal validity. However, they are the most prominent ones that you are likely to encounter when critically appraising studies that purport to test the effectiveness of an intervention, program, or policy. We examine some additional threats in the next chapter, which deals with the critical appraisal of experiments. Then, in Chapter 6, which deals with critically appraising quasi-experiments, we discuss some alternatives to random assignment for controlling for threats to internal validity. Let's turn now to the second question posed at the outset of this chapter: Was outcome measured in a valid and unbiased manner?

MEASUREMENT ISSUES

Even if a study controls for threats to internal validity via random assignment and other rigorous design features, the credibility of its results can be destroyed if its measurement procedures are unreliable, invalid, or seriously biased. For example, imagine the following scenario taking place in the office of a researcher in an American city.

The researcher is meeting with clients one at a time to have them complete a scale a week after each of them has completed his or her final treatment session provided by a nearby psychotherapist. The purpose is to evaluate the effectiveness of a new intervention the therapist has devised. It was not possible to administer a pretest before the start of the treatment, but because a large number of clients were assigned randomly to the treatment condition and a no-treatment control condition, it was safe to assume that the average pretest scores of the two groups were equivalent. Thus, significant differences in their posttest scores favoring the treatment group would be sufficient to indicate the effectiveness of the intervention.

A cheery little middle-aged man, who finished his final treatment session a week earlier, enters the researcher's office. The tall researcher, who looks a lot like the comedic actor Will Ferrell, explains the purpose of the evaluation and then hands the jovial client the scale with the instruction to answer each item in terms of his behavior during the past week.

The smiling little man, pencil in hand, starts reading the first item, then looks perplexed, scans through the remaining items, and then looks up at the researcher, and says, "You must have handed me the wrong scale. This one is in Chinese."

Researcher: "Please just respond to the items as best you can."
Client: (still unperturbed) "But it's in *Chinese*."
Researcher: "Please just respond to the items as best you can."

Client: (now beginning to become flustered) "Now, how in heaven's name can I answer this; as I *said*, it's in bloody *Chinese!*"
Researcher: "I'm sorry, but I can't tell you how to answer it; it would bias the research."

The client and researcher go back and forth like this for a couple of minutes, and as the researcher keeps responding the same way, the client gets increasingly agitated. Eventually, the client says, "This is freaking *ridiculous*, and it's really ticking me *off!*"

Researcher: (looking a bit frightened) "Now, now, remember your therapy."
Client: "I thought you weren't supposed to bias my responses!"
Researcher: "Yes, yes, please forget that I said that."
Client: "Now what?"
Researcher: "Please try to complete the scale."
Client: "At what circus did you get *your* research training? Okay, you clown, I'll complete it!"

The client then quickly completes the scale by just haphazardly checking response boxes having no idea what he's checking, muttering insulting wisecracks about the researcher the whole time. He then hands his completed scale to the researcher. The researcher examines his answers, shakes his head in disapproval, and says, "Tsk, tsk, it appears that the therapy didn't help *you* at all."

At that point, the client grabs a nearby pitcher of iced water, pours it inside the front of the researcher's trousers, dumps the researcher's large glass of iced tea over the researcher's head, and storms out of the office, slamming the door so hard on the way out that the office pictures fall off the wall. The researcher, looking unperturbed and not at all surprised, just shakes his head and utters to himself, "There goes another one; that therapist really needs to come up with a more effective anger management intervention."

As you can probably surmise, the point of this wacky story is that if an intervention is evaluated using an unreliable (and therefore invalid) measurement instrument, there is no reason to expect that the instrument will detect treatment success even after a successful treatment. Another extreme example of this point would be to evaluate an intervention to enhance anger management by using a scale that the client understands and can answer reliably, but which does not really measure anger management. Why should the scale detect improvement if it's not really measuring the problem that the treatment aimed to improve? In the real world of practice research, the examples of unreliable and invalid measurement are far less extreme than in the previous examples. But they do exist.

Therefore, whenever you read a study with results that fail to support the effectiveness of an evaluated intervention, one question you should ask is whether the study report supplies good evidence about the reliability and validity of the outcome measure.

If, however, the study reports results that support the effectiveness of the intervention, there is much less reason to wonder about the reliability and validity of the outcome measure. That's because if the measure were not reliable and valid, it would have had little chance of detecting treatment success. But measurement *bias* is a very different concern. Biased measurement typically increases the chance of obtaining results that erroneously depict treatment success.

For example, suppose the developer of an anger management intervention stands to gain fame and fortune if he can convince society that his is by far the most effective anger management intervention ever created. Suppose, instead of administering a valid self-report scale to his anger management group and a no-treatment control group, he does the following (I'll get extreme again to make the point clear).

After the final anger management session, the developer conducts an individual interview with each client. He begins the interview by telling each client that the purpose of the interview is to hopefully show that the clients who received the intervention that he invented are doing better in managing their anger than the control group participants. He then asks each client questions about how well they are managing their anger, smiling and nodding after each answer that he hopes to hear. At the end of the interview, he uses his own "judgment" to give each client a score from 1 to 10 according to how well he thinks they are handling their anger. He also interviews control group clients and uses his "judgment" to rate their anger management, but does so without the biasing introductory remarks or the reinforcing smiles or nods when they say they are doing well. With this much bias in measurement, it wouldn't matter how well designed the study was in other respects. The measurement bias would be egregious, and thus would constitute a fatal flaw in the research.

Admittedly, it's pretty hard to find published treatment outcome studies whose measurement is as egregiously flawed as in the previous example. But it's not as hard as you might imagine to find studies with fatal measurement flaws. In many studies, for example, clinicians assess progress face-to-face with their clients. Their clients would have to have cat litter for brains not to realize what their clinician wants them to say even if the clinician makes no biasing statements or facial expressions.

A former student of mine, as part of her internship, once observed an evaluation in which the practitioner administered a validated scale to the treatment group at posttest, but in introducing the scale urged the group to answer it in ways that showed that they made more progress than the control group. Years later, after the outcome study was published with results supporting the effectiveness of the intervention, the student told me what happened. I then reread the published article that reported the study. The article noted that a strength of the study was its use of a validated measurement instrument, but no mention was made of the inherent bias in the way it was administered.

This experience illustrates how biasing comments or expressions—or merely a biasing data collection context—can trump the fact that an instrument is valid. Suppose, for example, you ask me to complete the Beck Depression Inventory—a valid measure of depression—and tell me that you'll give me $10 for every point I score on it. Because a higher score indicates more depression and I have a son attending a very expensive college these days, I'll be sure to select the most depressed response category for every item on the inventory. The fact that the scale was shown to be valid when administered in an unbiased fashion would have no bearing on the validity of my answers.

Okay, okay, I used another extreme example. But you get my point: Even without any biasing expressions, if a clinician has a client complete a "valid" scale in her presence, the answers might be biased and invalid if the client is aware that the purpose of completing the scale is to show his clinician whether he has been a successful client or she has been a successful therapist.

Right now you might be asking yourself, "Can outcome measurement *ever* be valid and unbiased?" Yes, it can, and the key is to use a valid measurement approach that cannot be influenced by people who have a stake in the nature of the outcome. One way to do that is through the use of research assistants who administer measures without knowing what treatment group the participants are in. Better yet, the folks administering the measures could be kept uninformed as to the purpose of the study or the desired results. Studies using this ideal measurement approach typically use the term *blind* when referring to those administering the measures. That is, they are blind to the treatment status of the people they are assessing. This "blindness" is particularly important when using raters who will assign scores themselves based on what they observe. When they don't know the treatment status of the folks they are rating, they are referred to as *blind raters,* and their ratings are called *blind ratings.*

When critically appraising the measurement used in the studies you examine, you should remember that—as discussed in Chapter 2—studies are not either flawless or fatally flawed. There are many shades of gray, and reasonable people sometimes can disagree about whether a particular measurement flaw is so egregious that it destroys the credibility of a study. Many studies won't supply enough information for you to be sure. For example, they might report that research assistants administered validated self-report measures, but fail to report whether the assistants were "blind" and fail to mention whether any special precautions were taken to avoid making biasing comments when administering the measures.

To further illustrate what I mean by shades of gray in measurement, as well as to distinguish between fatal and nonfatal flaws, consider the following two scenarios. In scenario one, the therapist treating disaster survivors asks clients repeatedly at different points in each treatment session to rate from 0 to 10 how distressful it is when they bring up a mental image of the trauma. To assess treatment effectiveness, the therapist compares the first rating each client gave—at the start of treatment—to the last rating given at the conclusion of the final treatment session. If the final ratings are significantly better than the beginning ratings, then the therapist concludes that the treatment was effective. The therapist might also utilize a wait-list control group and ask its participants one time as a pretest to supply the same rating and then weeks later to do the same as a posttest. For this scenario, we might be predisposed to deem the bias egregious and perhaps fatal, even if the therapist used a control group. That's because throughout the therapy sessions the clients repeatedly get cues that even without saying may make them think that the therapist wants to see an improvement and that they are "failures" as clients if they do not report substantially better ratings. The control group participants, however, get no such repeated cues and have no reason to feel like failures or that they are disappointing their therapist if their ratings do not improve.

In scenario two, using the same study design, outcome is instead measured by the therapist having each treatment group and control group participant complete a validated scale measuring trauma symptoms before and after the treatment period. Suppose the report of the study mentions that the therapist made no biasing verbal or nonverbal expressions whatsoever, urged the client to answer candidly, and even had clients complete the scale in her waiting room rather than in her presence. Although we cannot rule out the possibility that the therapist's clients might still have been predisposed to please her (or themselves) with their scale answers, we probably would not depict this flaw as so egregious that the study's findings have too little credibility to guide our practice. Of course, if we found one or more other studies that were at least as strong as this one in all other respects while having much stronger measurement, we'd probably choose to be guided by them instead of by this one. If, however, this one was the best we could find for answering our particular evidence-based practice (EBP) question, and the most relevant to our particular practice context, its measurement flaw probably would not be a sufficient reason to dissuade us from recommending its intervention to our client.

STATISTICAL CHANCE

As you may recall from the beginning of this chapter, the third key question to ask when critically appraising an effectiveness study is: "What is the probability that the apparent effectiveness, or lack thereof, can be attributed to statistical chance?" We ask that question because we know that sometimes flukes in random assignment can be the reason why one group's outcome is better than another's. Most studies will rule out chance (also called *sampling error*) as a plausible explanation for differences if its probability is no more than .05 (five times out of 100). When the probability of chance is that low, the differences are called **statistically significant.**

They choose .05 merely because it's a traditional cutoff point in the social sciences for calling a finding *statistically significant;* there is no mathematical basis for it. For reasons we will see soon, some researchers might choose .10 instead of .05 as the cutoff point when their sample size is very small, but .05 is by far what you will see in most published studies. Researchers calculate the probability that chance explains their findings by using tests of statistical significance, such as *t*-tests, chi-square, and the like. You don't need to know about all that, but you should understand what it means (and does not mean) when a research report calls a finding *statistically significant.*

I've found that one of the best ways to illustrate the concepts of chance and statistical significance is by means of some fictional examples, each containing an extremely small number of fictional clients. Keeping the number of clients small enables us to visualize the need to assess chance and the meaning of statistical significance. Let's begin with the smallest number of clients that can possibly be assigned to a treatment group and a control group: one client per group.

Imagine that we have developed an innovative individual therapy intervention to prevent drug addiction among musicians. We've been providing the intervention for about a year, and it seems to be effective. So we decide to try to recruit musicians for a randomized experiment in which half of them will be assigned to our innovative intervention, and the other half will receive an older treatment approach. However, we are able to recruit only two participants for our experiment, whose names are John and Paul.

John is a rebellious lad whose friends are heavy drug users. He does not want to become addicted, but is at very high risk given his personality and peer influences. Chances are, no matter what intervention he receives, he'll eventually succumb to drug addiction. In contrast, Paul is not rebellious, has a healthy personality, and avoids bad influences. Still, being a young musician, he wants to make sure he doesn't succumb to the drug culture. Chances are, even without any intervention, Paul will continue to avoid drugs.

Using a coin toss to assign the two to treatment conditions, Paul gets assigned to our innovative intervention, and John gets assigned to the control (old treatment) condition. We assess outcome in terms of whether the participants become addicted to drugs. Paul does not, but John does. Thus, we have had a 100% successful outcome for our innovative intervention, and the control condition had a 100% failure rate. However, we cannot rule out chance as the explanation because with only two research participants we had a 50% chance of obtaining our results just due to the luck of the coin toss (heads or tails). In fact, we also had a 50% chance of obtaining the opposite results, which would have depicted our treatment as harmful. In all, then, with only two participants we had a 100% chance of obtaining a big difference in outcome between the two groups just due to the luck of the coin toss.

Now let's suppose that we were able to recruit four participants for our experiment. In addition to John and Paul, we recruited George and Ringo. George is a lot like John, and Ringo is a lot like Paul. No matter what intervention John and George receive, they'll probably succumb to drug addiction. Conversely, no matter what intervention Paul and Ringo receive, they'll probably avoid drug addiction. In fact, that's what eventually happens. Paul and Ringo have successful outcomes and John and George are treatment failures. If we use coin tosses to divide the four lads into our two treatment conditions—two per condition—the six possible outcomes of our random assignment are displayed in Table 4.1. The two treatment successes (Paul and Ringo) are in caps and the names of the two failures (John and George) are in italics.

Notice that of the 6 possible outcomes in Table 4.1, the first shows that both successful clients went to our innovative intervention and both failures went to the old (control condition). The odds of this happening due to chance are 1 in 6 (.167) because there is only one such result out of a total of 6 possible outcomes. In none of the other 5 possible outcomes did our innovative group do better than the control group. That is, there was a 50% success/failure rate in each of the outcomes 2 through 5, and in outcome 6 the control group did better than the innovative group. Thus, had our experiment attained the outcome 1 results, the fact that it had a

Table 4.1　Possible Random Assignment Outcomes of Four Research Participants to Two Treatment Conditions

Treatment Condition	Possible Random Assignment Outcomes					
	1	2	3	4	5	6
Innovative	PAUL RINGO	PAUL *John*	PAUL *George*	RINGO *John*	RINGO *George*	*John* *George*
Old	*John* *George*	RINGO *George*	RINGO *John*	PAUL *George*	PAUL *John*	PAUL RINGO

Note: The names of participants who avoid drug addiction are all caps. The names of those who eventually succumb to drug addiction are italicized.

.167 probability (1 in 6) of occurring due to the luck of the coin tosses would keep us from ruling out the plausibility of chance as the explanation for our results, even though we would have 100% successes for our innovative treatment compared to 100% failures for the old treatment.

Next, let's suppose that we were able to recruit six participants for our experiment—the above four plus two others. One of the 2 others (Bruce) was just like Paul and Ringo, and had a successful outcome. The other (Elvis) was just like John and George and had an unsuccessful outcome. We now would get 20 possible outcomes using our random assignment procedure. Looking over Table 4.2, we can see that in outcome 1, we would get a 100% success rate in our innovative group versus a 0% success rate in our control group. The odds of that happening due to chance are 1 in 20, or .05 (because there is only one such result out of a total of 20 possible outcomes). Therefore, if we had that result, we could deem our results statistically significant, and thus rule out the plausibility of chance.

Notice that in outcomes 2 through 10 we would get a 67% (2 out of 3) success rate in our innovative group versus a 33% (1 out of 3) success rate in our control group. That's not too shabby a difference. Many program developers would be delighted to make that much of a difference in preventing substance abuse or some other problem. However, because that outcome could occur 9 times out of 20 just due to the luck of the coin tosses, the probability that the difference in success rates could be explained by chance would be .45 (9 divided by 20). In fact, a test of statistical significance would come up with a probability of .50, because it would be based on the odds of getting *at least* that much of a difference between the two groups. That is, it would add outcome 1 to outcomes 2 through 10 and then divide 10 by 20. (It would do this by means of statistical formulas; not by creating a table like Table 4.2. But the meaning of the calculations would be the same as the meaning illustrated in Table 4.2.)

Understanding the essence of the foregoing discussion of statistical significance should keep you from being overwhelmed by the statistics you encounter when you are critically appraising an effectiveness study. No matter how unfamiliar you are with the specific test of statistical significance reported, and no matter how complicated it is, it will ultimately report a probability (p) value, usually in the form of $p < .05$ or $p > .05$, and that p value will refer to the probability that the results were due to chance, as explained above. (The symbol < means less than, and the symbol > means greater than.)

These examples also illustrate something else that's important to remember—the influence of sample size on the chances of getting statistically significant results. Recall that in our examples with only two participants and only four participants it was impossible to obtain an outcome that had as low as a .05 probability of being attributed to chance.

Table 4.2   Possible Random Assignment Outcomes of Six Research Participants to Two Treatment Conditions

Possible Random Assignment Outcomes	Treatment Condition	
	Innovative	Old
1	PAUL	*John*
	RINGO	*George*
	BRUCE	*Elvis*
2	PAUL	BRUCE
	RINGO	*George*
	John	*Elvis*
3	PAUL	BRUCE
	RINGO	*John*
	George	*Elvis*
4	PAUL	BRUCE
	RINGO	*Paul*
	Elvis	*George*
5	PAUL	RINGO
	BRUCE	*George*
	John	*Elvis*
6	PAUL	RINGO
	BRUCE	*John*
	George	*Elvis*
7	PAUL	RINGO
	BRUCE	*Paul*
	Elvis	*George*
8	RINGO	PAUL
	BRUCE	*George*
	John	*Elvis*
9	RINGO	PAUL
	BRUCE	*John*
	George	*Elvis*
10	RINGO	PAUL
	BRUCE	*John*
	Elvis	*George*
11	PAUL	RINGO
	John	BRUCE
	George	*Elvis*
12	PAUL	RINGO
	John	BRUCE
	Elvis	*George*
13	PAUL	RINGO
	George	BRUCE
	Elvis	*John*

Table 4.2   *(Continued)*

Possible Random Assignment Outcomes	Treatment Condition	
	Innovative	Old
14	RINGO *Paul* *George*	PAUL BRUCE *Elvis*
15	RINGO *John* *Elvis*	PAUL BRUCE *George*
16	RINGO *George* *Elvis*	PAUL BRUCE *John*
17	BRUCE *Paul* *George*	PAUL RINGO *Elvis*
18	BRUCE *John* *Elvis*	PAUL RINGO *George*
19	BRUCE *George* *Elvis*	PAUL RINGO *John*
20	*John* *George* *Elvis*	PAUL RINGO BRUCE

Note: The names of participants who avoid drug addiction are all caps. The names of those who eventually succumb to drug addiction are italicized.

With two participants, chance had a .50 probability of explaining the best possible outcome. With four participants, chance had a .167 probability of explaining the best possible outcome. However, with six participants, it became possible to obtain a statistically significant outcome—that is, outcome 1 with its .05 probability. But to get that significant outcome, we would have had to have a 100% success rate in our innovative group versus a 0% success rate in the control group. That much of a difference is virtually unheard of in the real world of practice. Still, at least we would have had some chance of getting a statistically significant result, compared to no chance with our other two (smaller) samples. With each increment of increase in sample size, the probability becomes smaller and smaller that a meaningful difference in outcome between groups could have been produced merely by chance.

Two practical implications of the influence of sample size are as follows. First, when reading a report of a study that failed to get statistically significant results, you should take into account its sample size. If the sample size is small, but the results seem potentially meaningful, the intervention should not be dismissed as necessarily ineffective. Second, if the sample size is very large, results that are trivial from a practical standpoint can attain statistical significance.

One rule of thumb you can use regarding sample size is to consider a sample containing considerably fewer than 80 participants (or much less than 40 per group when two groups are being compared) as small. An adequate sample size will usually contain 80 or more participants. A very large sample size might involve many hundreds of participants. (The basis for this rule thumb involves complex statistics that go way beyond the scope and purpose of this practitioner-oriented book.)

For example, with a sample of 10,000 participants divided evenly into two groups, the probability of finding only a 4% difference in success rates between the two groups is less than .001. With a sample of 100 participants divided evenly into two groups, the probability of finding a 20% difference in success rates between the two groups is higher, albeit still significant at less than .05. With only 20 participants divided evenly into two groups, the probability of finding the same 20% difference in success rates between the two groups is greater than .05 (not significant).

There is one more thing you should keep in mind about statistical significance. It *only* pertains to the plausibility of chance as an alternative explanation for obtained results. It does not trump other plausible explanations (history, passage of time, and so on), and it does not trump measurement bias. For example, one sure way for an unethical researcher to guarantee obtaining statistically significant results would be to egregiously bias his or her measurement procedures.

EXTERNAL VALIDITY

As mentioned at the start of this chapter, the fourth key question to ask when critically appraising studies that evaluate intervention effectiveness is: "Do the study participants, intervention procedures, and results seem applicable to your practice context?" That question pertains to the **external validity** of the study. An outcome study has external validity to the extent that the inferences it makes about the effectiveness of the evaluated intervention apply to settings other than the research setting and to clients other than the study participants. If, for example, the clinicians providing the intervention had very lengthy and expensive training in it that most real world agencies can't afford to provide their clinicians, and if their caseloads were much smaller than in most real world agencies, then the study would have very little external validity for most real world agencies. Likewise, if the characteristics of the research participants are unlike the characteristics of the clients in a particular agency, then that, too, would restrict the external validity of the study for that agency.

For the individual practitioner engaged in EBP, the main concern regarding external validity is not how representative a particular study is regarding the broader population of clients and practice settings. Instead, the individual practitioner is concerned with whether the findings of a particular study can be generalized to the client or practice setting pertaining to the EBP question being asked. For example, suppose you are searching for and appraising studies to find an intervention with the best evidence for treating depressive symptoms in a 100-year-old woman who recently emigrated from Timbuktu and who resides in a very expensive, assisted-living facility. Suppose you find a methodologically sound study that took place in a similar assisted-care facility with depressed female residents over 100 years old who recently emigrated from Timbuktu. Suppose the study shows that the evaluated intervention was very effective in alleviating the depressive symptoms of those women.

From the standpoint of the population of practitioners who treat the depressed elderly, that study would have very little external validity, because most of their clients are much less than 100 years old, don't hail from Timbuktu, are not recent immigrants, and cannot afford to reside in very expensive, assisted-living facilities. From your standpoint, however, that study might have excellent external validity because the facility and clients appear to be just like your client and her facility. However, you might have second thoughts if you learn that to be effective in providing the intervention you have to undergo 3 months of training in Timbuktu at the cost of $10,000 plus travel and living expenses.

We'll be returning to the basic concepts discussed in this chapter throughout the remainder of this book. We'll also delve into additional aspects of those concepts. What you learned in this chapter should help as you read each remaining chapter. Beginning here, and at the end of subsequent chapters in this book, you'll see two synopses of research studies germane to the chapter's purpose that you can critically appraise. I encourage you to read each synopsis and jot down what you think are the strengths, reasonable flaws, and fatal flaws of the study. You might also indicate whether and how it could be used to guide decisions about evidence-based practice. The appendixes at the end of this book provide my brief appraisal of each study to which you can compare your appraisal. Appendix A pertains to the synopses in this chapter. Although some of the fictional synopses may resemble real studies that have been completed and published; all were created to clearly exemplify chapter concepts. (I've also fabricated the citations in the fictional synopses.)

SYNOPSES OF RESEARCH STUDIES

Study 1 Synopsis

This study evaluated the effectiveness of the Road to Redemption (RTR) program in preventing re-arrest and increasing victim empathy among male inmates in correctional facilities in Texas. RTR is a (fictional) faith-based in-prison program that brings victim volunteers into the prison for 12 weekly sessions to meet face-to-face in small groups with prison inmates who are soon to be released. The purpose of the group sessions was to prevent future criminal behavior by encouraging prisoners to become born-again Christians who follow the teachings of Jesus Christ and by enhancing their empathy regarding the effect of crime on victims.

Each 2-hour RTR group session began and ended with the singing of a biblical hymn, a prayer, and with the group leader reciting a bible excerpt about God's forgiveness. In between, victims took turns telling the story of their victimization to inmates who have hurt others like them. Group facilitators encouraged the inmates to acknowledge the consequences of their behavior, express their sense of guilt, take responsibility for their crimes, and experience a "change of heart." Group leaders framed each discussion in terms of spiritual principles such as compassion, forgiveness, responsibility, restitution, and the notion that previous bad behavior does not necessarily imply irreversible bad character. Each week, inmates participating in RTR were given required homework that involved reading scriptures related to the forthcoming RTR weekly topic. During the final session, inmates were required to read aloud two letters that they had written: one to a victim of the their crime and another to a family member who suffered as a result of the crime.

Prerelease inmates with a pending release within 9 months were invited to participate voluntarily in the RTR program by the chaplains in each prison in Texas. Over the course of 1 year, 1,000 prerelease inmates completed the 12-week RTR program, and their outcomes were compared to the 5,000 inmates who opted not to participate. Outcomes for each of the 6,000 inmates were assessed according to two variables: (1) level of empathy for crime victims, and (2) whether they were re-arrested during 3 years after release.

Level of empathy was measured using the Feel Your Pain Empathy Scale, which has been shown in numerous studies to have a high level of reliability, validity, and cultural sensitivity (Clinton, 2006; Rodham, 2007). The written self-report scale was completed by each inmate in the prison chaplain's office 10 months before prison release and again 1 day before release. Although the chaplains recruited the 1,000 RTR participants, they also attempted to recruit the 5,000 inmates who opted not to participate. With each chaplain having attempted to recruit approximately 300 inmates, it was assumed that they would not remember which inmates did and did not participate in RTR. The chaplains did not take part in the RTR sessions and were not informed as to which inmates chose to participate.

Whether the inmates were re-arrested during the 3 years after release from prison was determined by examining the computerized records of the Texas Department of Criminal Justice. The difference in re-arrest rates between the two groups was statistically significant ($p < .001$), with only 10% of the RTR participants re-arrested, as compared to 40% of the inmates who did not participate in RTR.

The difference in increases in empathy levels also was statistically significant ($p < .05$). Possible scores on the Feel Your Pain Empathy Scale could range from 0 to 100. The RTR participants' scores increased from an average of 40 to 46, whereas the other inmates average scores remained unchanged; it was 20 at both pretest and posttest.

The findings of this study show that RTR is an evidence-based practice. It effectively increases victim empathy and prevents recidivism among soon-to-be-released prisoners.

Study 2 Synopsis

This (fictional) study evaluated the effectiveness of the RTR program in preventing re-arrest and increasing victim empathy among Spanish-speaking Mexican American male inmates in one correctional facility in Arizona. The RTR program was provided in the same way as described in the synopsis of Study 1. In this study, however, 20 inmates who volunteered to participate were randomly assigned to two groups: 10 to RTR and 10 to a no-treatment control condition. As in the previous study, pre-release inmates with a pending release within 9 months were invited to participate voluntarily in the RTR program by the prison chaplain.

Outcomes for each of the 20 inmates were assessed according to two variables: (1) level of empathy for crime victims, and (2) whether they were re-arrested during 3 years after release. Level of empathy was measured using the Feel Your Pain Empathy Scale, which has been shown in numerous studies to have a high level of reliability, validity, and cultural sensitivity (Clinton, 2006; Rodham, 2007). However, because the study participants did not speak English, the scale was translated and administered orally by the bilingual prison chaplain during individual interviews in his office. The pretest interviews were conducted 1 week before the 20 inmates were randomly divided into the two groups. The posttest interviews were conducted 1 day before they were released from prison.

Whether the inmates were re-arrested during the 3 years after release from prison was determined by examining the computerized records of the Arizona Department of Criminal Justice. The difference in re-arrest rates between the two groups was not statistically significant, with 2 of the 10 RTR participants re-arrested, as compared to 4 of the 10 inmates who did not participate in RTR.

The difference in increases in empathy level, however, was statistically significant ($p < .001$). The RTR participants' scores increased from an average of 30 to 80, whereas the other inmates' average score remained unchanged; it was 30 at both pretest and posttest.

The findings of this study show that although RTR is very effective in increasing victim empathy among prisoners, it fails to reduce re-arrest rates. Practitioners who seek to increase victim empathy can consider RTR to be an evidence-based intervention for that purpose, but if they seek to prevent recidivism, they should try to find or develop a more effective intervention approach.

KEY CHAPTER CONCEPTS

- A study of the effectiveness of an intervention (or a program or policy) has internal validity to the extent that its design arrangements enable us to ascertain logically whether the observed outcome really reflects the effectiveness (or lack thereof) of our intervention versus some alternative explanation.
- History is one of several threats to internal validity. It refers to the possibility that other events may have coincided with the provision of the intervention and may be the real cause of the observed outcome.
- Other key threats to internal validity include maturation or the passage of time, statistical regression to the mean, and selectivity biases.
- Randomly assigning clients to different treatment conditions controls for history, maturation or the passage of time, statistical regression to the mean, and selectivity biases.
- Even if a study controls for threats to internal validity via random assignment and other rigorous design features, the credibility of its results can be destroyed if its measurement procedures are unreliable, invalid, or seriously biased.
- Statistical chance refers to flukes in random assignment that can be the reason why one group's outcome is better than another's.
- Most studies will rule out chance (also called *sampling error*) as a plausible explanation for differences if its probability is no more than .05 (5 times out of 100). When the probability of chance is that low, the differences are called *statistically significant*.

- There is no mathematical basis for the .05 cutoff point. It is merely a tradition. Some researchers might choose .10 instead of .05 as the cutoff point when their sample size is very small, but .05 is by far what you will see in most published studies.
- When reading a report of a study that failed to get statistically significant results, you should take into account its sample size. If the sample size is small, but the results seem potentially meaningful, the intervention should not be dismissed as necessarily ineffective. If the sample size is very large, results that are trivial from a practical standpoint can attain statistical significance.
- Statistical significance pertains only to the plausibility of chance as an alternative explanation for obtained results. It does not trump other plausible explanations such as threats to internal validity and measurement bias.
- The external validity of a study pertains to whether the study participants, intervention procedures, and results seem applicable to the evidence-based practitioner's practice context.

Review Exercises

1. *Shortly after George W. Bush was elected president of the United States in 2000, the national news media were abuzz about his interest in funding faith-based social services. The director of a bible studies program that operated in various prisons soon appeared on several cable news programs and extolled the effectiveness of his faith-based program, claiming that only 14% of the prisoners who participated in it got re-arrested after release from prison, as compared to a re-arrest rate of 41% among the nonparticipants. None of the news moderators asked him tough questions about the research design that produced those rates. If you were the moderator, what questions would you have asked pertaining to the internal validity of his design? Explain why, from an internal validity standpoint, you might be suspicious about the effectiveness of his program in preventing re-arrest, despite the impressive figures he cited.*
2. *Your colleague tells you about a new intervention about which he is very excited. The basis of his excitement is a study he read*

that had a very large sample and obtained statistically significant results supporting the effectiveness of the intervention. Despite the statistical significance, what additional study details would you need to help you judge how effective the intervention really appears to be?

3. *Two of your colleagues, Jack and Jill, are disagreeing about the meaning of the results of a study they conducted to compare the effectiveness of two interventions designed to prevent high school dropout. In their study, two of the ten students who received Intervention A dropped out, while none of the ten students who received Intervention B dropped out. Jack argues that Intervention B is more effective because it had no dropouts, as compared to the 20% dropout rate for Intervention A. Jill argues that there is no difference in the effectiveness of the two interventions because the results were not statistically significant at the .05 level. What would you tell them to explain why both of their arguments are incorrect?*

ADDITIONAL READINGS

Campbell, D., & Stanley, J. (1963). *Experimental and quasi-experimental designs for research.* Chicago: Rand McNally.

Rubin, A. (2007). *Statistics for evidence-based practice and evaluation.* Belmont, CA: Thompson Brooks/Cole.

Chapter 5

CRITICALLY APPRAISING EXPERIMENTS

As you know from the preceding chapters, the distinguishing feature of research experiments related to evidence-based practice (EBP) is the random assignment of research participants into different intervention conditions. How many different conditions they get assigned to and the nature of those conditions varies in different studies.

Some studies compare an intervention group to a no-treatment control condition. Denying clients any treatment is sometimes deemed unethical or pragmatically unacceptable; therefore, some studies compare a group receiving an intervention that is predicted to be more effective than routine treatment to a group receiving routine treatment as usual. Some studies do this not for ethical or pragmatic reasons, but because they want to see not just whether a new treatment is effective, but whether it is *more* effective than ongoing practices.

Some studies want to compare the relative effectiveness of two promising new treatments and thus randomly assign clients to one or the other promising treatment. Other studies with the same aim might randomly assign clients to three groups: one or the other promising new treatment or to a no treatment (or routine treatment as usual) control condition.

Some studies add a placebo group to the mix to assess the extent to which the superior results for a tested intervention can be attributed to the power of suggestion or the impact of the client's thinking that he or she is receiving something special. Finally, some studies randomly assign clients to various groups that receive different combinations of the components of a multifaceted intervention, to see which components most account for the intervention's effects and which components might not even be needed.

In this chapter, we examine the design logic for each of these types of experiments. We also consider additional types of flaws not yet discussed in previous chapters that you should be on the lookout for when you critically appraise experiments. Although rigorous experiments reside high on the evidentiary hierarchy regarding intervention effectiveness in EBP, as noted in Chapter 3, some experiments can be so flawed that they lack sufficient credibility to guide practice decisions. Let's begin by examining the different types of experimental designs and their logic.

CLASSIC PRETEST-POSTTEST CONTROL GROUP DESIGN

Randomized experiments are far outnumbered in the outcome research literature by studies lower on the evidentiary hierarchy and with less internal validity than experiments. But among the experiments you do find, perhaps the most common will use the **classic pretest-posttest control group design.** The diagram for that design is as follows:

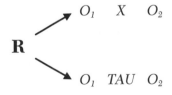

Where:
  R signifies random assignment,
  O_1 stands for the pretest,
  X signifies the intervention,

TAU represents treatment as usual (or perhaps no treatment), and O_2 stands for the posttest.

Figure 5.1 diagrams this design in more detail and illustrates two kinds of results: one that supports the effectiveness of the intervention and one that doesn't. Notice that in the first set of results, the experimental

Figure 5.1   Classic Pretest-Posttest Control Group Design with Two Kinds of Results

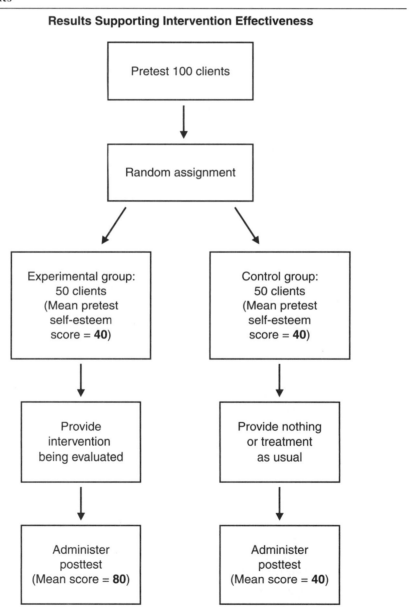

Figure 5.1   *(Continued)*

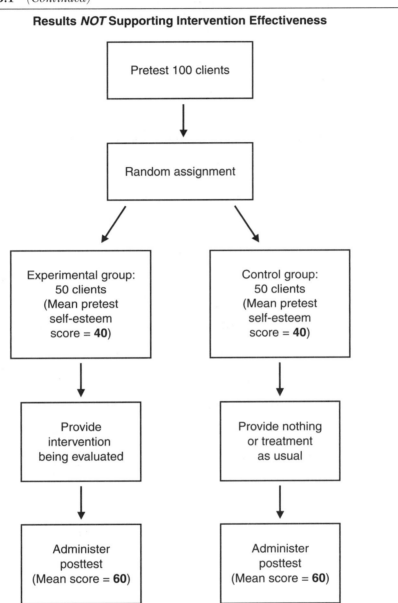

Results *NOT* Supporting Intervention Effectiveness

group's level of self-esteem doubles, while the control group's level remains unchanged, thus supporting the effectiveness of the intervention.

Notice in the second set of results that even though the experimental group's level of self-esteem increases, the control group's level increases by the same amount. Consequently, it would be illogical to attribute the improvement to the effects of the intervention. Instead, the logical interpretation is to attribute the improvement to some alternative explanation, such as history or the passage of time. Thus, there is no evidence supporting the notion that the intervention is effective despite the improvement in self-esteem among the intervention recipients.

Before we move on to the next type of experimental design, one more point should be clarified. Just because an experimental design controls for things like history, does not mean that the design eliminates the possibility that contemporaneous events (history) can affect things. Instead, it only means that the design enables us logically to ascertain whether history (or other threats to internal validity) represent plausible explanations for the obtained findings.

POSTTEST-ONLY CONTROL GROUP DESIGN

In some studies, conducting pretests is impractical or simply makes no sense. One example of such a study would be an experiment evaluating a program that aims to prevent re-arrest of prison inmates after their release and that evaluates outcome only in terms of re-arrest rates. Because the inmates are in prison to begin with, a pretest on being arrested is inconceivable. Every inmate in the study has been arrested and is in prison, regardless of whether they get assigned to the experimental or control group. It only makes sense to have a posttest, which would have a dichotomous yes or no result regarding whether the released inmate gets re-arrested. Moreover, we know that there is no pretest difference between the groups to begin with; that is, everyone starts out in prison. Likewise, we don't need to compare the degree of change from pretest to posttest because no increments of change are involved—they are either re-arrested or they are not. The same logic applies to countless other types of dichotomous prevention outcomes, such as when interventions are evaluated to see if they prevent school dropout, child abuse, and so on.

When the classic experimental design is conducted without a pretest, it is called the **posttest-only control group design.** The diagram for that design is as follows:

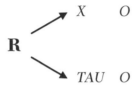

Where:

 R signifies random assignment,

 X signifies the intervention,

TAU represents treatment as usual (or perhaps no treatment), and

O stands for the posttest.

Sometimes this design is used when pretests are conceivable, but impossible to administer due to some pragmatic obstacle. Sometimes it is used in order to avoid the effects of testing. For example, if teenage parents participating in a parent education program take a pretest, they might learn from the pretest and might even look up answers to it later, which in turn might improve their posttest scores. Also, having taken the pretest might help them retain more from the educational intervention. Consequently, if their posttest scores are higher, that might be due at least in part to the effects of taking the pretest.

The logical assumption of the posttest-only control group design is that random assignment provides a reasonable basis for supposing that both groups would have had very similar pretest scores, and that therefore the difference at posttest represents treatment effects. Although that is a reasonable assumption and although this design is considered to be rigorous and high on the EBP evidentiary hierarchy for effectiveness studies, not having a pretest can be a problem when the study sample is quite small. With only about 10 or 20 participants per group, for example, the assumption that random assignment will produce equivalent groups is more dubious than with larger samples. Comparing the pretest scores of the two groups would give some indication as to whether the two groups really do appear to be equivalent.

SOLOMON FOUR-GROUP DESIGN

Some rare studies control for testing effects without sacrificing pretests by using a complex design called the *Solomon four-group design*. This design contains two groups that fit the pretest-posttest format and two groups that fit the posttest-only format. By comparing the results across all four groups, it becomes possible to separate out testing effects from intervention effects, as illustrated in Figure 5.2. The first set of results in Figure 5.2 supports the conclusion that the posttest differences between the experimental and control groups are totally a function of intervention effects and that there were no testing effects. That's because both the experimental group that got tested twice and the experimental group that only received a posttest had the same posttest scores and did better than their treatment-as-usual (TAU) control group counterparts. The second set of results supports the conclusion that the posttest comparisons reflect some testing effects and some intervention effects. That's because the experimental group that got tested twice scored the highest at posttest, while the experimental group that only received a posttest scored higher at posttest than both TAU control groups, but lower than the experimental group that got tested twice. The third set of results supports the conclusion that the intervention had no effect, but that testing had some effect. That's because the experimental group and the TAU control group that were tested twice both improved to the same degree, while the experimental group that only received a posttest had the same average posttest score as the control group that only received a posttest.

Figure 5.2   Three Sets of Results in an Imaginary Experiment Using a Solomon Four-Group Design to Evaluate the Effectiveness of a Parent Education Program

Set 1: Intervention Effective, No Testing Effects
(Scores reflect knowledge of good parenting)

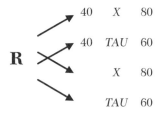

Set 2: Intervention Effective, Some Testing Effects
(Scores reflect knowledge of good parenting)

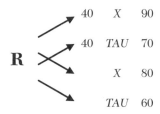

Set 3: Intervention Ineffective, Some Testing Effects
(Scores reflect knowledge of good parenting)

$$R \begin{matrix} 40 & X & 60 \\ 40 & TAU & 60 \\ & X & 50 \\ & TAU & 50 \end{matrix}$$

ALTERNATIVE TREATMENT DESIGNS

Alternative treatment designs are used in experiments that compare the relative effectiveness of two promising new treatments. Sometimes these designs involve randomly assigning clients to one or the other promising treatments, only without assigning any clients to a control group. When no control group is included, the diagram for these designs is as follows:

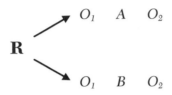

Where:

R signifies random assignment,
O_1 stands for the pretest,
A signifies Intervention A,
B represents Intervention B, and
O_2 stands for the posttest.

If the recipients of one intervention improve significantly more than the recipients of the alternative intervention, then this design provides strong evidence supporting the superior effectiveness of the intervention with the significantly greater improvement.

Although this design can also be used without any pretests, it's better to use pretests if possible in case both groups improve to the same degree. That is, if both groups have equal scores at posttest without any pretest, there would be no evidence supporting the notion that both interventions might be equally effective as opposed to the possibility that they both might be equally ineffective. But even with pretests, if both groups improve at the same rate, we can't be certain that the interventions caused the improvement. Without a control group, we cannot rule out history or passage of time as the cause of the improvement in *both* groups. That's why the following design is preferable:

$$\begin{array}{ccc} & O_1 & A & O_2 \\ \mathbf{R} \longrightarrow & O_1 & B & O_2 \\ & O_1 & TAU & O_2 \end{array}$$

Where:

R signifies random assignment,

O_1 stands for the pretest,

A signifies the Intervention A,

B signifies the Intervention B,

TAU represents treatment as usual (or perhaps no treatment), and

O_2 stands for the posttest.

If both intervention groups improve by the same amount while improving significantly more than the control group, it is safe to rule out history and the passage of time and thus infer that they both interventions are equally effective.

DISMANTLING DESIGNS

Sometimes debate emerges about whether certain—perhaps controversial—treatment components are really needed in an intervention that appears to be effective. Such debate currently rages over whether the main distinguishing treatment component of eye movement desensitization and reprocessing (EMDR)—dual attention stimulation (usually in the form of rapid eye movements)—has anything whatsoever to do with the effectiveness of EMDR. Some critics of EMDR argue that the rapid eye movements (or other forms of dual attention stimulation) are merely a marketing gimmick employed to make EMDR look different from exposure therapy or cognitive restructuring. To test their contention, they've conducted some studies using **dismantling designs.**

Dismantling designs randomly assign clients to various groups that receive different combinations of the components of a multifaceted intervention, to see which components most account for the intervention's effects and which components might not even be needed. The general diagram for dismantling designs is as follows:

$$
\mathbf{R} \diagdown \!\!\!\! \diagup
\begin{matrix}
O_1 & AB & O_2 \\
O_1 & A & O_2 \\
O_1 & B & O_2 \\
O_1 & TAU & O_2
\end{matrix}
$$

Where:

R signifies random assignment,

O_1 stands for the pretest,

AB signifies the intervention that includes both components A and B,

A signifies treatment component A,

B signifies treatment component B,

TAU represents treatment as usual (or perhaps no treatment), and

O_2 stands for the posttest.

The number of rows in the previous design can be modified, depending on how many treatment components are being compared. For example, suppose a dismantling study that is used to see whether the eye movement component of EMDR is really necessary obtains the following results, plugging in trauma symptom scores for O_1 and O_2 (lower scores are better):

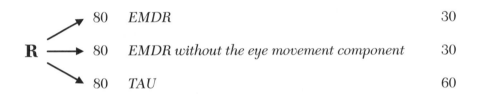

	80	*EMDR*	30
R	80	*EMDR without the eye movement component*	30
	80	*TAU*	60

These fictional results would suggest that the eye movement component contributes nothing to the effectiveness of EMDR. That's because the treatment group without the eye movement component improved just as much as the one with that component. Had the EMDR group with the eye movement component improved significantly more than the group without it, then the results would have supported the argument that EMDR is more effective with the eye movement component than without it. At the same time, such results would support the notion that even without the eye movement component EMDR is more effective than treatment as usual because the middle group improved much more than the control group. Dismantling studies regarding EMDR that actually have been carried out and published have had inconsistent results regarding the necessity of the dual attention stimulation component. Some have found it to be associated with better outcomes, and others have found it to be completely unnecessary (Rubin, 2004).

PLACEBO CONTROL GROUP DESIGNS

All of the foregoing experimental designs have relatively high degrees of internal validity and consequently reside high on the evidentiary hierarchy regarding intervention effectiveness in EBP. Nevertheless, each can be vulnerable to threats to their validity that fall under the rubric of **research reactivity**—a term that refers to various ways in which research procedures, as opposed to the tested intervention, can influence the dependent variable and thus confound the results of outcome studies.

One form of research reactivity of common concern in outcome studies is called *placebo effects*. You've probably encountered that term when reading about pharmaceutical studies that administer a pill that contains no active ingredients—a pill called a *placebo*—to see if the mere notion that they are getting some special treatment might induce as much improvement in patients as does the new drug being tested. **Placebo effects** occur when the desired improvement in a dependent variable results from client perceptions that they are getting special attention or a special treatment. In other words, the desired improvement might be attributed in part—or in total—to the power of suggestion, as opposed to the intervention being evaluated.

Another form of research reactivity—one that closely resembles placebo effects—is called **novelty and disruption effects.** Novelty and disruption effects occur when the introduction of an innovative intervention in a setting that is unused to innovation stimulates excitement, energy, and enthusiasm in the setting. Suppose, for example, a nursing home that has provided only minimal, perfunctory care for its residents gets an enthusiastic and innovative new director whose first act is to introduce a therapy dog to an experimental group of residents in the home. Suppose patient morale improves significantly after the residents are introduced to the happy, affectionate dog. Suppose further that no such improvement occurred in a control group. Did the concept of a therapy dog cause the improvement? Or was it merely the fact that something novel happened that disrupted the patients' normal, dull routine? To control for the possibility of novelty or disruption effects, some other novel innovation could be introduced to a second control group. Perhaps instead of a therapy dog, the control patients could be given a plant to care for or perhaps some new books to read. If the morale of this group of patients improves as much as the morale of the therapy dog patients, and more so than the control patients who receive nothing, that would indicate that there is nothing about the therapy dog intervention per se that causes improvement. Rather, it is merely the idea of doing something—perhaps anything—novel to break the dull routine of the home.

Thus, to control for novelty and disruption effects—or for placebo effects—two different control groups are used: one that receives nothing unusual and one that receives a placebo or some form of novel innovation. The latter group typically is called the *placebo group*. The diagram for this design is as follows:

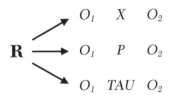

$$\mathbf{R} \longrightarrow \begin{array}{ccc} O_1 & X & O_2 \\ O_1 & P & O_2 \\ O_1 & TAU & O_2 \end{array}$$

Where:

    R signifies random assignment,

    O_1 stands for the pretest,

    X signifies the intervention,

    P signifies the placebo,

    TAU represents treatment as usual (or perhaps no treatment), and

    O_2 stands for the posttest.

The effects of the intervention are reflected in the degree to which the amount of improvement among its recipients exceeds the amount of improvement in the placebo group (assuming that it also significantly exceeds the amount of improvement in the TAU control group).

Adding a placebo group can significantly strengthen the validity of an experiment. However, the lack of a placebo group typically should not be deemed a fatal flaw in an otherwise rigorous experiment. Unlike pharmaceutical experiments, conditions in real-world settings in human services practice rarely are amenable to placebo group designs. Assigning clients to conditions in which they are deceived into thinking they are receiving a special treatment raises ethical and pragmatic concerns. Instead of disparaging otherwise strong experiments just because they lack a placebo group, we should view that lack as an acceptable limitation in light of feasibility and ethical constraints. Nevertheless, if other rigorous experiments evaluating the same intervention are able to control for placebo effects, then their findings will probably have more value for guiding practice decisions than the findings of experiments that lack controls for placebo effects.

Placebo effects and novelty and disruption effects are not the only forms of research reactivity that can limit the findings of outcome studies. Let's now turn to some other forms or research reactivity, some of which can be so extreme that they destroy the credibility of an otherwise well-designed experiment.

EXPERIMENTAL DEMAND AND EXPERIMENTER EXPECTANCIES

Chapter 4 discussed how the use of random assignment and control groups does not guard against biased measurement procedures. Illustrations of fatal biases were used in which practitioner-researchers with vested interests in getting positive results use their own "judgment" to subjectively rate client outcomes. Even if practitioners don't intend to bias the measurement of outcome, they might tacitly connote in some fashion to clients their hopes for how clients will respond to outcome measures. In an early study of the effectiveness of EMDR, for example, outcome was assessed by the therapist (who invented EMDR) asking her clients to rate their degree of distress on a 10-point scale at the start of treatment and at the end of treatment (Shapiro, 1989). They would do so when thinking of a core traumatic incident. In between, throughout the treatment, and as part of the treatment protocol, she would ask the clients at different points in each treatment session to think of that incident and rate how distressed they were at each point. Even if she said nothing directly to the clients about her expectations, repeatedly asking for the ratings implied those expectations and thus presumably unintentionally pressured clients to report less distress at the end of treatment than at the start.

The previous scenario does not necessarily mean that the clients were pressured to lie about their true perceived level of distress. Their perceived level might really have changed. But that change in perception might have been caused by the **experimental demand** or **experimenter expectancies** and not by the treatment. That is, not lowering their perceived distress may have meant not only disappointing their therapist, but disappointing themselves—perhaps not wanting to feel like "unworthy" clients or that they had wasted their time and had their hopes for a "cure" crushed. The difference between consciously lying about their true perceived level of distress versus actually perceiving less distress represents a difference between measurement bias and research reactivity. With reactivity, the perceptions really do change, but they do so because of the research protocol, not the treatment.

Nevertheless, the distinction between measurement bias and the influence of experimenter expectancies or experimental demand is fuzzy. As an evidenced-based practitioner, the term you use for these flaws is much less important than your ability to detect such flaws in research reports. You should also realize that using control groups does not prevent these flaws, especially if the degree of expectancy and demand for a better outcome is greater in the experimental group than in the control group. Rather than using some logical diagram to determine whether experimenter expectancies or experimental demand represents a minor or fatal flaw, we must use our judgment in examining the details of the reported research and treatment protocol. For example, separating measurement procedures from treatment procedures might alleviate the problem. Thus, had the previous EMDR study not repeatedly had the therapist asking for the same rating throughout the treatment and instead used unbiased and blind research assistants getting the rating just once before and once after treatment, then the impact of experimenter expectancies or experimental demand would have been much less and certainly far from fatal.

OBTRUSIVE VERSUS UNOBTRUSIVE OBSERVATION

Another form of research reactivity—one that overlaps with the concepts of measurement bias and experimenter expectancies—is called **obtrusive observation.** This flaw is most relevant to studies that measure outcome by observing behavior. Observation is obtrusive to the extent that clients are aware that they are being observed and why. Obtrusive observation can influence clients to behave in socially desirable ways that misrepresent their typical behavior patterns. Suppose a school counselor or social worker is treating a client for his disruptive classroom behavior. Suppose she tells him she will drop in on his classes from time to time to observe the progress he is making. That would represent an egregious form of obtrusive observation because we would have no reason to suppose that his behavior while the therapist is in the classroom represents how he behaves when she is not watching.

As an alternative, suppose the therapist monitors progress by examining school records of the student's conduct grades, academic performance, and disciplinary reports. Because the student is behaving under normal conditions, without any therapist or researcher watching him, that alternative would be called **unobtrusive observation.**

Whether observation is obtrusive or unobtrusive is not an all-or-nothing issue. The degree of obtrusiveness is relative. For example, suppose instead of coming to the student's classes to observe him, the therapist asks teachers to complete and submit a brief rating of the student's conduct after each class session (or perhaps at the end of each week). The student knows the teacher is observing him, but that's a far cry from having his therapist show up in the classroom. He may not know that the teacher is completing the rating form after dismissing the class, but even if he does know, it is being done in a way that does not change the classroom routine. The degree to which the student is likely to be influenced by the observation process would be much less than with his therapist present. Thus, some degree of obtrusiveness is not necessarily a fatal flaw. Again, we must use our judgment in deeming whether the *degree* of obtrusiveness egregiously destroys the credibility of the study's findings.

COMPENSATORY EQUALIZATION AND COMPENSATORY RIVALRY

So far we've been emphasizing reactivity flaws that stack the deck in favor of obtaining misleading findings that depict an intervention to be more effective than it really is. Sometimes, however, flaws can bias a study's results in the opposite direction. Two such flaws are **compensatory equalization** and **compensatory rivalry.**

Compensatory equalization occurs when practitioners or clients in treatment-as-usual control groups seek to offset a perceived inequality in service provision by exceeding the routine treatment regimen. Compensatory rivalry occurs when practitioners or clients in a treatment-as-usual control group compete with their counterparts in the experimental group. For example, control group practitioners might seek additional training or may read more in an effort to increase their effectiveness. Or they might spend more time on each case—not for the purpose of offsetting inequality in service provision, but rather to show that they can be just as effective as the experimental group practitioners who may have received special training in the intervention being evaluated. Clients, too, might rival their experimental group counterparts. Annoyed that they did not get assigned to the special treatment, they might become more motivated to work harder to improve.

Although these two flaws are worth noting, they are hard to avoid in real world outcome experiments, and consequently are unlikely to be viewed as unacceptable or fatal. And since they work against obtaining findings that support the effectiveness of the tested intervention, they would not cast doubt on conclusions that an intervention is effective.

RESENTFUL DEMORALIZATION

If clients or practitioners are disappointed about being assigned to routine treatment instead of the special intervention being tested, they might react in a way that is the opposite of compensatory rivalry. Such a reaction, called **resentful demoralization,** would bias the study in favor of obtaining misleading results that support the effectiveness of the tested intervention. Resentful demoralization occurs among clients when their confidence or motivation declines because they were excluded from the special treatment group, and that diminished confidence or motivation might be the real cause of finding poorer outcomes among the control group. Resentful demoralization can also affect treatment-as-usual practitioners. Their enthusiasm, confidence, or efforts might wane because they feel less valued or feel stuck providing a treatment that seems less promising than the one being evaluated.

TREATMENT DIFFUSION

Let's turn now to a type of flaw that, when applicable, will always work in the direction of underestimating an intervention's true degree of effectiveness, no matter how pristine an experiment might be in other respects. That flaw—**treatment diffusion**—occurs when practitioners in the treatment-as-usual control condition happen to learn about and incorporate aspects of the intervention being provided to the experimental group. When that happens, the planned difference in treatment between the two groups will be compromised. The unanticipated similarity in treatment will threaten to yield outcomes between the two groups that are more similar than they should be if the tested intervention truly is more effective than routine treatment without the aspects of the tested intervention.

Although the impact of treatment diffusion can be similar to the impact of compensatory equalization or compensatory rivalry, it is different from those flaws. With treatment diffusion, the control group practitioners are not trying to compete or equalize. Instead, they merely are engaging in their usual treatment, which includes aspects of the tested intervention just by happenstance. Thus, treatment diffusion is most likely to occur with interventions that have already received much attention in the professional literature or other communications. It might also occur when experimental group and control group practitioners work in the same facility and interact with each other.

Suppose, for example, an experiment is conducted to test the effectiveness of exposure therapy for rape victims experiencing posttraumatic stress disorder (PTSD). Suppose that the experimental group practitioners are trained in and instructed to provide a manualized form of exposure therapy as explained in the well-known book by Foa and Rothbaum (1998). Suppose that the control group practitioners are experienced in working with rape victims, take an eclectic treatment approach, and are instructed to provide treatment as usual. Chances are that some or all of the control group practitioners will already have read (or perhaps will soon read as a result of their chats with experimental group practitioners) the Foa and Rothbaum book and have incorporated some (perhaps many) of its exposure therapy techniques in their eclectic armamentarium. If so, their results might more closely resemble the experimental group results than if they had not incorporated those exposure techniques.

As was the case with compensatory equalization and compensatory rivalry, the effects of treatment diffusion work against obtaining findings that support the effectiveness of the tested intervention. Consequently, when you read a report of a study with findings supporting the effectiveness of an intervention, treatment diffusion would be a nonissue. It would be a relevant consideration, however, when a study uses treatment as usual for the control condition and either fails to support the effectiveness of the tested intervention or suggests that its effects are weak. In that case, you should see whether the study's authors identify ways in which they attempted to avoid treatment diffusion or assess its possible occurrence. Did they, for example, take steps to prevent interactions between control group and experimental group practitioners, such as by geographically separating the two treatment conditions? Did they monitor the fidelity of the control condition by interviewing control group practitioners about how they intervene and perhaps by videotaping randomly selected treatment sessions?

TREATMENT FIDELITY

In addition to monitoring the fidelity of the control condition, researchers should monitor whether the tested intervention is being implemented skillfully and as intended. This is known as monitoring **treatment fidelity.** If the tested intervention is provided in an unskillful manner or in a way that deviates significantly from the way it is supposed to be implemented, then findings can underestimate an intervention's true degree of effectiveness.

When you read a report of a study that either fails to support the effectiveness of the tested intervention or suggests that its effects are weak, you should examine whether the authors adequately resolve doubts about treatment fidelity. Were the experimental group's practitioners well trained for the tested intervention and experienced in delivering it? What were their professional credentials? Were they well supervised by experts in the tested intervention? Was there turnover among them? Most importantly, did independent experts in the tested intervention observe (perhaps by videotape) and rate the fidelity of a representative sample of their work? Was more than one rater used, and did their ratings agree? Were the raters external to the study (i.e., not the study authors) and—most importantly—were they unbiased?

To illustrate problematic rater bias, suppose that a study's findings depict an intervention to be ineffective and that experts with vested interests in that intervention who already know that the findings are negative are asked to rate treatment fidelity. Those experts would likely be biased to give poor ratings of treatment fidelity so as to suggest that the findings mean that the intervention was implemented improperly, and thus would have no bearing on the intervention's true value.

PRACTITIONER EQUIVALENCE

Somewhat like the treatment fidelity issue is the question of whether the practitioners providing the different interventions in the groups being compared are really equivalent in factors such as professional education, experience, skillfulness, and other background characteristics (such as gender or ethnicity, and so on). The best random assignment of clients won't prevent bias if the practitioners providing the tested intervention are known to be much more experienced and skillful in general than those providing treatment as usual or some alternative intervention. The same applies if one group has a better match between client and practitioner gender and ethnicity than the other.

The focus here is not on the training and skillfulness of experimental group practitioners in providing the tested intervention. For purposes of treatment fidelity, it's okay for the practitioners providing that intervention to be better trained and skillful in it. Instead, the focus is whether they are more experienced, better trained, and more skillful across areas of practice other than in the tested intervention. If they are, then we wouldn't know if their client outcomes were due to the tested intervention or to practitioner differences. For example, we know that across treatment modalities, therapists who are more empathic and better able to form therapeutic alliances with clients are more likely to be more effective than therapists who are less skillful in those respects.

In some practice settings, it's hard to resolve this issue. For example, if a study is conducted in a small agency, with a small number of practitioners of varying background characteristics, it might not be possible to divide the practitioners into equivalent groups, even if the dividing is done randomly. Other concerns might make dividing the practitioners into two groups inadvisable or infeasible. Doing so, for example, might severely alienate the few practitioners who do not get chosen for the special training. Consequently, the researcher might decide or be required to provide the training to all of the agency's practitioners and then ask them to provide the tested intervention (perhaps in addition to treatment as usual) to their clients who get randomly assigned to the experimental condition, while withholding the tested intervention from their clients who get randomly assigned to the treatment-as-usual, only condition. Taking this route, the researcher avoids the possibility of practitioner inequivalence. However, the same practitioner might be more enthusiastic with those clients who receive the tested intervention than with the other clients. The alternative would be to have different practitioners provide the two treatment conditions, but at the cost of the potential inequivalence and alienation problems mentioned previously.

Either option is undesirable, but there may be no other way to conduct the study in such an agency. In either case, the research report should discuss the issue and provide information helping you decide whether the problem is fatal or not. Unless the difference is blatant and egregious regarding practitioner characteristics or their enthusiasm, then flaws like this probably should be viewed as understandable real-world feasibility limitations that are not fatal. If, however, another study has the same degree of methodological rigor plus the ability to ensure practitioner equivalence, its evidence should be deemed stronger.

DIFFERENTIAL ATTRITION

Let's now examine one more potential problem that can undermine the value of an experiment: the problem of **differential attrition.** Like some of the other problems that we've been considering, this problem cannot be controlled by the logic of experimental design. Also known as *experimental mortality,* the term *attrition* refers to participants dropping out of an experiment before it has been completed.

Attrition can be particularly problematic when a much larger proportion of experimental group participants drop out than do control group participants. That's because of the possibility that many of those dropping out of an experimental treatment do so because they feel they are not benefiting from the intervention or because their willingness or ability to complete the (perhaps demanding) treatment protocol is impeded by their poor functioning or lack of motivation to change.

Suppose, for example, that the intervention being evaluated is a therapeutic community for substance abusers. Therapeutic communities place heavy demands on their residents. Consequently, many of the poorly motivated residents or the most dysfunctional residents have difficulty meeting those demands and graduating from the program. If the dropouts cannot be found at posttest, or if they are excluded from the study because they did not complete the intervention, then only the experimental group clients who were the most functional and motivated to begin with will complete posttests. In contrast, control group participants will not face the same treatment demands and therefore may be less likely to drop out of the study. Thus, a greater proportion of control group clients who were the least functional and motivated to begin with will complete posttests. If so, this differential attrition rate would stack the deck in favor of getting better posttest results from experimental group clients even if the intervention was ineffective.

Some investigators might argue that excluding treatment dropouts from the posttests is justified even when the dropouts are available and willing to complete posttests. Their reasoning is that the effectiveness of the intervention will be underestimated if the outcomes of clients who did not complete the treatment protocol are included in the experimental group results. They might believe that it is unfair to judge the effectiveness of an intervention based on cases that did not receive the entire intervention as intended. Although such reasoning is understandable, it does not resolve the bias resulting from significant differences in attrition between the groups. Moreover, it overlooks the notion that failing to retain clients in treatment can be viewed as the way in which the intervention was ineffective with those clients.

Differential attrition also can be a serious flaw when a much larger proportion of control group participants drop out of an experiment.

Maybe the control group dropouts were the least motivated or most poorly functioning clients from the beginning. If so, that might stack the deck against getting more favorable results from the experimental group even if the intervention is really effective.

Most studies will have at least a small amount of attrition. When the amount of attrition is small, and especially when there is little difference in attrition rates between groups, the degree of attrition should be viewed as an acceptable limitation. Unfortunately, no formula or cutoff point exists that you can use to judge whether the degree of attrition in a study is a fatal flaw that renders the findings unworthy of guiding your practice decision. You'll have to rely on your own judgment for that. As with some of the other flaws discussed in this chapter, the important thing is that you be aware of the significance of the issue of attrition and consider it when you appraise the evidence emanating from an experiment.

Before moving on to the next chapter on critically appraising quasi-experiments, a bit of clarification is in order regarding the notion of whether a flaw is fatal. No matter how pristine an experiment might appear to be in other respects, it takes only one egregious flaw to wreck the credibility of a study's findings and render it unworthy of guiding your practice. The strengths of random assignment and sophisticated logical design arrangements are trumped by egregiously biased measurement, egregiously biased differences in attrition, egregious lapses in treatment fidelity, egregiously obtrusive observation, and so on. You'll need to use your own judgment to decide whether a flaw is egregious and fatal. Hopefully, the examples in this book will enhance your confidence in making that judgment.

I also hope that you'll *not* appraise studies using a summated rating scheme that some who write about EBP propose. In such schemes, a checklist is provided for all methodological issues, and the evidence-based practitioner is advised to rate (perhaps on a scale from 1 to 5) each methodological aspect of a study. Then the practitioner is instructed to sum the ratings to depict the overall quality of the evidence supplied by that study. If you take that approach, a study with one fatal flaw—such as ridiculously obtrusive and biased measurement—could get a very high score if it has no other serious flaws. If you do use such a checklist—perhaps as a reminder of all things to consider—rather than just be influenced by your summed ratings, I advise that you simply determine whether at least one of the methodological aspects is so egregiously flawed that the study's "evidence" is weaker than another study that contains no fatal flaws—even if the latter study's overall summed rating score might be lower. I offer this advice not only for appraising experiments, but also for appraising all of the types of studies discussed in the remaining chapters of this book.

SYNOPSES OF RESEARCH STUDIES

Study 1 Synopsis

A special field placement unit was set up in a child welfare agency for a group of four students in their final year of work toward their master's degree in social work. The aim of the unit was to provide and evaluate the effectiveness of an innovative new intervention (we'll call it Intervention X) designed to promote positive parenting and prevent child neglect and abuse among teen parents who are at high risk for child abuse or neglect.

Each student was able to carry a caseload of five clients, for a total of 20 clients who would receive their intervention. Forty teenage parents were recruited for the study and were randomly assigned: half to the student unit and half to the treatment-as-usual unit. Treatment as usual was provided by the agency's full-time clinical practitioners, who were instructed to provide the same routine treatment regimen that they normally provide to teen parents referred for their services.

In both groups, treatment was to consist of 10 weekly sessions per client. Outcome was measured in two ways. On completion of treatment, the service providers completed the Child Welfare League of America's Family Risk Scale, which consists of a checklist of items that practitioners rate. The sum of the item ratings is thought to depict how well the parents are functioning and the degree of risk for child abuse or neglect. In addition, agency records were analyzed 1 year after completion of treatment to ascertain whether the study participants were referred during the interim for child abuse or neglect.

All of the 20 clients referred for Intervention X completed the 10 sessions of treatment. Fourteen of the control group clients completed the 10 sessions of routine treatment, and 6 dropped out after only one or two sessions. The Family Risk Scale was not completed for the routine treatment dropouts because they were not willing to be assessed. The mean posttest score on the Family Risk Scale for Intervention X was better than the mean for the control group, but the difference was not statistically significant ($p = .08$). Agency records showed that during the year following treatment, 2 (10%) of the 20 Intervention X treatment completers had been referred for child abuse or neglect, as compared to 5 (36%) of the 14 routine treatment completers. Again, however, the difference was not statistically significant ($p = .08$).

Because neither finding was statistically significant, the report of the research, which was published in a prestigious child welfare journal, concluded that Intervention X is not more effective than routine treatment. It therefore recommended that child welfare practitioners should refrain from implementing Intervention X and instead should seek or try to develop interventions that are more effective than Intervention X.

Study 2 Synopsis

This synopsis is inspired by an actual study reported by Brannen and Rubin (1996). It has been modified quite a bit, however, for the purpose of illustrating some of the key concepts in this chapter.

This study was conducted in two unconnected agencies that are located far from each other in a very large city. Both agencies specialize in treating court-referred perpetrators of nonlife-threatening and relatively moderate forms of spouse or partner abuse. Both agencies use a group treatment modality. Agency A treats the perpetrators and victims in separate groups. In Agency B, the victim and perpetrator pairs are treated together in the same groups. The purpose of the study was to see whether one approach has better outcomes than the other regarding future referrals for abuse and a validated self-report measure that victims and perpetrators complete independent of one another as to the recent behavior of the perpetrator.

Each group intervention consisted of 10 weekly sessions. During the course of the study's treatment period, 200 court-ordered cases were randomly assigned with an equal number (100) referred to each agency. Posttests were conducted at the end of the 10 weeks for each group cohort. Court records were examined regarding whether study participants had future referrals for abuse during a 2-year period following the completion of the 10-week treatment for each cohort.

Five cases in each agency dropped out of treatment before completing 10 sessions, and refused to complete the posttest. Although these 10 cases therefore had to be excluded from the pretest-posttest analysis, they were included in the analysis of court records regarding future abuse.

Each of the practitioners providing the intervention in each agency had received advanced trained in its group intervention and had at least 3 years of experience providing it. The average types and amounts of practitioner training and experience in the two agencies were virtually identical. So were other practitioner characteristics. The intervention models in the two agencies were similar, with the exception that one was adapted for treating perpetrators and victims in separate groups and the other was adapted for treating the perpetrator and victim pairs together.

Treatment fidelity was assessed by videotaping two randomly selected group treatment sessions per therapist, and then having the quality of the treatment depicted in each video rated by two national experts in each treatment modality who were blind to the study's results and to the other's ratings. Each pair of raters had a high level of agreement (inter-rater reliability) in their ratings.

The validated self-report measure of perpetrator behavior was administered at pretest and posttest by research assistants who were trained in administering self-report measures and who were blind as to the study's purpose and to the group status of the client. Each group's mean pretest scores were virtually identical, as were their mean posttest scores. Although there was no difference in outcome between the groups, the posttest scores were much better on average than the pretest scores, reflecting the same dramatic and statistically significant degree of improvement in each group. In addition, the scores of the victim and perpetrator pairs correlated highly at both pretest and posttest.

Two years after the completion of the intervention, the number of future referrals for abuse had dropped significantly by the same amount in each group. In light of that finding and in light of the same dramatic improvement in self-report scale scores in each group, the study concludes that both intervention approaches are equally effective.

KEY CHAPTER CONCEPTS

- By definition, all experiments randomly assign participants to treatment conditions; however, they vary according to the number and types of conditions they use and whether pretests are used in addition to posttests.
- In some studies, pretests are not feasible. The lack of a pretest can be a problem when the study sample is quite small because the assumption that random assignment will produce equivalent groups is more dubious than with larger samples. Comparing the pretest scores of the two groups would give some indication as to whether the two groups really do appear to be equivalent.
- The alternative treatment design can compare two treatment groups without using a third control group; however, if both groups improve at the same rate, we can't be certain that the interventions caused the improvement. Without a control group, we cannot rule out history or passage of time as the cause of the improvement in *both* groups.
- Dismantling designs randomly assign clients to various groups that receive different combinations of the components of a multifaceted intervention, to see which components account most for the intervention's effects and which components might not even be needed.
- Research reactivity refers to various ways in which research procedures—as opposed to the tested intervention—can influence the dependent variable and thus confound the results of outcome studies.

(continued)

- Two common forms of research reactivity include *placebo effects*, which occur when the desired improvement in a dependent variable results from client perceptions that they are getting special attention or a special treatment, and *novelty and disruption effects*, which occur when the introduction of an innovative intervention in a setting that is unused to innovation stimulates excitement, energy, and enthusiasm in the setting. These effects are controlled for by using two different control groups: one that receives nothing unusual and one that receives a placebo or some form of novel innovation.
- Although experimental designs rank high on the EBP hierarchy for evaluating intervention effectiveness, any given experiment can have serious and perhaps fatal flaws that are not controlled by random assignment. These include measurement bias, the influence of experimenter expectancies or experimental demand, obtrusive observation, compensatory equalization, and compensatory rivalry, resentful demoralization, treatment diffusion, inadequate treatment fidelity, and lack of equivalence between treatment conditions regarding practitioner characteristics or client attrition.

Review Exercises

1. *Develop a synopsis of an experiment to evaluate the effectiveness of a program, policy, or intervention that piques your interest. Include in it the steps that would be taken to try to minimize the problems of measurement bias; the influence of experimenter expectancies or experimental demand, obtrusive observation, compensatory equalization and compensatory rivalry, resentful demoralization, treatment diffusion, inadequate treatment fidelity; and the lack of equivalence between treatment conditions regarding practitioner characteristics.*

2. *Use the Internet to find two studies that employed experimental designs to evaluate the effectiveness of a program, policy, or intervention. Compare and contrast the two studies regarding their vulnerability to the problems of measurement bias; the influence of experimenter expectancies or experimental demand, obtrusive observation, compensatory equalization and compensatory rivalry, resentful demoralization, treatment diffusion, inadequate treatment fidelity; and the lack of equivalence*

*between treatment conditions regarding practitioner charac-
teristics. Explain your reasoning.*

3. *Suppose you conduct an experiment evaluating the effectiveness of an intervention for people with the comorbid diagnoses
of schizophrenia and substance abuse. Treatment outcome is
measured based on whether they get arrested for substance
abuse or get psychiatrically hospitalized during a specified
time period. Suppose your experimental group has a high rate
of attrition. Of the 50 clients assigned to that group, 10 clients
drop out very early in treatment, 5 drop out in the middle of
treatment, and 5 drop out near the completion of treatment. In
contrast, none of your control group participants drop out of
the study. Answer the following questions:*

   a. *What rationale could be cited be for including the dropouts
in the analysis of outcome data?*

   b. *What rationale could be cited be for excluding the dropouts
from that analysis?*

   c. *What rationale could be cited be for including some of the
dropouts in the analysis and excluding others?*

   d. *Which of the three dropout data analysis options (in a, b,
and c) would you choose? Why?*

ADDITIONAL READINGS

Campbell, D., & Stanley, J. (1963). *Experimental and quasi-experimental designs for
research.* Chicago: Rand McNally.

Cook, T. D., & Campbell, D. T. (1979). *Quasi-experimentation: Design and analysis issues for field settings.* Chicago: Rand McNally.

Shadish, W. R., Cook T. D., & Campbell D. T. (2001). *Experimental and quasi-
experimental designs for generalized causal inference.* New York: Houghton Mifflin.

Chapter 6

CRITICALLY APPRAISING QUASI-EXPERIMENTS: NONEQUIVALENT COMPARISON GROUPS DESIGNS

In the real world of practice, it usually is not feasible to use random procedures to assign clients to different treatment conditions. Administrators might refuse to approve random assignment for several reasons. Practitioners and clients might complain about it. Board members might hear of it and not like or understand it. If some clients are assigned to a no-treatment control group or wait list, they might go elsewhere for service, and this might have undesirable fiscal effects on the agency. Administrators and practitioners alike might view random assignment as unethical, even if it is just to alternate forms of treatment and not to a no-treatment group. Assigning clients to treatment conditions on any basis other than an assessment as to what seems best for the client might be utterly unacceptable.

Fortunately, there are designs for conducting internally valid evaluations of the effectiveness of interventions, programs, and policies without using random assignment. Although these designs are less desirable than using random assignment from an internal validity standpoint, when employed properly, they can be almost as desirable. Such designs are called **quasi-experimental.** Quasi-experimental designs come in two major forms, each of which employs features that attempt to attain a credible degree of internal validity in the absence of random assignment to treatment conditions. One form is called the **nonequivalent comparison groups design.** The other form is *time-series designs.* This chapter focuses on critically appraising nonequivalent comparison groups designs. Chapter 7 focuses on time-series designs. Let's begin by examining the nature and logic of nonequivalent comparison groups designs.

NONEQUIVALENT COMPARISON GROUPS DESIGNS

Nonequivalent comparison groups designs mirror experimental designs, but without the random assignment. That is, different treatment conditions (including perhaps a no-treatment condition) are compared, but the clients are not assigned to each condition randomly. The basis for forming each condition can vary. One option, for example, is to compare two different sites that seem comparable in all key respects except for the type of intervention, program, or policy in place in each. Thus, the morale of residents in a nursing home that provides a particular intervention can be compared to the morale of similar residents in a similar nursing home without that intervention. Or, the degree of change achieved by the first X number of clients who fill the caseload capacity of a new program can be compared to the degree of change of the next X number of clients who are placed on a waiting list until the first cohort has completed treatment. Likewise, each new case could be referred either to an innovative new treatment unit or to a routine treatment-as-usual unit depending on which unit has a caseload opening at the time of referral. The basic diagram for this design is the same as the pretest-posttest control group experiment except that it lacks the R for random assignment. It is as follows:

$$O_1 \quad X \quad O_2$$
$$O_1 \qquad\quad O_2$$

The blank space in the second row of the diagram between O_1 and O_2 represents the withholding of the tested intervention from comparison group clients. You can imagine the symbol *TAU* there for studies in which the comparison group receives treatment as usual instead of no treatment or delayed treatment.

Are the Groups Comparable?

As you may have already surmised, the key issue in judging whether a study using this type of design achieves a credible degree of internal validity is the extent to which its authors provide a persuasive case for assuming that the groups being compared are really comparable. Are they really equivalent? This might strike you as a contradiction in terms. On the one hand, these are called *nonequivalent* comparison groups designs. On the other hand, the groups should be *equivalent*. What gives? Was the person who came up with this design label smoking something unusual?

The reasoning behind this seeming contradiction is as follows: The lack of random assignment weakens the basis for assuming that the groups are equivalent. Therefore, we call them *nonequivalent*. Nevertheless, researchers should try to come up with groups that *seem* to be equivalent, and they should provide evidence supporting the notion that maybe they really are equivalent. But we still use the label *nonequivalent* comparison groups designs, so that we remain vigilant in critically appraising the persuasiveness of the argument and evidence for assuming that they are equivalent, for remembering that random assignment would have been a preferred basis for assuming equivalence, and for viewing their results with an appropriate degree of caution.

Some of the studies you read that use this type of design will compare groups that strike you as not at all equivalent. Some others will compare groups that strike you as perhaps equivalent, but you'll have some nagging doubts. Others still will compare groups that clearly seem to be equivalent, but may not be truly equivalent for reasons that are not apparent. If the study does not provide you with information that persuades you that the groups really do seem to be equivalent and thus really deserve to be compared, then you probably should be very skeptical about their comparability. After all, in light of the importance of this issue, what competent researcher would omit providing information that would make his or her study look more valid and useful? Likewise, what competent journal editors would approve the publication of a study that did not provide such information and did not alert the reader to the serious implications of its absence?

Grounds for Assuming Comparability

Various grounds can be cited in attempting to persuade you that the groups are equivalent. One is to present data comparing the groups on attributes that seem to be potentially relevant to the possibility of a selectivity bias. (Recall from previous chapters that the main role of random assignment is to control for a potential selectivity bias.) For example, are the clients in each group similar in regard to age, gender, ethnicity, socioeconomic status, diagnosis, degree of impairment or well-being, pretest scores, and other such attributes? If different facilities are being compared, are they similar in regard to things like practitioner characteristics, caseload size, and so on? To the extent that a study using this type of design provides comprehensive and persuasive data supporting the comparability of the groups with regard to such attributes, and especially if there is no meaningful difference between the average pretest scores of the groups, then although the risk of a selectivity bias still exists, it probably would not be severe enough to deem the study unworthy of guiding your practice.

In addition to citing the attributes of the groups being compared, authors could argue on logical grounds that the threat of a selectivity bias is unlikely. For example, one type of nonequivalent comparison groups design is called the *overflow design.* In this design, the assignment of each new case depends on which condition has a caseload opening at the time of referral. Suppose a small demonstration project using an innovative service delivery approach is conducted in a larger agency offering routine services. Each new case is referred either to the demonstration project unit or to the routine services depending solely on whether the demonstration project's caseload is full at the time of referral. It seems unlikely to suppose that a selectivity bias might be operating to cause clients referred on October 3, for example, to be different in relevant ways from clients referred on October 10, or to cause clients referred on April 12 to be different than those referred on April 19, and so on.

As mentioned earlier, published studies using nonequivalent comparison groups designs vary in how well they support the comparability of the groups. Some studies provide much more evidence than others supporting the notion of comparability. Some authors offering weak or no evidence in support of comparability nevertheless draw conclusions as if there were no threat of a selectivity bias whatsoever. Sometimes they do this in studies comparing groups that don't seem at all equivalent. Thus, it bears repeating that you should be vigilant in your critical appraisal of the potential for a selectivity bias in studies using nonequivalent comparison groups designs.

ADDITIONAL LOGICAL ARRANGEMENTS TO CONTROL FOR POTENTIAL SELECTIVITY BIASES

Even in studies that cite persuasive evidence and logical grounds for assuming that the threat of a selectivity bias seems to be far-fetched, such a bias is not impossible. Perhaps some critical attribute was overlooked. Perhaps data weren't available to compare the groups on that attribute. Perhaps two groups with comparable pretest scores and comparable background characteristics are not equally motivated to change. Perhaps referral sources in an overflow design study knew when demonstration project caseloads were open or full and let that knowledge influence them to delay referring the most needy cases until there was a caseload opening. Fortunately, Shadish, Cook, and Campbell (2001) have suggested additional logical arrangements that can be employed in nonequivalent comparison groups designs—arrangements that further control for the threat of a selectivity bias. Use of these arrangements can make using a nonequivalent comparison groups design almost as strong as a randomized experiment from an internal validity standpoint. Thus, when you appraise studies using this type of design, you should examine whether any of these features were used. Let's now look at the logic of each such arrangement.

Multiple Pretests

There are various ways in which groups in a nonequivalent comparison groups design can lack comparability. Perhaps the most important way they can differ is when one group is more motivated to change than the other and therefore is already engaged in an ongoing change process before the tested intervention is introduced. Comparing background characteristics and scores on a pretest might not detect such a difference. However, comparing scores on **multiple pretests** can help. If one group is already changing before the intervention begins, then a study that administers the same pretest on multiple occasions to each group before the onset of the intervention can detect that ongoing change process. There is no set number of pretests that should be used, but two or three is probably the most you can expect to find. With three pretests, the diagram for adding multiple pretests to the nonequivalent comparison groups design is as follows:

$$O_1 \quad O_2 \quad O_3 \quad X \quad O_4$$
$$O_1 \quad O_2 \quad O_3 \quad TAU \quad O_4$$

Where:

O_1 is the first pretest,

O_2 is the second pretest,

O_3 is the third pretest,

X is the intervention being evaluated,

TAU is routine treatment as usual (a blank space would signify no treatment), and

O_4 is the posttest.

Suppose two groups of substance abusers are being compared. Suppose further that their scores on a measure of the frequency or severity of substance abuse (the lower the score, the better) are as follows for the previous design:

50	45	40	X	35
50	51	50	TAU	51

Despite the improvement from 50 to 35 in the experimental group, and the lack of improvement in the comparison group, these results do not imply that the evaluated intervention (X) was effective. Instead, they imply that a selectivity bias was operating in which the improvement in the experimental group can be attributed to a change process that was ongoing before the onset of treatment.

In contrast, suppose the results are as follows:

50	49	52	X	35
50	51	50	TAU	51

These results would provide strong evidence that the difference in improvement between the two groups cannot be attributed to a change process that was ongoing before the onset of treatment.

Switching Replications

Another way to improve control for a selectivity bias in a nonequivalent comparisons group design is by providing the tested intervention to the comparison groups after the posttest has been completed and then—following that intervention—by administering a second posttest. Suppose, after the comparison group completes the intervention, its degree of improvement is similar to the degree of improvement initially observed at the first posttest in the experimental group. Such a result would imply that it is the intervention, and not a selectivity bias, that explains the improvement in both groups. If, on the other hand, the experimental group's improvement is not replicated, then the experimental group's improvement can be attributed to a selectivity bias. The diagram for adding the **switching replications** component to the nonequivalent comparison groups design is as follows:

O_1	X	O_2		O_3
O_1	TAU	O_2	X	O_3

Where:

O_1 is the pretest,

O_2 is the first posttest,

O_3 is the second posttest,

X is the intervention, and

TAU is routine treatment as usual.

Suppose a study using this design obtains the following results for an intervention that aims to increase scores on a measure of self-esteem:

30	X	60		60
30	TAU	30	X	60

These results would provide strong evidence that the difference in improvement between the two groups at the first posttest cannot be attributed to a change process that was ongoing before the onset of treatment or some other form of a selectivity bias. That's because the comparison group should not have had a similar improvement at the second posttest (after receiving the intervention) if the reason for the difference at the first posttest was merely the fact that the two groups were dissimilar. In contrast, if the comparison group's second posttest score did not improve like the experimental group improved at the first posttest, as illustrated next, then that result would imply that the first posttest difference probably really was attributable to a selectivity bias:

30	X	60		60
30	TAU	30	X	30

Nonequivalent Dependent Variables

A more problematic way to try to improve the control for a selectivity bias in a nonequivalent comparison groups design is by using a **nonequivalent dependent variable.** A nonequivalent dependent variable has two key features. One is that it represents a possible change that is not targeted by the intervention being evaluated, and that therefore should not change as a result of that intervention. The other feature is that it should be something that is likely to change if the reason for the change in the targeted variable is merely an ongoing change process of self-betterment.

Suppose a study evaluates the effectiveness of an educational intervention that aims to prevent smoking and tobacco chewing among adolescents. Suppose the focus of the intervention is on all the nasty effects of those habits and includes hideous pictures of various forms of lung cancer and gum cancer. Outcome is measured by administering at pretest and posttest a measure of knowledge about the harmful effects of those habits and attitudes about engaging in them. Suppose that an additional measure is administered at pretest and posttest that assesses knowledge about the effects of alcohol abuse and attitudes about drinking. Finally, suppose that no part of the intervention addressed the alcohol issue.

If the adolescents receiving the tested educational intervention were to improve their knowledge and attitudes about problem drinking to roughly the same degree as they improved their attitudes about tobacco, that would suggest that perhaps the targeted improvement came about as part of an ongoing self-improvement change process, and not as a result of the intervention. Because the intervention only targeted tobacco, it should not have had roughly the same impact on alcohol.

In contrast, suppose the knowledge and attitudes about tobacco improved significantly in the experimental group (and not in the comparison group), but the knowledge and attitudes about alcohol had little or no improvement. That set of results would support the notion that the intervention caused the improvement. Again, the reasoning would be that if a selectivity bias—in the form of an ongoing self-betterment process—explained the improvement, then improvement should have been detected in similar areas of self-betterment not specifically targeted by the intervention.

Recall that I referred to the use of nonequivalent dependent variables as a *more problematic* way to try to improve the control for a selectivity bias in a nonequivalent comparison groups design. It is more problematic because an effective intervention with one target can spill over onto other problems not specifically targeted by an intervention. Thus, if both the tobacco and the alcohol measure show roughly the same degree of improvement, perhaps that occurred because the effective tobacco prevention intervention stimulated some teens to read up on their own about other nasty habits that perhaps they should avoid or quit. Consequently, improvement on both measures would not necessarily imply a selectivity bias; it just would fail to rule out such a bias. However, if improvement occurred only on the targeted measure, that would support the effectiveness of the intervention and would make the notion of a selectivity bias less plausible.

Although the inclusion of one or more of these three logical arrangements can significantly strengthen the internal validity of a nonequivalent comparison groups design—by making the threat of a selectivity bias seem far-fetched—you should not assume that the absence of these logical arrangements necessarily wrecks the internal validity and credibility of a study. Although the addition of one or more of these arrangements is highly desirable, it is not always feasible to add them, and some studies can provide a persuasive case as to the comparability of groups without adding these arrangements. The important thing is for you to be vigilant about the issue of the comparability of the groups when you appraise studies using a nonequivalent comparison groups design.

Stressing the need to be more vigilant about the potential for a selectivity bias in a nonequivalent comparison groups design than in a randomized experiment does not mean that such a bias is the only thing about which you need to be vigilant. All of the other threats to the validity of an experiment apply equally to a nonequivalent comparison groups design. Thus, you should additionally be vigilant in appraising the potential for biased measurement, poor treatment fidelity, practitioner inequivalence, different attrition rates, and various forms of reactivity (placebo effects, experimenter expectancies, resentful demoralization, and so on). Although the need to remain vigilant about all of these things might seem a bit overwhelming to you right now, as you appraise more and more studies as part of the evidence-based practice (EBP) process, it will eventually become second nature to look for and spot problems in these areas of concern. As you start engaging in EBP, however, you may want to use the list in Table 6.1 as a guide to remind you of what to look for when appraising studies using a nonequivalent comparison groups design. (You can also use Part II of the list as a reminder of things to look for when appraising randomized experiments.)

Although you should be vigilant about the potential flaws germane to the items listed in Table 6.1, you should not demand that a study be perfect with regard to everything on the list. As discussed earlier in this chapter and in Chapter 5, some items are more important than others. Also, one strong feature—such as using switching replications—can be enough to control for a selectivity bias. It's not necessary to use all of them. Remember, no study—not even a randomized experiment—is flawless. Remember also that you should not merely ask whether a study has more strengths than weaknesses. Instead, the key is to appraise whether any of the weaknesses—even just one—is so egregious that in your judgment it becomes fatal and thus wrecks the credibility of a study that might be strong in other respects. Imperfect studies that lack any fatal flaws can merit guiding your practice—assuming, of course, the absence of stronger studies that fit your idiosyncratic practice situation and client characteristics.

STATISTICAL CONTROLS FOR POTENTIAL SELECTIVITY BIASES

Notice that item I D in Table 6.1 mentions the use of multivariate data analysis procedures to control statistically for possible differences between groups that might explain away differences in outcome. Let's now look at how that works.

Suppose the two groups being compared differ in regard to some background characteristic such as age, ethnicity, socioeconomic status, diagnosis, degree of impairment, or well-being. To assess whether any such variation might explain away differences in outcome, a study can assess

Table 6.1   Guide for Appraising Studies using a Nonequivalent Comparison Groups Design

---

I. Does the study do one or more of the following to alleviate doubt about a selectivity bias and provide a persuasive case for assuming that the groups being compared are really comparable:

   A. Does it present data comparing the groups on client attributes such as age, ethnicity, socioeconomic status, diagnosis, degree of impairment or well-being, pretest scores, and so on?

   B. Does it provide information showing that the facilities being compared are similar in regard to things like practitioner characteristics, caseload size, and so on?

   C. Does it provide logical grounds for deeming the threat of a selectivity bias to be far-fetched, such as by using:

      1. An overflow design?

      2. Multiple pretests?

      3. Switching replications?

      4. A nonequivalent dependent variable?

   D. Does the study use multivariate data analysis procedures to control statistically for possible differences between groups that might explain away differences in outcome?

II. Does the study adequately handle potential problems in the following areas (that are equally applicable to randomized experiments):

   A. Measurement bias and obtrusive observation?

   B. Treatment diffusion?

   C. Treatment fidelity?

   D. Differential attrition?

   E. Practitioner equivalence?

   F. Research reactivity:

      1. Placebo effects?

      2. Compensatory equalization?

      3. Compensatory rivalry?

      4. Resentful demoralization?

   G. Did the study include or exclude people with diagnoses or other characteristics like the client(s) pertaining to your EBP question?

---

differences in outcome separately for each category of the background characteristic.

When the Outcome Variable Is Categorical

For example, suppose you are critically appraising a study that compares the effectiveness of two approaches to dropout prevention. Each approach was provided in a different high school, and the two schools seem to be comparable. However, 60% of the 100 students participating in Program

Table 6.2   Outcome Data for a Fictional Evaluation of Two Dropout Prevention Programs Showing No Difference in Program Effectiveness

Outcome	Number of Males		Number of Females	
	Program A	Program B	Program A	Program B
Graduated	30 (50%)	20 (50%)	40 (100%)	60 (100%)
Dropped out	30 (50%)	20 (50%)	0 (0%)	0 (0%)
Total	60 (100%)	40 (100%)	40 (100%)	60 (100%)

A are male, whereas 60% of the 100 students in Program B are female. The students participating in each program had been deemed to be at high risk of dropping out on entering the program. The study finds that the dropout rate in Program A is 30% as compared to only 20% in Program B.

To control statistically for the possibility that the difference in gender, and not the difference in treatment approach, explains the difference in dropout rates, the study could present the multivariate statistical table illustrated in Table 6.2. In analyzing a table like this, we compare the two programs once for males only and then for females only. Notice how there is no difference in dropout rates for the two programs when we look at the males only. It is 50% for both programs (30 out of 60 for Program A and 20 out of 40 for Program B). Likewise, we find no difference in outcome between the programs when we look at the females only (a 0% dropout rate for both programs). Thus, the original difference in dropout rates of 30% versus 20% is explained away by the fact that only males dropped out and that Program A had a higher percentage of males than Program B.

In contrast, suppose the results had been like those presented in Table 6.3. There we see that the difference in dropout rates between programs holds for each gender. Although the overall 10-point difference in dropout rates (30% versus 20%) is not the same when each gender is compared separately, a difference between programs is still found. That between-program difference is 8 percentage points for each gender, at 33% versus 25% for males and 25% versus 17% for females. Table 6.3

Table 6.3   Outcome Data for a Fictional Evaluation of Two Dropout Prevention Programs Showing that Program B Is More Effective than Program A

Outcome	Number of Males		Number of Females	
	Program A	Program B	Program A	Program B
Graduated	40 (67%)	30 (75%)	30 (75%)	50 (83%)
Dropped out	20 (33%)	10 (25%)	10 (25%)	10 (17%)
Total	60 (100%)	40 (100%)	40 (100%)	60 (100%)

would show that the difference between the two programs regarding gender does not explain away the difference in outcome. This conclusion is based on the percentages, not just the raw numbers. The fact that an equal number of females (10) dropped out in each program is not relevant because, in Program A, that raw number comprised 25% of the 40 females in that program, whereas the 10 female dropouts in Program B comprised 17% of the 60 females in that program.

Notice in Table 6.3 that although there is a difference of 8 percentage points between Program A and Program B for each gender category, the data correspond to an overall difference of 10 percentage points when gender is eliminated from the comparison. Thus, combining the males and females for Program A would yield 30 (30%) dropouts out of the 100 cases in that program, and doing the same for Program B would yield 20 (20%) of the 100 cases in that program. The point differential changes when gender is controlled because males have a higher dropout rate than females in the data and there is a higher proportion of males in Program A (60%) than in Program B (40%).

Most studies that use multivariate statistical controls report their multivariate findings in more statistically advanced ways than illustrated in Tables 6.2 and 6.3. However, no matter how sophisticated their statistical procedure is—even if you never heard of it and have no idea what it means—it is likely to be based on the same reasoning displayed in these two tables. That is, it likely uses a statistically complex way of comparing outcome when various categories of other variables are held constant. (Holding another variable constant means analyzing the relationship between two variables separately for different categories of the other variable, as was done in Tables 6.2 and 6.3, which analyzed the relationship between type of program and dropout rate separately for males and for females. Thus, gender was held constant.) Many studies control for many other variables. For example, in addition to controlling for gender, they might simultaneously control for ethnicity, age, diagnosis, and other variables. Although you might not be able to interpret the complex statistics yourself, the study should translate what it means in terms of whether there are outcome differences between treatment conditions after other characteristics are controlled.

When the Outcome Variable Is Quantitative

When studies do report multivariate tables of findings that you can interpret, the tables often compare means instead of the head counts (frequencies) that are displayed in Tables 6.2 and 6.3. The type of data displayed depends on the measurement level of the outcome variable. For example, if the outcome data are categorical in the form of yes or no regarding things like dropout, re-arrest, relapse, and so on, then they can only be displayed in terms of proportions. On one hand, if the outcome variable is whether a parent gets referred again for child neglect or abuse, the parent does not get an average (mean) child abuse score. It's either yes or no, and therefore the data are displayed as proportions. On the other hand, suppose the outcome variable is quantitative—like the family's summed score on a scale containing many items measuring family risk of child neglect or abuse. In that case, the outcomes between groups can be displayed in terms of differences in average (mean) scores of each group.

Suppose, for example, an innovative program to prevent child neglect or abuse is compared to a routine program in terms of scores on a Family Risk Scale. Suppose further that a greater proportion of substance-abusing clients are in the innovative program. Let's say that the proportion is 50%, as compared to only 20% in the routine program. In other words, the selectivity bias might be working against the innovative program, assuming that substance-abusing parents are at greater risk of child neglect or abuse than other parents. Let's also suppose that the mean outcome scores of both the innovative and routine programs are the same, at 30, with higher scores indicating a greater risk of child maltreatment. Finally, let's suppose that the mean outcome score for the substance-abusing parents is 60, whereas the mean for the other parents is only 14. Table 6.4 shows how, by controlling for whether parents are substance abusers, we could find that the innovative program actually is more effective than the routine program, despite its having the same mean outcome scores overall before controlling for substance abuse.

You may be wondering how these numbers all correspond. If you multiply the number of cases in the first cell by that cell's mean score, and then add that to the multiplicand in the adjacent cell, and then divide by the total number of cases for that row or column, you'll get the mean that appears in the Total cell for that row or column. Looking at the first row, for example, 50 times 50 equals 2,500, and 10 times 50 equals 500. Thus, the total for the row is 3,000, and when we divide that by the total number of cases in that row (100), we get a row mean of 30.

Table 6.4   Mean Outcome Scores on a Family Risk Scale for a Fictional Evaluation, Controlling for Parental Substance Abuse

Type of Program	Substance Abuse Mean Score (n)	No Substance Abuse Mean Score (n)	Total Mean Score (n)
Innovative	50 (50)	10 (50)	30 (100)
Routine	85 (20)	16 (80)	30 (100)
Total	60 (70)	14 (130)	30 (200)

Note: n signifies number of cases per cell.

Table 6.5   Mean Pretest and Posttest Scores on a Family Risk Scale for a Fictional Evaluation

Type of Program	Mean Score	
	Pretest	Posttest
Innovative	40	10
Routine	50	20

The essence of Table 6.4 is that because the substance abusers had worse outcome scores and were more numerous in the innovative program, the innovative program's overall mean (30) was the same as the overall mean for the routine program, despite the fact that the innovative program's mean scores were better than the means for the routine program when we compare those program means separately for substance-abusing parents and nonsubstance-abusing parents. Thus, Table 6.4 shows how controlling for another variable can show an innovative program to be more effective than a routine program even if there was no difference in outcome between the programs when that additional variable was not controlled.

When a study has both pretest and posttest scores, it should not just compare the posttest scores. Instead, it should examine the difference in improvement between the two groups from pretest to posttest. Table 6.5 illustrates this point. Notice that although the innovative program's mean posttest score is lower (better) than the routine program's mean, so was its pretest mean. Both groups improved by 30 points. Thus, despite its better posttest score, the innovative program does not show any more improvement than does the routine program. Most studies that examine pretest to posttest improvement will use a statistical procedure that controls for pretest scores when comparing posttest scores and then will report whether the difference between the programs or interventions in the degree of improvement is statistically significant. The studies also should address the magnitude of the difference and whether that magnitude is meaningful and important from a clinical or societal standpoint.

PILOT STUDIES

In your search for evidence, you are likely to encounter quite a few studies with weak designs. Some of them will imply that their findings are more conclusive than they really are. Others will carefully alert the reader as to how limited and tentative their findings are. When viewed with appropriate caution, the findings of some studies with weak designs can have significant value.

Suppose, for example, that you develop a new way to treat a target population of sex offenders for whom there are no known effective treatments and for whom the recidivism rate is known to be very high. Suppose the reality of your practice context and your lack of resources makes it impossible to include any kind of control or comparison group in your study. Nevertheless, you decide to examine descriptively and on a pilot basis the recidivism rate of the offenders treated with your new intervention 5 years after each is discharged. If it turns out to be about the same as the known recidivism rate for the target population, you'll have little grounds for optimism about the effectiveness of your intervention. Conversely, if it turns out to be dramatically lower than the known recidivism rate for the target population, you'll be encouraged about its possible effectiveness.

In either outcome, you would not be able to make a causal inference. If there is little or no difference in recidivism rates, perhaps that's because somehow the offenders who received your intervention were much more difficult cases than most offenders. If your recidivism rate is dramatically lower, perhaps that's because somehow the offenders who received your intervention were much more motivated to rehabilitate themselves than most offenders. Nevertheless, a dramatically lower rate will provide you or others with a basis for seeking the resources for conducting a well-controlled evaluation of your intervention. Thus, your study would have significant value in stimulating further investigation of an intervention that might be shown to be very effective. Moreover, if someone treating this population reads your study, even with all of its limitations, they would have grounds to test out your intervention in their setting in light of the dearth of any evidence supporting the effectiveness of any alternative intervention.

Given that you conducted your study fully aware of its limitations and because you just needed to break the ice and get some preliminary data to guide decisions about whether your intervention merits further study, it would be appropriate to call your investigation a *pilot study.* Another common occasion for conducting a pilot study is when researchers plan to obtain the resources for a more tightly controlled investigation, but first want to try their research in a less controlled and preliminary manner with a small sample just to detect unanticipated pitfalls in implementing their investigation so they can debug those kinks for their larger study.

Some pilot studies use quasi-experimental designs highly vulnerable to selectivity biases or other flaws—problems that they intend to correct when they obtain the wherewithal to conduct their larger, better controlled study. Despite their utility on a pilot basis, authors of these studies should not interpret their findings as if they provide a basis for causal inferences about the effectiveness of the interventions, programs, or policies that they evaluate. You should be vigilant in spotting the inappropriateness of such interpretations when you read reports of such limited studies.

Other pilot studies use no comparison group and just assess outcome for the one group that receives the intervention. These studies, too, sometimes are reported with interpretations of findings that are worded as if they provide more support for causal inferences than their designs warrant. For example, if they find significant improvement from pretest to posttest, they might conclude that the findings provide a tentative basis for deeming the tested intervention to be evidenced based. Tentative indeed! Too tentative! Instead, they should just interpret their tentative findings as encouraging and as providing a basis for conducting more well-controlled outcome studies in the future. Calling their study a *pilot study* might justify having conducted it despite its limitations, but it does not give them license to interpret their findings as if their design were stronger. You should be vigilant about such misleading claims.

Being vigilant, however, does not imply dismissing the potential value of pilot studies. If you cannot find better evidence supporting some other intervention (or some other policy or program) for your practice question, then the evidence from a pilot study might provide grounds for testing out its intervention in your setting. On the other hand, if you can find stronger evidence (from a more well-controlled study) supporting some other intervention, and if that evidence appears to be equally applicable to your practice context, then that other intervention could become your Plan A. The intervention supported by the pilot study could be your Plan B, to be tested out in case the desired outcome is not attained after you implement Plan A.

One more thing to be vigilant about is the misuse of the term *quasi-experiment*. Authors of some published reports call their studies *quasi-experimental* even when the study did not include a nonequivalent comparison groups or a time-series design. (The next chapter discusses the latter type of design.) Because the main distinction between an experiment and a quasi-experiment is whether random assignment is used, some authors apparently think that *any* study not using random assignment qualifies as a quasi-experiment, even if it just involved one group or was merely correlational in nature. Consequently, if you read a study deemed quasi-experimental by its authors, do not assume that it deserves the stature of a real quasi-experiment on the EBP evidentiary hierarchy. Read it carefully, using your critical thinking perspective, and make that judgment for yourself. And remember, even if it really is quasi-experimental (or even experimental for that matter), it might still contain a fatal flaw. Nevertheless, if despite its limitations it provides the best evidence you can find that is applicable to your practice context, you might still want to consider implementing it and (in the final EBP phase) monitoring whether a desired level of progress follows its implementation.

SYNOPSES OF RESEARCH STUDIES

Study 1 Synopsis

Conventional wisdom assumes that substance abuse programs that strive to be culturally competent are more effective in treating minority populations than substance abuse programs that make no special efforts to be culturally competent. However, that assumption has never been empirically tested. This study tested that notion by comparing two substance-abuse treatment programs for teens. The programs are both located in Los Angeles, California. Both programs have the same staff-client ratios, offer the same services, have staff members with comparable educational degrees, and have caseloads that are comparable regarding age, gender, and ethnicity. More than 95% of the clients in each program are Mexican American. (Assume tables of data support claims of comparability on these variables.)

What distinguishes the two programs is that Program A requires all of its staff members to be Mexican American, bilingual, and trained in culturally competent practice with Mexican Americans. Program B has some (not all) staff members who share one or more of these attributes, but does not require them.

All of the 500 clients entering each program during a 1-year period were included in the study, for a total sample size of 1,000. Outcome was assessed by comparing the arrest rates of the two groups of clients over the 3 years after each client entered treatment. For Program A, only 10% of the clients were arrested, as compared to 16% for Program B. This difference was extremely significant ($p < .01$). This finding supports the notion that substance-abuse programs for Mexican American teens are much more effective when they make special efforts to be culturally competent.

Study 2 Synopsis

This study evaluated the effectiveness of a continuing education workshop that trained experienced social work practitioners in the EBP process and aimed to improve their attitudes about EBP and the extent to which they appropriately engaged in EBP in their actual practice. It was not possible to randomly assign practitioners who signed up for the workshop to different treatment conditions. Therefore, a nonequivalent comparison groups design was employed.

The workshop was provided in two Texas cities: in Dallas in early February 2007 and in Houston in late March 2007. Twenty licensed social workers enrolled in the workshop in each city, for a total sample size of

40. The Houston cohort signed up well in advance—at the same time as the Dallas cohort, so that they could be pretested at the same time the Dallas cohort was pretested.

A self-report scale was constructed to measure the participants' attitudes about every aspect of the EBP process and their perceptions as to how likely they were to engage in those aspects. Higher scale scores signified a more favorable attitude about EBP and a greater propensity to engage in it. Scores could range from 0 to 100. The scale was mailed to all of the Dallas and Houston participants 3 weeks before the Dallas workshop took place, and received from all 40 of them before the Dallas workshop took place.

Two weeks after the conclusion of the Dallas workshop, the scale was mailed to all 40 Dallas and Houston participants as the first posttest. All 20 Houston participants completed and returned the scale, and 18 of the 20 Dallas participants did so. Three follow-up mailings and two follow-up telephone calls to the two Dallas nonrespondents were unsuccessful in obtaining the posttests from them.

Two weeks after the conclusion of the Houston workshop, the scale was again mailed to all 40 Dallas and Houston participants as the second posttest. Eighteen of the 20 Houston participants completed and returned the scale, and the same 18 of the 20 Dallas participants who completed the first posttest did so. Again, three follow-up mailings and two follow-up telephone calls to the two Houston nonrespondents were unsuccessful in obtaining the posttests from them.

The study results displayed in Table 6.6 show that the workshop was effective. The mean score at pretest was higher for the Dallas cohort than for the Houston cohort, but at the first posttest the difference between the two cohorts was significantly greater than at the pretest ($p < .05$). The effectiveness of the workshop was further supported by a significant increase ($p < .05$) in the Houston cohort's mean score on the second posttest. That is, the Houston cohort improved after it received the workshop (on the second posttest) by approximately the same degree as the Dallas cohort had improved at the first posttest.

Table 6.6 Participants' Mean Pretest and Posttest Scores before and after Receiving Workshop Training

Cohort	Pretest Mean	Action	Posttest 1 Mean	Action	Posttest 2 Mean
Dallas	20	Workshop	93	Nothing	72
Houston	15	Nothing	15	Workshop	91

KEY CHAPTER CONCEPTS

- Quasi-experimental designs attempt to attain a credible degree of internal validity in the absence of random assignment to treatment conditions.
- Nonequivalent comparison groups designs mirror experimental designs, but without the random assignment. The key issue in judging whether a study using this type of design achieves a credible degree of internal validity is the extent to which its authors provide a persuasive case for assuming that the groups being compared are really comparable.
- One type of nonequivalent comparison groups design is called the *overflow design.* In this design, by assigning each new case based on which treatment condition has a caseload opening at the time of referral, the plausibility of a selectivity bias is reduced.
- The plausibility of a selectivity bias can be further reduced by employing design features such as multiple pretests, switching replications, and nonequivalent dependent variables.
- Multivariate data analysis procedures can control statistically for possible differences between groups that might explain away differences in outcome.
- Pilot studies with serious design limitations can have utility, but they need to be read and interpreted cautiously. Some authors of pilot studies imply that their findings are more conclusive than they really are.
- Some studies deemed quasi-experimental by their authors are not really quasi-experimental. Do not automatically assume that they deserve the stature of a real quasi-experiment on the EBP evidentiary hierarchy. Read them carefully, using your critical thinking perspective and make that judgment for yourself. And remember, even if a study is quasi-experimental (or even experimental for that matter), it might still contain a fatal flaw.

Review Exercises

1. *Write a synopsis (like the ones in this book) of a study that you create that uses a nonequivalent comparison groups design for evaluating the effectiveness of an intervention in which you are interested. Include in it features that would assure readers that the threat of a selectivity bias seems far-fetched.*

2. *Use the Internet to find two studies that employed nonequivalent comparison groups designs to evaluate the effectiveness of a program, policy, or intervention: one in which a selectivity bias seems far-fetched, and one in which the threat of such a bias is egregious, perhaps representing a fatal flaw. Explain your reasoning.*

ADDITIONAL READINGS

Cook, T. D., & Campbell, D. T. (1979). *Quasi-experimentation: Design and analysis issues for field settings.* Chicago: Rand McNally.

Shadish, W. R., Cook, T. D., & Campbell, D. T. (2001). *Experimental and quasi-experimental designs for generalized causal inference.* New York: Houghton Mifflin.

Chapter 7 ———————————————————

CRITICALLY APPRAISING QUASI-EXPERIMENTS: TIME-SERIES DESIGNS AND SINGLE-CASE DESIGNS

Chapter 6 mentioned that quasi-experimental designs come in two major forms. In this chapter, we examine the second form: *time-series designs.* The key feature of time-series designs is their use of multiple data points before as well as after a new intervention, program, or policy is introduced. The multiple data points might be in the form of pretests and posttests, or they might in the form of observations or data from available records. Using available records, for example, a state might evaluate the impact of a speed limit change by graphing the number of highway traffic fatalities in the state for each year before the change and each year after the change. By graphing a sufficient number of data points both before and after a new intervention, program, or policy is introduced, time-series designs can offer a reasonable degree of internal validity without requiring a control or comparison group.

Time-series designs are most commonly used when it is not feasible to obtain a comparison group. When no comparison group is included, they are called **simple time-series designs.** Some time-series studies attempt to strengthen their internal validity by including both an experimental and comparison group in their time-series analyses, and thus are called **multiple time-series designs.** Some studies apply the logic of time-series designs to a single case, such as an individual client. Although they apply time-series logic, and thus represent a variant of time-series designs, their designs typically are called *single-case, single system,* or *single-subject designs.* To simplify things, I refer to them as **single-case designs.** Most evidence-based practice (EBP) research hierarchies list single-case designs below quasi-experiments because, by being limited to a single-case, they have less external validity. Nevertheless I cover them in this chapter because they really are time-series designs with less external validity. Let's begin by examining the logic of simple time-series designs.

SIMPLE TIME-SERIES DESIGNS

As mentioned, simple time-series designs supplant the need for a control or comparison group by graphing multiple data points both before and after a new intervention, program, or policy is introduced. Recall the discussion in Chapter 6 of the use of multiple pretests to control for the possibility that one group might already be engaged in a change process before a new intervention is introduced. Simple (as well as multiple) time-series designs extend that logic to control for maturation (or the passage of time) and statistical regression to the mean. By graphing a sufficient number of data points both before and after a new intervention, program, or policy is introduced, time-series designs control for maturation (passage of time) by showing whether the pattern of improvement over time after the change simply is an extension of an improving trend that predated the change. Likewise, the use of multiple data points shows whether any particular data points appear to be aberrant blips. Thus, time-series designs can depict whether improvement from an atypically bad data point appears to be a function of regression to the mean. Moreover, as we'll see shortly, with enough data points, these designs can also reduce the plausibility of history as a threat to internal validity. (Recall the discussion in Chapter 4 of these threats to internal validity.)

To illustrate the logic of simple time-series designs, let's begin by examining their notation, as follows:

$$O_1 \quad O_2 \quad O_3 \quad O_4 \quad O_5 \quad X \quad O_6 \quad O_7 \quad O_8 \quad O_9 \quad O_{10}$$

Each O in the notation represents a different data point. The X represents the change in the policy, program, or intervention. Although this notation includes five data points before the intervention is introduced and five after the intervention is introduced, no set number of data points is required for this design. But saying that there is no set number does not mean that anything goes. The more data points included in a time-series study, the more control it has for the three threats to internal validity mentioned previously: passage of time (maturation), regression to the mean, and (to a lesser extent) history.

Suppose, for example, that a state's child welfare policy changed in the year 2000 to an emphasis on family preservation. That change would have meant putting a greater emphasis on working more intensively with referred families to prevent future neglect or abuse in an effort to avoid having to remove the child from the home and thus to keep children living with their biological parents and siblings. In the past, the policy put more emphasis on removing children for out-of-home placements to protect them. Suppose further that in the year before the policy change the state had a total of 1,000 children removed for out-of-home placements and that in the year of the policy change that number dropped to 900.

Although the 2-year data show a 10% drop from 1999 to 2000, they offer no control for threats to internal validity. Perhaps the number had been dropping by about the same rate for quite a few years before 1999 (passage of time). Perhaps 1999 was an atypically bad year for child abuse, and the years that preceded it all hovered near the 900 figure that occurred in 2000 (regression to the mean). Similarly, perhaps 2000 was simply an atypically good year, and in the years that followed 2000 it went back up to around 1,000 out-of-home placements (regression to the mean following the change). Perhaps the number of out-of-home placements fluctuated from year to year before and after the change, depending on whether the news media in a given year reported tragic deaths from child abuse and thus put more pressure on the child welfare agency to remove children from the home under conditions of even the slightest doubt about whether to do so (history).

Now let's look at the following four alternative data patterns for simple time-series designs for the previous scenario (Table 7.1), this time using 5 years of (fictional) data before and after the state's child welfare policy change.

Table 7.1   Four Alternative Data Patterns for Simple Time-Series Designs

Pattern	1995	1996	1997	1998	1999		2000	2001	2002	2003	2004
A	1400	1300	1200	1100	1000	X	900	850	800	750	700
B	900	890	910	900	1000	X	900	910	890	905	900
C	900	1100	910	890	1000	X	900	890	910	1100	960
D	1000	1010	995	1020	1000	X	900	850	800	750	700

Which of the four data patterns strikes you as offering the most plausible evidence that the policy change made a difference? If you answer Pattern D, you win the prize. Why is that?

To begin, Pattern A merely suggests passage of time as the explanation for the decreases after the policy change because similar (and somewhat greater) decreases were occurring consistently every year preceding the policy change. Pattern B merely depicts regression to the mean as the most plausible explanation for the decrease in the year 2000 because 1999 was an atypically high year, and the years preceding it were just like the years after 1999. Pattern C suggests history as the most plausible explanation for the decrease in 2000 because we see several years where the numbers shift up or down both before and after the policy change, with no apparent pattern. The absence of a pattern seems consistent with the notion that extraneous events might cause the number to rise in some years and fall in others. The drop from 1,000 in 1999 to 900 in 2000 thus seems to be attributable to history because we see a similar drop between 1996 and 1997 and between 2003 and 2004, not to mention the fact that the drop in 2000 was not sustained and in fact reversed in 2003.

Pattern D, however, shows no diminishing trend before the policy change, and then a consistent diminishing trend every year after the change. The data points before the policy change is implemented comprise the **baseline** phase. The data points after the policy change is implemented comprise the **intervention** phase. It's important that Pattern D has more than just a couple of data points per phase. With fewer data points, it's harder (perhaps impossible) to detect improving baseline trends, statistical regression, or various up and down years in baseline and intervention phases that seem to be suggesting the influence of extraneous events.

With enough data points, Pattern D offers plausible evidence supporting the notion that the policy change was effective in diminishing out-of-home placements. Nevertheless, the simple time-series design's control for history is limited. Perhaps the economy improved significantly in 2000 and kept on improving through 2004. Maybe that had an impact on the stress levels in many high-risk families, which in turn contributed to sustained decreases in child abuse and neglect from 2000 on. Perhaps some other change occurred in 2000, and we don't realize that it had a sustained impact on incidents of child abuse and neglect. For example, maybe a national news story exposed some false reporting of abuse in a preschool that ruined the careers (and perhaps lives) of those falsely accused, and as more and more people learned of the story, they became more reluctant to report suspected abuse to the authorities. Therefore, we cannot rule history out entirely just because the change in the data pattern coincides with the policy change. That's why some time-series studies bolster their control for history by adding a comparison group. Adding the comparison group makes them *multiple time-series designs*.

MULTIPLE TIME-SERIES DESIGNS

Multiple time-series designs combine time-series logic with the logic of the nonequivalent comparison groups design. The shorthand notation for this design is:

$$O_1 \quad O_2 \quad O_3 \quad O_4 \quad O_5 \quad X \quad O_6 \quad O_7 \quad O_8 \quad O_9 \quad O_{10}$$
$$O_1 \quad O_2 \quad O_3 \quad O_4 \quad O_5 \quad \quad O_6 \quad O_7 \quad O_8 \quad O_9 \quad O_{10}$$

Again, each O in the notation represents a different data point. The X represents the change in the policy, program, or intervention. The blank represents no change in the policy, program, or intervention. Thus, both an experimental group and a nonequivalent comparison group are measured at multiple points in time before and after the experimental group experiences a change in policy, program, or intervention.

To illustrate how adding the comparison group improves control for history, let's reexamine the fictional data from Pattern D, but this time Table 7.2 compares it to the data points for a comparison group over the same baseline and intervention years.

Notice how this comparison makes history seem a lot less plausible than in the simple time-series design's data pattern. In Table 7.2, two adjacent and similar states, known for their relatively liberal social policies, have very different data patterns. Wisconsin, which changes its policy in 2000, immediately experiences a continuing reduction in out-of-home placements from the start of its intervention phase onward. Minnesota, which does not change its policy (which we'll assume was the same as the Wisconsin baseline policy), experiences no change in its data pattern during those same years. To suppose that history explains the difference, we would have to imagine some extraneous event that affects child abuse and neglect rates occurring in 2000 in Wisconsin and *not* in Minnesota (such as Wisconsin's economy strengthening and Minnesota's remaining unchanged).

Again, however, we have further reduced the plausibility of history but not eliminated it entirely. We might still have some nagging doubt, albeit perhaps slight, that despite the similarity of these two adjacent states, some relevant extraneous event might have occurred in one state and not in the other. What design feature could be added to make history so far-

Table 7.2   Data Points for a Comparison Group over the Same Baseline and Intervention Years

State	1995	1996	1997	1998	1999		2000	2001	2002	2003	2004
Wisconsin	1000	1010	995	1020	1000	X	900	850	800	750	700
Minnesota	1005	1015	1000	1030	1010		1015	1050	1020	1025	1030

fetched as a rival explanation that it would be safe to rule out its plausibility entirely? If you reexamine the outline at the start of Chapter 6, you'll probably come up with the answer (if you haven't figured it out already.)

The answer is to add a switching replication to the design. Suppose in 2005 Minnesota changes its policy, making the same change that Wisconsin did in 2000. Let's consider two possible outcomes. First, what if after making the change, Minnesota's intervention phase data from 2005 through 2009 show no improvement from its data from 1996 through 2004. That would support the notion that the improvement in Wisconsin really might have been due to history because, if its new policy explained the improvement, it stands to reason that it should have had a similar impact in Minnesota when that state adopted the same new policy.

What if after making the change, Minnesota's intervention phase data from 2005 through 2009 showed the same pattern of sustained improvement as was found in Wisconsin after its policy change? That would support the notion that the improvement in Wisconsin really was caused by the policy change. Why should Minnesota's child abuse data change after adopting the same policy if the earlier difference between the two states' data patterns was a function of the lack of comparability between the two states?

"Wait a minute!" you might exclaim. "Maybe Minnesota's economy began a sustained improvement in 2005, just like Wisconsin's did in 2000!" Yes, *maybe*. But it seems very improbable to suppose that over a 15-year period, Minnesota's economy started improving only when the Wisconsin policy was adopted and that Wisconsin's economy started improving only after it adopted the same policy 5 years earlier. Not impossible, but far-fetched.

But, hey, maybe you are hard to impress. Well, that's where replication comes into play. Recall that in Chapter 3 we saw that systematic reviews and meta-analyses reside above experiments and quasi-experiments on the evidentiary hierarchy for answering questions about the effectiveness of programs, policies, or interventions. If various studies evaluate the effectiveness of the (fictional) Wisconsin policy change as implemented in other states, and if those studies consistently come up with roughly the same results as in our Wisconsin/Minnesota study, we have significantly more evidence for deeming that policy to be effective. The next chapter is devoted to systematic reviews and meta-analyses. But before we go there, we need to examine another time-series designs category: single-case designs.

SINGLE-CASE DESIGNS

As I mentioned at the outset of this chapter, single-case designs apply the logic of time-series designs to a single case. That single case might be an individual client, a family, or a larger grouping. Recognizing that these designs can be applied to large groups, such as an entire program or organization, some prefer the term *single-system* designs. Disagreeing about the label, however, has always struck me as rather silly. After all, the entire program or system can pertain to a state and its new policy, in which case the broader term, *time-series design,* would apply. Regardless of what we call them, there are four major types of single-case designs: AB designs, ABAB designs, multiple baseline designs, and multiple component designs. Let's look at the logic of each of them, starting with the simplest: AB designs.

AB Designs

The **AB design** is merely a simple time-series design applied to a single case. The A refers to the baseline phase, and the B refers to the intervention phase. Using the same logic as in the simple time-series design, if a shift in the data pattern dramatically coincides with the introduction of the intervention in the B phase, then the plausibility of maturation (or passage of time), regression to the mean, and (to a lesser extent) history is reduced as rival explanations for the improvement.

If you read a study reporting the use of an AB design, its results typically will be in the form of a graph, such as the one in Figure 7.1. The graphed data pattern is considered to be *visually significant* when the results support the inference that the intervention, and not some threat to internal validity (maturation, passage of time, etc.), caused the improvement in the B phase. **Visual significance** means that you can rule out the plausibility of rival explanations (threats to internal validity) for the improvement merely by *eyeballing* the graph, as is the case in Figure 7.1.

For a graph of AB design results that lack visual significance, examine Figure 7.2. Notice how the improvement in that graph's B phase merely

Figure 7.1   A Visually Significant Data Pattern for an Intervention Seeking to Reduce a Client's Undesirable Behaviors

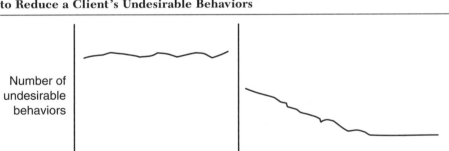

**Figure 7.2   A Data Pattern That Lacks Visual Significance for an
Intervention Seeking to Reduce a Client's Undesirable Behaviors**

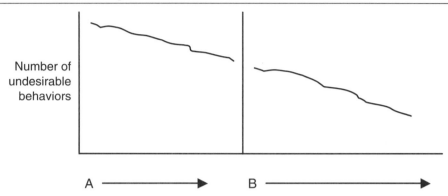

continues the A phase's improving trend, thus suggesting that passage of
time (or maturation) is a much more plausible explanation for the improvement than is the intervention.

ABAB Designs

To improve the control for history in single-case designs, additional baseline and intervention phases can be added. The logic is to see whether the
data pattern consistently shifts in ways that coincide with the introduction and withdrawal of the intervention. If a visually significant AB pattern can be replicated at different times, then the plausibility of history
as a rival explanation becomes improbable. One way to add more phases is
to use an **ABAB design,** which also can be called a *withdrawal/reversal
design.* Using this design, after an improving trend in the first B phase,
the intervention is temporarily withdrawn at a point when the practitioner deems it clinically sound and ethical to do so. That withdrawal
phase can be very short (for clinical and ethical reasons), and it is followed
by a second B phase, when the intervention is reintroduced. The results
are deemed visually significant when the graph shows that improvement
occurs in each B phase, but not in the A phases. It makes no sense to suppose that extraneous events (history) repeatedly occur at different times
to cause changes in outcome only when the intervention is introduced.

Figure 7.3 illustrates an ABAB graph with visually significant results.
In contrast, the data pattern in Figure 7.4 lacks visual significance. That's
because the change in the first A to B shift did not get replicated in the
second A to B shift. Data patterns like the one in Figure 7.4 are deemed
inconclusive. On the one hand, history is a plausible rival explanation
for the first A to B improvement because the failure to replicate that

Figure 7.3   A Visually Significant Data Pattern for an Intervention Seeking to Reduce a Client's Undesirable Behaviors, Using an ABAB Design

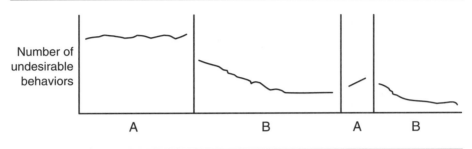

improvement fails to make history more far-fetched as a rival explanation for the original improvement. On the other hand, perhaps the intervention had long-lasting or irreversible effects that persisted regardless of whether the intervention was withdrawn or reintroduced. The latter possibility would be desirable from a clinical standpoint, but more studies would be needed to determine if it's the more plausible explanation. If the data pattern in Figure 7.4 were to be replicated with additional clients at other points in time, we could infer that the intervention is effective. That's because it is improbable to suppose that across different clients, at different points in time, extraneous events affect the target problem only when the first B phase commences.

Multiple Baseline Designs

An alternative way to see if an AB data pattern replicates is to use a multiple baseline design. Instead of withdrawing and reintroducing the intervention, multiple baseline designs introduce the intervention to different

Figure 7.4   An Inconclusive Data Pattern for an Intervention Seeking to Reduce a Client's Undesirable Behaviors, Using an ABAB Design

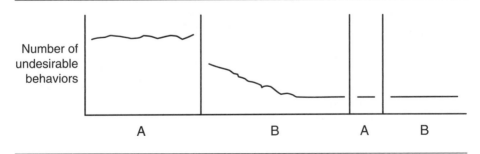

target problems, different situations, or different clients at different time points. With **multiple baseline designs,** each A phase can begin at the same time, but the introduction of the B phase is staggered. If improvement consistently coincides with the introduction of the B phase, then history becomes far-fetched, using the same logic as discussed previously.

To illustrate this logic, consider the data patterns in the multiple baseline graphs displayed in Figures 7.5 and 7.6. In Figure 7.5, each of three boys in a residential treatment center improves his behavior only after the intervention is introduced. Because the intervention was introduced at a different point for each boy, it makes no sense to suppose that extraneous events are causing the improvement. In Figure 7.6, however, all three boys improve their behavior when the intervention is introduced to the first boy, even though the other two are still in baseline.

After seeing the results in Figure 7.6, our first impulse might be to conclude that some extraneous event (history) is the most plausible explanation for the improvement in all three boys. Perhaps something changed in the environment of the residential treatment center to cause the improvement (a new and more competent cottage parent, perhaps). But what if the three boys are in frequent contact with each other? Perhaps they even all reside in the same cabin. If so, then the improvement in the first boy's behavior could influence the others to improve. This possibility, known as *generalization of effects,* would then rival history as an equally plausible explanation for the data pattern in Figure 7.6. That is, perhaps the intervention really was effective, and its effects spilled over to the other two boys to the degree that the desired degree of behavior change occurred before the other two boys entered their B phases.

If generalization of effects seems plausible, then results like those in Figure 7.6 should be interpreted as being inconclusive. But what if the three boys don't know each other, reside in different cabins, and never have any contact with each other? Then generalization of effects would no longer be a plausible explanation for data patterns like the one in Figure 7.6. Instead, history would be the more plausible explanation. Perhaps some extraneous change in the environment, in the seasons, in the academic calendar, or some other change was the reason.

As mentioned, multiple baseline designs can also involve just one client. In that case, the introduction of the intervention would be staggered across different target problems or situations. For example, Tom could have a cognitive-behavioral intervention applied to angry outbursts in his cabin after the first baseline, then have the same intervention applied to his fighting in the playground after the second baseline, and then have the intervention applied to clowning around in class after the third baseline. When multiple baseline designs are used in this manner, generalization of effects becomes much more likely than when the multiple baselines involve different clients.

Figure 7.5   A Visually Significant Multiple Baseline Data Pattern for an Intervention Seeking to Reduce Undesirable Behaviors by Three Boys in a Residential Treatment Center

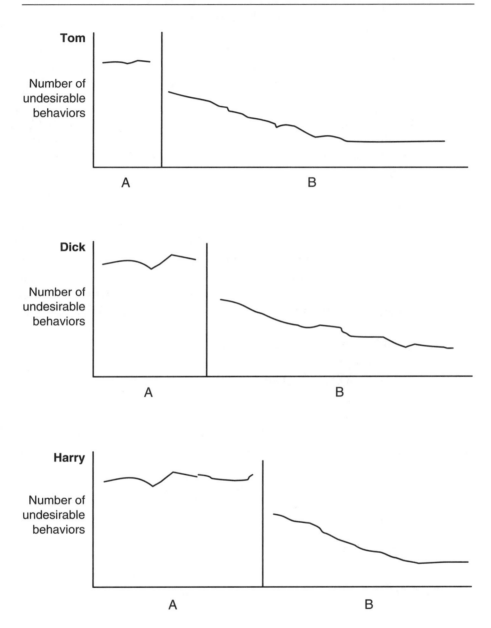

Figure 7.6   An Inconclusive Multiple Baseline Data Pattern for an Intervention Seeking to Reduce Undesirable Behaviors by Three Boys in a Residential Treatment Center

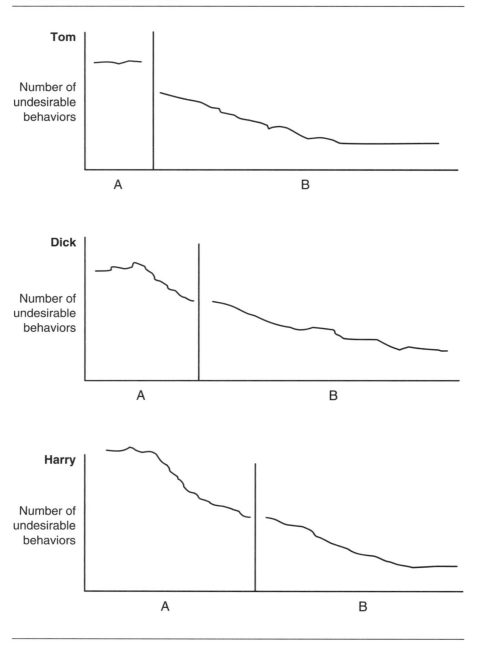

Multiple Component Designs

The final single-case design we'll consider is **multiple component designs.** Unlike the preceding two designs, the main purpose of this design is to ascertain whether any part of an intervention is unnecessary and whether any part is most responsible for the intervention's effects.

Consider the controversy discussed earlier regarding eye movement desensitization and reprocessing (EMDR), for example. Are the eye movements really necessary? Or is it just the elements of EMDR in which the client recalls the traumatic incident, discusses feelings and cognitions associated with it, and so on? One way to try to answer those questions would be to use a design like the one displayed in Figure 7.7. After the first baseline, the intervention package is provided without any eye movements. A brief second baseline follows, and after that the intervention package is reintroduced, this time including the eye movements. If the results look like the graph in Figure 7.7, it is reasonable to conclude that at least for one client the eye movements aren't needed; they add nothing to the intervention's effects. The opposite conclusion would be reached if the results look like the graph in Figure 7.8.

External Validity

A key limitation in all single-case designs, no matter how well they control for history or other threats to internal validity, is their extremely restricted external validity. There is virtually no basis whatsoever for supposing that one case is representative of a population of people with the same target problem. Consequently, it's tempting to conclude that single-case studies have no value in guiding practice decisions or in the development of scientific knowledge in general. But people who do so in regard to scientific knowledge overlook the importance of Pavlov's single case—

Figure 7.7   A Multiple Component Design Data Pattern Suggesting that the Eye Movement Component of EMDR Is Not Needed to Reduce a Client's Trauma Symptoms

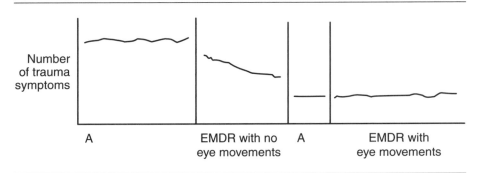

Figure 7.8   A Multiple Component Design Data Pattern Suggesting That the Eye Movement Component of EMDR Is Needed to Reduce a Client's Trauma Symptoms

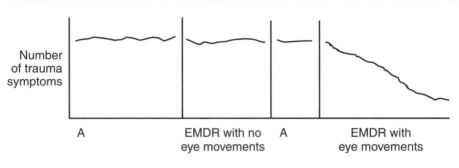

his dog—in the early development of learning theory. They also overlook the role of replication. If a new intervention appears to be effective in one single-case study, it can be evaluated in other single-case studies. To the extent that similar results are attained consistently as replications accumulate, external validity is strengthened.

Moreover, from the standpoint of guiding your EBP practice decision, you are searching for the best evidence applicable to your idiosyncratic practice situation. If you can find no interventions supported by experiments or quasi-experiments with clients like yours, it's conceivable that one or more single-case designs might be the best evidence you can find applicable to your situation. Although you cannot safely generalize the results to your client(s), the same can be said regarding studies with greater external validity. You'll need to monitor client progress with the intervention in Step 5 of the EBP process. If the best evidence you can find involves a single-case design that evaluated the effectiveness of an intervention that you had not yet considered, and if that intervention seems applicable to your situation, then you have good reason to suggest that intervention to your client(s) and see what happens.

In Chapter 12, we revisit single-case designs, but from a different perspective. Rather than focus on how to critically appraise the studies others have done using these designs, we focus on how you can utilize some feasible single-case design methods to monitor client progress in Step 5 of the EBP process. But before moving on, examine Table 7.3, which can serve as a handy guide when appraising studies using time-series designs. Among other uses, it will remind you that, just as was the case with experimental designs and nonequivalent comparison groups designs, controlling for history, passage of time, and regression to the mean aren't the only concerns. You should also critically appraise each study for possible measurement

Table 7.3   Questions for Appraising Studies Using Time-Series Designs

1. Were there sufficient data points in each phase to control for the plausibility of regression to the mean, passage of time, and (to a lesser extent) history?
2. Was a comparison group used to increase control for history?
3. If a comparison group was used, was a persuasive case made for its similarity to the experimental group?
4. If a comparison group was used, was history further controlled by adding a switching replication?
5. If a comparison group was used, and its outcome did not differ from the other group, was the potential for treatment diffusion addressed?
6. If a comparison group was used, did any of the following concerns seem problematic: Practitioner equivalence? Placebo effects? Compensatory equalization? Compensatory rivalry? Resentful demoralization?
7. If a single-case design was used, was it limited to the AB design, or did it increase its control for history by replicating baseline and intervention phases?
8. Were the measurement procedures unbiased and relatively unobtrusive?
9. Was treatment fidelity assessed and if so was it assessed in an unbiased manner?
10. Did the study include or exclude people with diagnoses or other characteristics like the client(s) pertaining to your EBP question?

bias, research reactivity, and other problems that are not prevented just by having control groups, many measurement points, or replicated baseline and intervention phases.

SYNOPSES OF RESEARCH STUDIES

I have made up both of the following two synopses. Although, the first one was inspired by a real study [Tolson, E. R. (1977). Alleviating marital communication problems. In W. R. Reid & L. Epstein (Eds.), *Task-centered practice* (pp. 100–112). New York: Columbia University Press], I have modified that study significantly to fit the purposes of these synopses.

Study 1 Synopsis

This study employed a multiple baseline design to evaluate the effectiveness of a marital therapy intervention for a couple who were experiencing marital dissatisfaction. To protect their identities, we call them Mr. and Mrs. T, which were not their real names. After a thorough assessment, which ruled out physical abuse, I (their therapist) suspected that the main cause of their dissatisfaction was in their undesirable communication patterns. So I asked Mr. and Mrs. T to videotape at home seven 30-minute normal conversations with each other—one per day for a week—and bring me the tapes.

They did so, and after viewing the tapes, I was able to identify what appeared to be three key related communication problems. First, Mr. T would tend to monopolize conversations and seem disinterested in hearing anything that Mrs. T might have to say. Second, Mrs. T would try to interrupt his monopolizations in an effort to make the conversation more balanced. Her interruptions were futile, however. Every time she tried to get a word in, Mr. T would respond angrily with the same line (that he had apparently picked up from watching his favorite TV show): "I pity the fool who tries to interrupt me!"

I added up the amount of time Mr. T monopolized each conversation in the videotape, the number of interruptions by Mrs. T, and the number of times Mr. T responded to her interruptions with his angry "I pity the fool . . ." line. Those counts became the three baselines for this study. Next, I informed Mr. and Mrs. T of these three problems and suggested a cognitive-behavioral package of three techniques for alleviating them, staggering the introduction of each technique so that I could have a multiple baseline design.

For the first graph in the multiple baseline design, after the baseline week I explained to Mr. T that he was monopolizing the conversations and suggested that he watch the videos they had made so that he would become more sensitive to that. After viewing the tapes, Mr. and Mrs. T made seven more daily videotaped conversations at home during the week and brought me the tapes. After they did so, I then suggested to Mrs. T that instead of interrupting Mr. T when he started monopolizing the conversation, she should just gently lift her hand a little bit to let him know he was monopolizing and that she wanted to speak. She and Mr. T then practiced the hand signal in my office. For the next week, after I suggested the hand signal, Mr. and Mrs. T made seven more daily videotaped 30-minute conversations. After that week, I addressed the dysfunctional nature of Mr. T's angry outbursts and provided Mr. T with an anger management technique that he could use to keep from angrily intimidating Mrs. T with his "I pity the fool . . ." line. Then seven more tapes were made during the subsequent week.

The results of the three baselines are displayed in the three graphs in Figure 7.9. These results show that the intervention package was ineffective. Although each target problem showed dramatic improvement, they all improved at the same time, when two of them (in the second and third graphs) were still in their baseline phases. Therefore, the improvements were due to history and not the intervention. Apparently, some extraneous event occurred after the first baseline and coincided with the onset of the first intervention phase to make all three target behaviors improve simultaneously.

Figure 7.9 Multiple Baseline Results

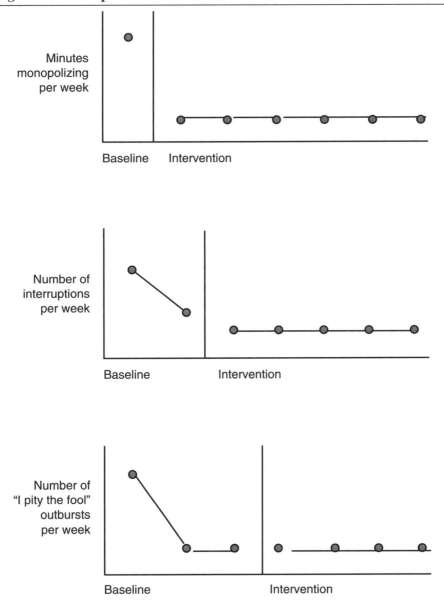

Study 2 Synopsis

This study employed a multiple time-series design to evaluate the effectiveness of a prerelease program for prisoners in a medium-security state prison located in central Pennsylvania. The prison psychologist and social worker co-led groups in which prisoners would meet with victims of other offenders and hear about the way that crimes hurt people. Each group met once a week for 12 weeks. Each group session lasted 2 hours. Attendance was required for each prisoner, beginning no more than 6 months before each was to be released. There were no dropouts.

The program was introduced in January 2002 and continued each year thereafter during the course of this study, which ran through 2006. In all, 400 prisoners completed the program. The main aim of the program was to prevent re-arrest by increasing prisoner empathy for crime victims. Annual re-arrest rates were graphed for all prisoners released from the prison for each of 5 years before the program was introduced and each of 5 years after it was introduced. Aggregated annual re-arrest rates also were graphed for all prisoners released from all other medium-security state prisons in Pennsylvania during the same 10-year period.

All re-arrest data were retrieved from the Pennsylvania Department of Corrections computerized files. The results are displayed in Figure 7.10. Those results clearly support the effectiveness of the program. It is recommended that the program be implemented in other prisons, and that this study be replicated in them to see if its results generalize to prisons in other areas.

Figure 7.10   Re-arrest Rates for Study Prison and Aggregated for All Other Prisons in Pennsylvania

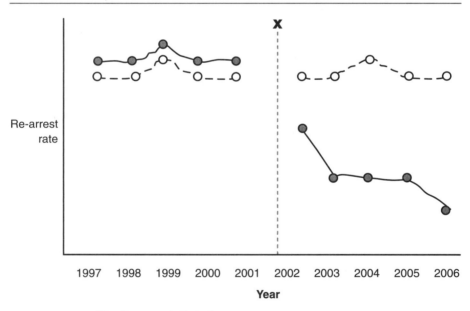

KEY CHAPTER CONCEPTS

- By graphing a sufficient number of data points both before and after a new intervention, program, or policy is introduced, time-series designs control for maturation (passage of time) by showing whether the pattern of improvement over time after the change simply is an extension of an improving trend that predated the change. Likewise, the use of multiple data points shows whether any particular data points appear to be aberrant blips. Thus, time-series designs can depict whether improvement from an atypically bad data point appears to be a function of regression to the mean.

- Some time-series studies attempt to strengthen their internal validity by including both an experimental and comparison group in their time-series analyses, and thus are called multiple time-series designs.

- Multiple time-series designs combine time-series logic with the logic of the nonequivalent comparison groups design.

- Single-case designs apply the logic of time-series designs to a single case. That single case might be an individual client, a family, or a larger grouping.

- Visual significance means that you can rule out the plausibility of rival explanations (threats to internal validity) for the improvement merely by eyeballing a graph of single-case results.

- To improve the control for history in single-case designs, additional baseline and intervention phases can be added.

- One way to add more phases is to use an ABAB design, which also can be called a withdrawal/reversal design. Using this design, after an improving trend in the first B phase, the intervention is temporarily withdrawn at a point when the practitioner deems it clinically sound and ethical to do so. Then it is reintroduced in the second B phase.

- An alternative way to add more phases is to use a multiple baseline design. Instead of withdrawing and reintroducing the intervention, multiple baseline designs involve introducing the intervention to different target problems, different situations, or different clients at different times. With multiple baseline designs, each A phase can begin at the same time, but the introduction of the B phase is staggered. If improvement consistently coincides with the introduction of the B phase, then history becomes far-fetched, using the same logic as discussed previously.

- Another design, the multiple component design, can be used when trying to ascertain whether any part of an intervention is unnecessary and whether any part is most responsible for the intervention's effects.
- A key limitation in all single-case designs is their extremely restricted external validity.

Review Exercises

1. *Use a database on the Internet (such as Google Scholar, PsycINFO, or Medline) to find a report of a time-series study that piques your interest. (Hint: Enter* time-series *as your search term for titles. If using Google Scholar, use its Advanced Scholar Search option and check the circle for limiting your search to the social sciences.) Critically appraise the study in terms of the issues emphasized in this chapter.*

2. *Use a database on the Internet (such as Google Scholar, PsycINFO, or Medline) to find a report of a study that used a single-case AB design and that piques your interest. (Hint: Enter* single-case *as your search term for titles. If using Google Scholar, use its Advanced Scholar Search option and check the circle for limiting your search to the social sciences.) Critically appraise the study in terms of the issues emphasized in this chapter.*

3. *Repeat Exercise 2, for studies using an ABAB design, a multiple-baseline design, and a multiple component design.*

4. *A time-series design obtains the following results for the number of time-outs for out-of-control behavior in group play therapy sessions before and after a behavioral contingency intervention is introduced:*

   Session 1: Six time-outs

   Session 2: Six time-outs

   X (behavioral contingency intervention is introduced)

   Session 3: Two time-outs

   Session 4: Two time-outs

   How would you interpret these results regarding the impact of introducing the behavioral contingency intervention?

   (continued)

5. A single-case ABAB design obtains the following results regarding number of temper tantrums per day:

A: 7   6   7   8   6   7   6   7
B: 2   3   2   1   2   3   1   2
A: 2   3   1   2   1   2   2   2
B: 2   1   3   2   1   2   2   1

How would you interpret these results regarding the effectiveness of the intervention?

6. A single-case, multiple-baseline design obtains the following results regarding number of disciplinary incidents per week among three boys in a residential treatment center (X signifies the onset of the intervention being evaluated):

Boy 1: 4   3   4 X   1   0   1   0   1   0   0   1   0   0
Boy 2: 3   4   3   1   0 X   0   1   0   1   0   0   1   0
Boy 3: 3   4   3   0   1   0   1 X   0   0   1   0   1   0

How would you interpret these results regarding the effectiveness of the intervention?

7. Discuss how replicating the studies in Exercises 4 through 6, and obtaining similar results, would influence your interpretation of those results.

ADDITIONAL READING

Bloom, M., Fischer, J., & Orme, J. G. (2003). *Evaluating practice: Guidelines for the accountable professional* (4th ed.). Boston: Allyn & Bacon.

Chapter 8 ———————————————

CRITICALLY APPRAISING SYSTEMATIC REVIEWS AND META-ANALYSES

As we saw in Chapter 3, systematic reviews and meta-analyses reside at the top of the evidentiary hierarchy for answering evidence-based practice (EBP) questions as to which intervention, program, or policy has the best effects. These two sources of evidence attempt to synthesize and develop conclusions from the diverse studies and their disparate findings. Thus, to the extent that they are accurate, unbiased, and therefore trustworthy, they can save you a great deal of time in searching for and appraising studies and in ascertaining which alternative interventions, programs, or policies tend to have the stronger and more beneficial effects.

You might ask, however, if systematic reviews and meta-analyses reside at the top of the evidentiary hierarchy for answering EBP questions about effectiveness, why did the chapters on experiments and quasi-experiments—two sources of evidence that reside immediately below systematic reviews and meta-analyses—precede this chapter? The answer is that we must first understand the logic, strengths, and possible flaws in those two sources of evidence before we can understand how to critically appraise the studies that claim to have adequately reviewed and synthesized them.

You might also wonder why systematic reviews of studies should reside above the best-controlled and most internally valid studies on the evidentiary hierarchy. Is that not like saying that a good review of some classic movies or classic novels is more valuable than the movies or novels themselves? Although it might be more valuable and enjoyable to watch a great movie or read a great novel than to read a review of either, you'll not be shocked to hear that outcome studies have a different purpose than movies or novels. Rather than entertain or enthrall you, they aim—often in a tedious way—to ascertain causation. Also, although it may be harder to complete a very rigorous experiment or quasi-experiment than to review it and some others, a good systematic review can be a better source of evidence for you than any one excellent study.

ADVANTAGES OF SYSTEMATIC REVIEWS AND META-ANALYSES

No matter how rigorous one particular outcome study might seem to be, if it is the only one implying that a particular intervention is effective, it could be misleading. Typically, the most internally valid experiments and quasi-experiments will have limited external validity. As discussed in Chapter 4, *external validity* refers to the extent that a study's inferences apply to settings other than the research setting and to clients other than the research study participants. Thus, a systematic review showing whether a particular intervention, program, or policy has been found to be effective by different independent researchers in different types of settings will give you better evidentiary grounds than just one study for supposing that it might be effective in your setting or with your client.

Aside from external validity, another advantage of systematic reviews is that any one study might have reached an erroneous or misleading conclusion about its own setting. At one extreme, for example, are unethical researchers who manipulate or falsify their data so they can report what they want to report. It is not unheard of in some very rare cases for authors to report a study that they never even conducted—manufacturing the whole thing to enhance their careers. More commonly, ethical researchers can unintentionally reach erroneous conclusions. Perhaps their small sample size prevented their findings from supporting a truly effective intervention. Perhaps they did not realize that their measurement approach was biased, invalid, or lacked sensitivity. Perhaps one of the other flaws discussed in previous chapters affected their results in a way they did not detect.

By informing you as to whether any particular study's outcome did or did not get consistently replicated across various independent studies, a good systematic review provides you with better evidence than any one of the studies by itself. Moreover, some of the best systematic reviews will be conducted by a panel of independent research experts, each of whom will scrutinize every study, looking for their methodological flaws. To the extent that the panel of reviewers really are experts and unbiased, then their scrutiny of a study may be more likely than yours (or any other single person's) to identify flaws that should undermine the credibility of that study's findings. In addition, such a panel will probably have much more time than you will to search for and critically appraise all the relevant studies evaluating the effectiveness of a particular intervention, program, or policy. That not only saves you time; it means that the panelists may have had more time to carefully scrutinize each study than you will if you attempt to find and read all the relevant studies that have been completed pertinent to your EBP question.

Systematic reviews also can help you make sense out of a bewildering array of different studies that used different methodologies and produced inconsistent results. Perhaps the most flawed studies found Intervention A to be more effective than Intervention B, while the least flawed studies found the opposite to be true. Perhaps the studies supporting the effectiveness of Intervention C all had eligibility requirements that prevented clients with comorbidity (such as a psychiatric diagnosis *plus* substance abuse) from participating in the study. That information would be of great value to you if you were looking for the most effective way to treat a client with a comorbid diagnosis.

One more advantage of systematic reviews is that they can apply statistical techniques that merge the findings of many different studies. Systematic reviews that apply statistical techniques are called *meta-analyses*. Those techniques can tell you how strong the effects of an intervention, program, or policy are on average. Perhaps Interventions D and E were consistently supported by studies with strong methodologies, but Intervention D had stronger effects on average. In addition, meta-analyses can statistically combine the results of various studies that used small samples and thus ascertain whether findings that were not statistically significant in any one or more of those studies become statistically significant in the aggregate analysis. We'll examine meta-analyses in more depth later in this chapter.

RISKS IN RELYING EXCLUSIVELY ON SYSTEMATIC REVIEWS AND META-ANALYSES

A debate rages among experts in EBP as to whether practitioners should be encouraged to rely primarily on systematic reviews and meta-analyses to answer their EBP questions, as opposed to reviewing the various individual studies themselves. Those favoring relying primarily on systematic reviews and meta-analyses cite the advantages of them, as discussed earlier, and emphasize the limited time practitioners typically have for searching for and critically appraising many individual studies. Those opposing such reliance cite the fact that some systematic reviews and meta-analyses are seriously biased or otherwise flawed. They also argue that one of the prime aims of EBP is to move away from a reliance on authority to dictate practice decisions and instead to use critical thinking and an independent search for and appraisal of scientific evidence as a guide. If practitioners merely rely on systematic reviews and meta-analyses to guide their practice, are they not just substituting one form of authority for another? The latter argument, however, is viewed by some as very nice but too idealistic. Busy practitioners don't always have the time and resources to find and critically appraise all the relevant studies bearing on their EBP question—especially not as thoroughly and meticulously as panels of independent expert scholars.

So, as a busy practitioner, what should *you* do? Just rely exclusively on reviews and meta-analyses? Find and critically appraise all the studies yourself relevant to your EBP question? The answer depends on several factors, including: How much time do you have? How much access do you have to literature databases that save you time in finding studies and letting you download them instead of looking for them in a library? How many relevant studies are out there for you to find and appraise? If your question involves a target problem for which very few interventions, programs, and policies have received rigorous evaluations, perhaps it will be feasible for you to find and appraise all the studies yourself. Moreover, perhaps no systematic review or meta-analysis has yet been conducted regarding your EBP question. And if one or two have been conducted, maybe they are biased or otherwise seriously flawed.

WHERE TO START

Perhaps the most reasonable way to proceed is as follows: Begin by looking for and appraising systematic reviews and meta-analyses relevant to your EBP question. If you find none, you'll need to look for the individual studies yourself. If you find some systematic reviews and meta-analyses, critically appraise them. You might suspect that they are so biased that you'll want to look for and appraise the individual studies yourself. If, however, the systematic reviews and meta-analyses seem trustworthy, the extent to which you go further will be based on feasibility considerations. Ideally, to the extent you can, you should conduct your own independent search and appraisal, rather than just rely on authority. If you have limited time however, you might just examine a sample of the reviewed studies to see if your critical appraisal of them matches what you read in the reviews. In short, do what you can. Now let's turn to what you should look for in critically appraising systematic reviews.

WHAT TO LOOK FOR WHEN CRITICALLY APPRAISING SYSTEMATIC REVIEWS

As I implied, some systematic reviews and meta-analyses are more trustworthy than others. You may have heard, for example, of biased reviews sponsored by cigarette companies that questioned the harmful effects of tobacco. You may also have heard of reviews sponsored by pharmaceutical companies that were biased in favor of a new medication they developed. Although less money may be at stake, vested interests can seriously bias reviews in the human services field, as well. For example, reviews have disagreed about the comparative effectiveness of exposure therapy versus eye movement desensitization and reprocessing (EMDR) in the treatment of posttraumatic stress disorder (PTSD). You probably won't be shocked to learn that some of the reviews were conducted by people whose reputations were connected to one or the other intervention approaches. Bias, however, is not the only reason why some reviews can be misleading. Sometimes an unbiased reviewer unintentionally makes serious mistakes. Remember, when a *type* of evidence resides high on the evidentiary hierarchy, that does not mean that all reviews or studies that seek to supply that type of evidence offer trustworthy evidence. Let's now look further at some of the things you should look for when considering whether a particular review is seriously flawed, beginning with bias.

Bias

Who sponsored, funded, or conducted the review? Were vested interests at stake? For example, if the review was conducted by a team of authors who reap financial or other career rewards from their books and workshops on EMDR, touch-field therapy (TFT), hypnotherapy, or any other form of intervention, then you should be particularly skeptical as to whether their review is biased and misleading.

Why was the review conducted? Several years ago, I was asked to participate in a symposium debate about the effectiveness of EMDR. The symposium was part of a national conference. The organizer of the debate asked me to argue the pro position (that EMDR has sufficient research support to be deemed effective), but expressed doubt as to whether he'd be able to find someone willing to argue the con position. Knowing the research on both sides of the issue and believing that more research was needed before the issue would be resolved, I offered to argue either the pro or con position—whichever he needed me for the most. Several weeks later he got back to me. As it turned out, he needed me to take the con position in the debate. I agreed, but after updating my review of the research, I could not honestly argue that EMDR is ineffective. Instead, I concluded that EMDR appears to be effective under certain conditions and discussed the target groups for whom more research is needed before we can deem it to be effective or ineffective.

When my review was published, it was attacked as biased by three coauthors, at least one of whom was affiliated with EMDR. Although I didn't intend for my review to be biased, their criticism had some basis in the fact that the reason I conducted my review was because I was asked to argue the con position in the debate. Had I been asked to argue the pro position, perhaps I would unintentionally have been less skeptical about the effectiveness of EMDR for some target groups. (I like to think I would have reached the same conclusions, but we all like to fancy ourselves as unbiased, and I am no exception!) Despite my possible bias, however, I perceived the attack on my review to have been much more biased than my review. The critics of my review earlier had conducted their own review on the effectiveness of EMDR, and in my review I had suggested that perhaps their conclusions were biased by their vested interests in EMDR.

If you'd like to read my review, their attack on it, and my response to their attack, see Rubin (2003), Maxfield, Lake, and Hyer (2004), and Rubin (2004). Regardless of how you might feel about those readings or about EMDR, my point is that despite my intention to conduct an unbiased review, I might have been biased. Thus, why a review is conducted can bias it even if money and fame are not at stake. And if money and fame are at stake, all the more reason to be wary of a review.

The Cochrane and Campbell Collaborations

In contrast, consider the relatively trustworthy reviews conducted by the Cochrane Collaboration and Campbell Collaborations. These are sibling international nonprofit organizations that recruit researchers, practitioners, and consumers into review groups. The **Cochrane Collaboration** (www.cochrane.org) provides reviews of research on the effects of health care interventions. The reviews of the **Campbell Collaboration** (www.campbellcollaboration.org) focus on social welfare, education, and crime and justice.

The trustworthiness and value of what you can find at these two sites are based on several considerations. One is in the heterogeneity of the individuals who comprise their review groups. That enhances the chances that their reviews will be comprehensive and relatively unbiased. Another is that their libraries, in addition to containing their reviews, contain comments and criticisms about their reviews. They also contain abstracts of other reviews, bibliographies of studies, links that might help facilitate conducting your own review, and information about the quality of their review systems.

Inclusion and Exclusion Criteria

Every review has criteria guiding which studies it will include and which it will exclude. Some reviews use methodological criteria, such as including only randomized experiments and excluding all other studies. Some reviews use criteria pertaining to the characteristics of study participants, such as including only those studies whose participants had the same diagnosis and excluding studies if some participants had comorbid diagnoses. For example, a review of the effectiveness of EMDR in treating PTSD might exclude studies of EMDR's effectiveness in treating panic disorder or studies of EMDR's effectiveness in treating PTSD if some participants suffered from both PTSD and substance abuse.

In appraising a review in terms of its inclusion/exclusion criteria, you might first ask: Did the review even identify those criteria? If not, it is highly suspect—if for no other reason—because failure to do so creates doubt about the overall competence of the review.

If methodological inclusion/exclusion criteria are identified, are they too narrow or too restrictive? If a review includes only randomized experiments, some of the quasi-experiments it excludes might have a high degree of internal validity. If the review simply takes the position that all randomized experiments are valid because of the status of that type of evidence on the evidentiary hierarchy, it might put too much stock in some studies with egregiously biased measurement procedures or other serious flaws, such as differential attrition. Perhaps some well-controlled quasi-experiments without the latter types of flaws provide better evidence. Conversely, if a review includes all types of studies, it might be putting too much stock in weakly controlled studies that have very little internal validity.

If participant characteristics criteria are identified, how do they compare to the characteristics of your clients—the ones for whom you are conducting your EBP search for evidence? A review that excludes studies involving clients with comorbid disorders will be less valuable to you than one that includes such studies if you are treating clients who have a comorbid disorder. If your client is a recent immigrant from a non-English-speaking country, a review that includes only those studies with English-speaking residents of North America will be less valuable to you than one that includes studies with clients like yours.

Does the Review Critically Appraise the Quality of Included Studies?

Regardless of a review's inclusion and exclusion criteria regarding research design, it should critically appraise the included studies. As discussed in previous chapters, for example, even studies employing designs at the top of the evidentiary hierarchy can have fatal flaws. The review should clarify which included studies were seriously flawed and which weren't. Also, it should sort the evidence accordingly. Thus, if 10 very strong studies fail to support the effectiveness of an intervention, and 10 fatally flawed studies support its effectiveness, the review should not just conclude that the evidence is mixed, with an equal number of studies supporting and not supporting the intervention's effectiveness.

Likewise, the review should sort the evidence according to client characteristics. For example, it should address whether different conclusions were obtained depending on client diagnosis, ethnicity, and so on. This will help you decide whether particular conclusions seem to apply to your practice situation and clients.

Comprehensiveness

Some reviews search for studies in a more comprehensive fashion than others. For example, some look only at published articles. Some might include additional types of publications, but not look for unpublished studies, such as dissertations, reports on web sites, reports of ongoing studies with preliminary findings, or recently completed studies reported in recent conference proceedings but not yet appearing in print.

You might wonder whether expecting authors of systematic reviews to search for unpublished works is asking too much. You might suppose that works that are not published are probably weaker or of narrower interest than published works. It's understandable that you might think so; however, studies have found that there is a publication bias among some journals in accepting articles reporting positive findings supporting the effectiveness of interventions in preference to articles that conclude that a particular intervention is ineffective (Epstein, 2004).

Likewise, there is general agreement among experts on intervention research that a similar bias exists—called the **file drawer effect**—in which researchers whose findings fail to support the effectiveness of an intervention are less likely to submit their studies for publication than researchers with positive findings (Vergano, 2001). They may choose to file their studies away in a file drawer because they assume that no one is interested in interventions that don't work or because they suspect that journals are only interested in publishing studies of things that do work. Or they might have a vested interest in the intervention they evaluated and therefore suppose that something must have been wrong with their study, deciding to wait for an opportunity to do a better study rather than "mislead" the field with negative findings about an intervention that they are convinced is the best thing to come along since sliced bread.

For example, in the late 1990s, I completed a study that was the first randomized experiment to evaluate the effectiveness of EMDR with children. I found no difference in outcome between the children who had received EMDR plus treatment as usual and the children who received only treatment as usual. I sent a copy of the draft of the report of my study—before submitting it for publication—to various colleagues who had contributed to the study in some way, requesting their reactions and suggestions. Two of them, both well known for their leadership in EMDR, urged me to delay submitting my report for publication. Their rationale was that some other randomized experiments evaluating the effectiveness of EMDR were ongoing and expecting results that would support the effectiveness of EMDR with children and that if my study got published first, everyone would conclude that EMDR is ineffective with children and would therefore pay less heed to the forthcoming (more positive) results. Since they were convinced that EMDR really is effective with children, they apparently reasoned that my results would be misleading and that this therefore would justify disregarding my sense that it is a violation of research ethics to stifle or delay the dissemination of findings just because those findings challenge conventional wisdom or threaten vested interests. (I did not delay submitting my study. If you'd like to read it, see Rubin et al., 2001.) Thus, it is important for researchers conducting systematic reviews to search for and to include those unpublished works that meet other inclusion criteria of their reviews. Otherwise, their reviews might be wrong in concluding that the studies supporting the effectiveness of a particular intervention far outnumber those that suggest that the intervention is ineffective.

Some reviews include only studies written in English. Some reviews use only one literature database, such as PsycINFO. Others scour one or more additional databases, such as Medline. In addition, most reviews will (and should!) widen their search by examining the studies cited in the materials that they have already found. Some also include going to specific web sites on the area of the search, such as the web site for the National Center for Post-Traumatic Stress (www.ncptsd.va.gov/facts/treatment/fs_treatment .html) if the focus of the search is on the treatment of PTSD (or some other issue related to PTSD). Some reviews will contact authors of some of the studies they review seeking additional information needed to appraise the methodological rigor of those studies or the meaning of their findings.

Of particular importance is whether a review considered only one type of intervention, as opposed to looking at a target population and then seeing which interventions have the best evidence regarding their effectiveness with that population. For example, when I assign students a term paper in which I instruct them to select a client or target population of interest and then critically appraise outcome studies bearing on how most effectively to intervene with that client or population, they commonly start out by looking for studies evaluating just one particular intervention approach, such as cognitive-behavioral therapy, play therapy, or some other approach. I then ask them, "How will you know if that's your *most* effective option, the one with the *best* evidence and *strongest* effects, if you don't include in your search studies of *other* various interventions that have been tested for your client or population?" Using the same reasoning, a review that merely looks for evidence supporting the effectiveness of Intervention A with problem X won't ascertain whether perhaps more and stronger evidence supports the effectiveness of Intervention B or Intervention C with the same problem.

Some reviews can start out too broad in scope. But that probably will be a feasibility headache for the reviewer more than an issue for practitioners who are critically appraising reviews that have already been completed. Nevertheless, if you encounter a review of research on PTSD in general or on depression in general, it might have less value to you than one on effective *treatments* for PTSD or depression (assuming the purpose of your search is to find the *intervention* whose effectiveness in treating either disorder has the best evidence.) On the other hand, if a *subsection* of a very broad review of PTSD in general focuses on the evidence pertaining to your particular EBP question, then the review might have significant value to you.

As long as the reviews—or subsections of the reviews—pertain to your particular EBP question—and assuming that the reviews are of equal merit in other respects, then a broader search pertaining to your EBP question probably deserves more confidence than a narrower one. Spelling out the comprehensiveness of the review's search process overlaps with the notion of spelling out inclusion and exclusion criteria and with the possibility of bias. If the review does not supply information assuring you that its search was comprehensive, that lack of information should be a red flag alerting you to the possibility that the reviewers may have selectively excluded some sources that don't fit their biases or vested interests. In a study of 280 articles in psychology journals, for example, Shadish (1995) found that relatively weak studies often get cited merely because they support the author's viewpoint.

Transparency

An overarching issue in critically appraising systematic reviews is **transparency.** Transparency means spelling out all the details regarding inclusion and exclusion criteria, how studies were collected, source of funding, reviewer backgrounds, whether different reviewers with different backgrounds (and perhaps different orientations) agreed about the review conclusions, and so on. By arming you with all this information, transparency enables you to make a more informed appraisal and decision about the evidence supplied in a review. A review that lacks transparency in regard to anything relevant to your critical appraisal of it should be viewed warily.

WHAT DISTINGUISHES A SYSTEMATIC REVIEW FROM OTHER TYPES OF REVIEWS?

You can find many reviews of studies that don't warrant the label *systematic*. What makes a review systematic is the extent to which it attempts to be comprehensive in finding relevant studies and unbiased in appraising, synthesizing, and developing conclusions from the diverse studies with their disparate findings. This is not an all-or-nothing distinction. As noted previously, some systematic reviews can be more comprehensive and unbiased than others. Thus, some reviews that claim to be systematic might strike you as less than truly systematic.

Other reviews might not even claim to be systematic. Some are merely called *literature reviews* by their authors. Or they might be called *narrative reviews.* Their authors may not try to show how their reviews were comprehensive and unbiased. They may merely state in vague terms that an examination of the literature on their topic published during a specified time period was examined. They might proceed to list the studies found, critically appraise each, and then synthesize them, and draw conclusions. While they may resemble systematic reviews in those respects, they do not provide you with ample information to gauge whether the review was adequately comprehensive, whether particular inclusion or exclusion criteria were used, what procedures were employed to minimize bias in the review, and so on. Thus, they might lack the transparency that should be evident in a good systematic review. Implicitly, they may be conveying the message, "I'm an expert; trust me." In contrast, systematic reviews represent a special type of literature review: they are literature reviews that are transparent about and attempt to incorporate the desired features of systematic reviews as discussed in this chapter.

Another distinction between systematic reviews and other literature reviews is the greater specificity in most systematic reviews regarding the question the review seeks to answer. For example, a literature review on PTSD might cover studies on its nature, etiology, and prevalence in addition to studies on the effectiveness of interventions to treat it. A systematic review, in contrast, will articulate a specific research question it seeks to answer. Rather than attempt to cover all there is worth knowing about a topic, a systematic review might ask such questions as: What interventions are most effective in treating combat-related PTSD among military veterans? What measurement instruments are the most valid and sensitive for assessing levels of depression among the frail elderly? What factors best predict desirable or undesirable outcomes among victims of child abuse?

Before moving on to discuss a particular type of systematic review called meta-analysis, you may want to examine Table 8.1, which summarizes questions to ask when critically appraising systematic reviews and meta-analyses.

WHAT TO LOOK FOR WHEN CRITICALLY APPRAISING META-ANALYSES

As mentioned earlier in this chapter and in Chapter 3, **meta-analyses** are systematic reviews that apply statistical techniques that merge the findings of many different studies. One technique calculates the aggregated statistical significance of the various studies, including those that may have failed to get statistically significant results due to their small sample

Table 8.1   Questions to Ask When Critically Appraising Systematic Reviews and Meta-Analyses

1. Does it specify a sufficiently narrow and well-defined question?
2. Is it transparent regarding the following questions?
3. Were its search procedures and inclusion criteria sufficiently comprehensive?
4. Were its exclusion criteria too restrictive?
5. Did those who sponsored, funded, or conducted the review have vested interests at stake in its conclusions? (Review authors should report whether any of them were involved in any studies included in the review and whether they have any sort of affiliation with or financial stake in any of the concerns being reviewed.)
6. Does it critically appraise the quality of included studies?
7. Does it sort the evidence according to study quality?
8. Does it sort the evidence according to client characteristics? If so, do its conclusions seem to apply to your clients?
9. Does it inappropriately lump together clinically meaningful outcome indicators and clinically insignificant ones?
10. Did it use at least two independent review authors to assess the quality of the studies and extract findings from the studies?
11. If yes to question 10, was there agreement between the assessments and findings of the review authors? If there were disagreements, how were they resolved?
12. Were strategies for dealing with missing data described?
13. Were steps taken to prevent bias in the review process?
14. Were clear and practical implications for practice articulated?

sizes. That technique is too technically complicated for this book. If you'd like to learn more about it, you can read the Lipsey and Wilson (2000) book listed in the additional readings section at the end of this chapter. The important thing for you to remember in this connection is the meaning of statistical significance in ruling out chance as an explanation for findings, as I discussed in Chapter 4.

Effect Size

Another, less complicated meta-analytic statistical technique calculates **effect size.** Effect-size statistics depict the average strength of the effects of an intervention across studies that use different types of outcome measures. It's important for you to understand the meaning of effect size. That understanding will help you decide which intervention has the strongest evidence even if you don't read any meta-analyses. That's because individual studies should report the effect sizes they found, and if they don't, you might find enough information in the study's report to easily calculate their effect sizes yourself.

Correlations

Effect size comes in two forms: correlations and z-scores. Correlations depict the strength of relationship between two variables in terms of a figure that can range from 0 (no correlation) to either +1.0 (a perfect positive correlation) or −1.0 (a perfect negative correlation). In a perfect correlation, regardless of whether it is positive or negative, knowing a person's characteristic on one variable enables us to predict with perfect accuracy his or her characteristic on another variable. (In a negative correlation, also called an *inverse correlation,* as one variable increases, the other decreases. An example would be a decrease in level of depression the more treatment sessions attended. In a positive correlation, both variables would move in the same direction, such as severity of symptoms increasing with increases in the number of traumas experienced.)

Suppose every control group client drops out of school and every experimental group client graduates. That would be a perfect correlation. Knowing that finding, if you were told which group each client was in and then asked to guess whether each dropped out or graduated, you could guess correctly every time.

Suppose 65 of 100 control group clients drop out versus 35 of 100 experimental group clients. Knowing that, if I paid you a dollar for every correct guess, you could guess dropout for every control group client and graduate for every experimental group client. You'd win $130, because you'd guess correctly 65 times for each group. There would be some correlation between the group variable and the dropout variable, but it wouldn't be a perfect correlation. If it were perfect, you'd guess correctly every time and thus win $200.

If you had no information about the group variable, but knew only that 100 clients graduated and 100 dropped out, you'd have no basis to predict either outcome, and your pure guesses would be correct about half the time. Thus, you'd win $100. Therefore, knowing that the group differences in dropout proportions were 65% versus 35% would enable to you to improve the accuracy of your predictions by 30% (being right 130 times knowing the different proportions instead of just 100 times without knowing the proportions). If you calculated a correlation coefficient on the difference in dropout rates between the two groups, it would be .30. If there was a perfect relationship in which all control group clients dropped out and all experimental group clients graduated, you'd improve the accuracy of your predictions by 100% (from being right 100 times to being right 200 times), which is consistent with the 1.0 correlation.

In treatment outcome studies, a correlation of .30 is not too shabby. For example, an intervention that reduces the dropout rate from 65% to 35% could be extremely valuable. You should keep that in mind when you read outcome studies because when those studies report correlations, they'll often square the correlations to depict in more complex statistical terms the amount of variance in one variable that is explained by the other variable. Thus, the above .30 correlation regarding the difference in dropout rates might get reported as a squared correlation of .09. That squared correlation seems quite low, but it really isn't. In fact, many meta-analyses have found that the average correlation found in studies reporting effective human service interventions is approximately .30 before squaring and .09 afterward ($.30 \times .30 = .09$). Ultimately, you should consider what any particular effect size means in practical terms. Doing so gets us into the realm of the *clinical significance* of a finding, which we'll delve into soon. For now, let's just say that the above .30 correlation regarding dropout rates probably would impress you as having more practical value (and thus being more clinically significant) than a .50 correlation in which 75% of experimental group students said they enjoyed their treatment sessions versus 25% who said they enjoyed the control routine treatment sessions.

The *d*-Index

As mentioned, effect sizes can also come in the form of *z*-scores. A *z*-score is calculated by dividing the difference between the experimental and control group means by the standard deviation. You've probably encountered the term *standard deviation* in the past, but let's take a moment to review in a simplified way what it means.

Suppose a study evaluates the effectiveness of Intervention A for treating conduct disorders. Suppose it measures outcome in terms of the number of temper tantrums in an experimental and control group, each made up of five children with the following results:

Number of Temper Tantrums

Experimental Group	Control Group
1	4
2	5
3	6
4	7
5	8

The mean of the experimental group is 3; the control group's mean is 6. Applying the formula for calculating standard deviations (which you don't need to know for our purposes here), and after rounding off, we'd find that the standard deviation in each group is 1.6. In simple terms, that indicates that on average the individual clients in each group tend to fall within approximately 1.6 points of that group's mean.

Next, suppose another study evaluates the effectiveness of Intervention B for the same type of children with conduct disorders, but in this study outcome is measured in terms of scores on a conduct disorder scale completed by parents. Suppose the scores for an experimental and control group each made up of five children are as follows (higher scores indicate worse behavior):

Conduct Disorder Scale Scores

Experimental Group	Control Group
10	20
30	40
50	60
70	80
90	100

The mean of the experimental group is 50; the control group's mean is 60. Rounding off, the standard deviation of each group is 32. In simple terms, that indicates that on average the individual clients in each group tend to fall within approximately 32 points of that group's mean.

Now that we see the means and standard deviations for each study, let's see how that information can enable us to compare the strength of the effects of Intervention A and Intervention B. To begin, notice that the difference in means for Intervention A was 3 temper tantrums (the difference between the means of 3 and 6). Next, notice that the difference in means for Intervention B was 10 points on a scale (the difference between the means of 50 and 60).

It wouldn't make any sense to conclude that Intervention B had stronger effects than Intervention A because its mean difference of 10 was larger than Intervention A's mean difference of 3. A difference in the number of temper tantrums does not mean the same thing as a difference in scale scores. Comparing those two mean differences is like comparing apples and oranges. But if we divide each study's mean difference by its standard deviation, a comparison of the strengths of the effects of the two interventions would make sense.

Dividing the difference of 3 for Intervention A by its standard deviation of 1.6 gives us a z-score of 1.9. Dividing the difference of 10 for Intervention B by its standard deviation of 32 gives us a z-score of 0.3. By dividing each study's difference by its standard deviation, we can standardize to a common scale very different outcome measures with very different score meanings. In other words, one study using a measure that involves very large numbers can be compared to another study using a measure with very small numbers, because the standard deviations will tend to be smaller in a scale that involves small numbers and larger in a scale that involves large numbers.

You can read more about z-scores in introductory statistics texts, such as one I wrote: *Statistics for Evidence-Based Practice and Evaluation* (Rubin, 2007). For now, suffice it to say that the foregoing examples of z-scores—ones that compare differences in means divided by standard deviations in outcome studies—are called *effect-size* statistics.

Although correlations also depict effect size (as already discussed), they are usually just called *correlations.* In contrast, the z-score calculation is often referred to by the term *effect size.* Its more precise term is the ***d-index*** or the d-statistic, but many studies will just call it the *effect size.*

As with correlations, many meta-analyses have calculated the average d-index found in studies reporting effective human service interventions. Although different meta-analyses don't all report the same results, their mean d-indexes tend to cluster around .50 to .60. Formulas exist to transform those statistics into correlations, and a d-index of about .60 corresponds to a correlation of about .30. Thus, both figures are considered to represent medium effects. Correlations of about .50 and d-indexes of about .80 are considered to represent strong effects. Correlations of about .10 and d-indexes of about .20 are considered to represent weak effects.

You can view the effect-size statistic of any particular study as weak, medium, or strong in terms of the approximate benchmarks developed by various meta-analyses. This knowledge can help you consider which intervention appears to have stronger effects even if you just appraise individual studies, and find no meta-analysis regarding your specific EBP question. If you do find and appraise a meta-analysis, however, this knowledge will help you appreciate and understand why and how meta-analyses can calculate and compare the average effect sizes associated with different interventions evaluated in many different studies using very different outcome measures.

The calculations of meta-analyses are a bit more complex than I've depicted so far. That's because they use a somewhat complicated formula to weight each effect size according to the sample size in each study. But if you understand my depiction, that should be enough to enable you to use the results of meta-analyses in helping you to answer your EBP questions.

Correlating Effect Size with Other Variables

As I've noted, meta-analyses can report the average effect size for a particular type of intervention with a particular target problem across the many studies that have evaluated its effectiveness with that problem. Likewise, any one meta-analysis can compare the average effect sizes of two or more different types of interventions for a particular target problem across the many studies that have evaluated each intervention with that target problem. Thus, if many well-controlled, methodologically sound studies support the effectiveness of Intervention A in treating PTSD among rape victims, and many other sound studies support the effectiveness of Intervention B in treating PTSD among rape victims, a meta-analysis might help you decide which intervention to choose by reporting which one's group of studies has the larger overall average weighted effect size.

In addition, meta-analyses can assess whether the effect sizes for one or more particular interventions are correlated with other study attributes. Suppose that Interventions A and B have very similar average effect sizes, but only Intervention A's effect sizes are strongly correlated with the number of treatment sessions provided: the more sessions, the stronger the effect size. Suppose further that for studies in which 10 or fewer treatment sessions are provided, Intervention B's average effect size is considerably greater than Intervention A's average effect size. If managed care pressures or other considerations make it difficult for you to provide more than 10 treatment sessions in your practice, the foregoing finding would probably tilt you toward choosing Intervention B (all other considerations being equal, of course.)

Sometimes doubt is expressed as to whether the relatively strong average effect size found for a particular type of intervention in a particular meta-analysis might have been influenced by the inclusion of some weakly controlled or biased studies in the meta-analysis. To anticipate and deal with such doubt, some researchers conducting meta-analyses rate the methodological strength of each study reviewed and then calculate the correlation of the studies' effect sizes with their methodological strength ratings. A strong positive correlation indicates that the intervention tends to appear most effective the stronger the study methodology. A strong negative (inverse) correlation indicates that the intervention tends to appear most effective the weaker and perhaps more biased the study methodology. Both correlations suggest that the overall average effect size is misleading. Depending on whether the correlation is positive or negative, the intervention's true effects might be stronger or weaker than depicted in the overall average. But if there is very little or no correlation between effect size and methodological rating, that would alleviate doubt as to whether the overall average effect size has been inflated by including some relatively weak studies in the meta-analysis.

In addition to—or perhaps instead of—reporting the correlation between methodological strength ratings and effect size, a meta-analysis can report average effect sizes separately for different groupings of studies. For example, it could compare the mean effect size of methodologically stronger studies with that of methodologically weaker studies. It could report similar comparisons according to the client characteristics of the reviewed studies. For example, perhaps an intervention has a stronger mean effect size with Caucasian clients than with other clients, perhaps its mean effect size is lower in studies that included clients with comorbid diagnoses, and so on.

Some Caveats

Recall that a meta-analysis is a type of systematic review. Despite its employment of impressive statistical procedures, it is not immune to the same sorts of flaws that can hamper the trustworthiness of other types of systematic reviews—flaws pertaining to bias, inclusion and exclusion criteria, comprehensiveness, and transparency. Don't let fancy statistics make you less vigilant in your critical appraisal regarding such flaws.

Even if a meta-analysis examines the correlation between effect sizes and ratings of methodological strength, and finds little or no correlation between them, you should remain vigilant. Reviewers with vested interests in a particular intervention can be biased not only in their inclusion criteria (such as by including methodologically weak studies that support their favored intervention), but also in the way they rate the methodological strength of each study they include.

Recall our fictional character Joe Schmo from Chapter 2, the guy who invented psychschmotherapy and who hopes it will make him rich and famous. Suppose he conducts a meta-analysis comparing the mean effect sizes of psychschmotherapy with some commonly used alternative intervention that he hopes to displace. Not only might he be biased in including weak studies supporting psychschmotherapy in his meta-analysis, he might be inclined to rate their methodologies as strong, knowing they supported his therapy. Likewise, he might be inclined to be much more critical in his ratings of the methodological strength of studies that found psychschmotherapy to be ineffective, studies that found the rival therapy to be effective, and especially studies that found the rival therapy to be *more* effective than psychschmotherapy.

This does not imply that Joe Schmo would *intentionally* bias his inclusion criteria or ratings. Vested interests can result in such biases even when people with a great deal of integrity think they are being objective. Being influenced by our biases doesn't imply intent. We are all vulnerable to self-deception in thinking that we are being unbiased and objective when we are really biased; it's not necessarily a conscious process. The fervent supporters of EMDR—including those who have vested interests in it—who argue that their meta-analyses are more valid than those that question EMDR's effectiveness probably really believe in the veracity of their case, and probably really believe that they and their meta-analyses are quite unbiased. And the same can be said of those who fervently believe in and argue for the superior effectiveness of exposure therapy or who fervently dispute the effectiveness of EMDR. Thus, if you read a meta-analysis that you think might be tainted by vested interests or other sources of bias, you are not necessarily impugning the integrity of its authors.

Bias is not the only reason that meta-analytic results can be misleading. Some misleading results can occur as a result of human error having nothing to do with bias. For example, an unbiased researcher conducting a meta-analysis might *unintentionally* let the effect sizes found in methodologically weak studies cancel out the effect sizes found in methodologically strong studies. Thus, if one weakly controlled study with biased measurement procedures reports a medium d-index of .50 for Intervention A, and one strong study reports a d-index of 0 for Intervention A, then the mean d-index of .25 will suggest that on average Intervention A has relatively weak effects. Such a meta-analysis could mislead you, because the strong study might be the better indicator of Intervention A's likely effects in your practice situation, and you might have been better off just being guided by that strong study than by the flawed meta-analysis.

For example, in a meta-analysis of studies on the treatment of chronic mentally ill clients, Videka-Sherman (1988) reported that shorter-term treatments were more effective than longer-term treatments. Hogarty (1989) responded to Videka-Sherman's article with a scathing critique. Throughout his career, Hogarty had conducted experimental research on the effectiveness of interventions for individuals with chronic mental illness. His findings, and those of other well-controlled experiments, consistently found that chronic mental illness tends to be a lifelong affliction requiring long-term care. Hogarty pointed out that Videka-Sherman's finding regarding the superior effects of short-term treatment resulted primarily from the inclusion in her meta-analysis of a nonexperimental study with inadequate internal validity that merely found that service users were much more likely to be rehospitalized than nonusers. That study had a very large negative d-index of -1.97. A negative d-index indicates harmful effects. Hogarty argued that that finding cancelled out the effect sizes of some stronger studies finding superior effects for long-term care. For example, if a weak study finds a negative d-index of -1.97 for long-term care, and a strong study finds a positive d-index of $+1.97$ for long-term care, the mean d-index of the two studies will be 0, suggesting that long-term care is completely ineffective.

Hogarty argued that the study reporting the -1.97 d-index was misleading because it interpreted no treatment as the shortest form of treatment and because that particular study had a selectivity bias in which the treatment was provided only to individuals with the most severe impairments. Thus, those who received no treatment did not receive "shorter-term" treatment, and they were more likely to have better outcomes because they were less impaired to begin with. Hogarty further showed how Videka-Sherman's meta-analysis would have reached the opposite conclusion had only strong experimental studies been included in it.

One more caveat regarding meta-analysis warrants special attention because it applies to your appraisal and use of individual studies as well as meta-analyses and other systematic reviews. It concerns a concept that I touched on earlier and one that we examine next: clinical significance.

Clinical Significance

If everything else is equal—such as the nature of the outcome indicator being measured and the degree of validity and objectivity in study design and measurement—a stronger effect size will indicate stronger and more meaningful intervention effects. But rarely is everything else equal in different outcome studies. Consequently, effect-size differences do not necessarily portray which intervention has stronger or more meaningful effects.

Suppose, for example, a meta-analysis averages the effect sizes of some studies that measured outcome in terms of how satisfied clients were with an intervention to prevent teen substance abuse and some studies that measured outcome in terms of actual frequency of substance abuse. Decades ago, I ran a drop-in center for teens at risk for substance abuse who resided in a middle-class neighborhood. At the start, our program philosophy was to be nondirective and let the teens who dropped in have autonomy in center activities that they developed. Early on, for example, they put on a performance of *Hair,* a hit show on Broadway at that time. As word of the center spread, however, the better functioning teens gradually got displaced by teens who were more troubled, more defiant, and more prone to substance abuse.

Eventually, we became concerned that our laid-back, unstructured approach to the center was having harmful effects. That is, we worried that the center had degenerated into a place where substance-abusing teens could have harmful influences on other teens and use the center as a base for their drug culture. While our unstructured approach was still in place, however, the teens seemed quite satisfied with the center. They came there voluntarily to hang out after school and seemed delighted to do so. Had we measured the effectiveness of our program at that time in terms of consumer satisfaction, perhaps comparing the mean satisfaction level of our teens with that of teens in a more structured program that attempted to educate them about substance abuse or perhaps confront them using therapeutic community techniques, I surmise our effect size would have been rather strong. But had we used actual substance abuse as our outcome measure, I surmise that our effect size would have been either quite weak or negative (indicating that our mean program's frequency of substance abuse was worse than the other program's).

Suppose a number of evaluations of programs like ours had been reported, half using client satisfaction as the outcome indicator and half using frequency of substance abuse as the outcome indicator. Chances are the studies using client satisfaction would have reported very strong effect sizes and the studies using frequency of substance abuse would have reported very weak effect sizes. If so, a meta-analysis of all the studies might conclude that programs like ours had, on average, medium beneficial effects. But such a meta-analysis would be misleading because it would not have taken the **clinical significance** of the different effect sizes into account.

The term *clinical significance* refers to the meaningfulness and practical value of a finding, and recognizes that statistically significant findings—even those with very strong effect sizes—can lack clinical significance. Although some scholars have devised statistical procedures that attempt to gauge clinical significance, those procedures are quite controversial (Rubin, 2007). You can disregard them in your consideration of clinical significance, instead interpreting clinical significance in terms of your clinical expertise and value judgments regarding the practical value and meaningfulness of a particular outcome indicator and its effect size. Thus, you'd probably agree with me that a medium effect size showing that Program A prevents actual substance abuse among teens has a lot more clinical significance than a very strong effect size showing that teens are a lot more satisfied with Program B. If so, then one of the things you should look for when appraising a meta-analysis is whether in calculating an average effect size for an intervention it lumped together clinically significant and clinically insignificant out-come measures. If it did, then its average effect size could be very mis-leading.

A finding can also lack clinical significance when it pertains to a very meaningful outcome indicator but lacks an adequate effect size. Recall that with a large sample size, a weak effect size can be statistically signif-icant. For example, a difference of only 4% in dropout rates or recidivism (52% versus 48%) would be statistically significant at $p < .001$ if a large-scale study included 5,000 clients in its experimental group and 5,000 in its control group. Although dropout or recidivism might be extremely meaningful outcome indicators, a difference that slight is not likely to ex-cite practitioners or others seeking to make a meaningful impact on re-cidivism and dropout rates.

Sometimes even a meaningful indicator with a strong effect size can lack clinical significance. We are unlikely to be satisfied, for example, with an intervention that reduces the number of times male batterers be-come violent from an average of 20 times per month to 10 times per month. Even though the intervention cut the frequency of battering in half, we'd probably be very eager to find a much more effective interven-tion, one with a much stronger effect size that reduced the battering to 0 or near 0 times per month on average. (The term *on average* is important here. We should not be satisfied with any amount of violent battering by an *individual*. But if the average among a *group* of batterers is near 0, that would mean that many individual batterers had dropped to 0.)

To reiterate an important point I made earlier, you should be consider-ing the issue of clinical significance not only when you appraise meta-analyses, but also when you appraise individual studies. If you find two studies of two different interventions, and both have acceptable designs and unbiased measurement procedures, and one reports a very strong ef-fect size for a clinically insignificant outcome indicator, and the other re-ports a medium effect size for a much more meaningful (clinically significant) outcome indicator, then that information should predispose you to favor the intervention with the weaker effect size.

You can find some excellent sources for unbiased systematic reviews and meta-analyses by re-examining Table 2.2 in Chapter 2. Let me also remind you that useful systematic reviews and meta-analyses can be found regarding EBP questions about the effectiveness of policies or programs—not just questions about clinical interventions. Petrosino and Soydan (2005), for example, conducted a meta-analysis that found that when program developers evaluated the programs they developed the effect sizes regarding criminal recidivism outcomes were much stronger (and more positive) than when the program evaluators were not the pro-gram developers. Petrosino and Soydan discussed two alternative pos-sible reasons for their findings. Perhaps the program developers were more biased in their evaluations, wanting to show that their programs were effective. Alternatively, perhaps their influence improved the fidelity of the evaluation.

Reports of meta-analyses about policies will probably use the term **substantive significance** instead of the term *clinical significance.* Substantive significance—like clinical significance—also refers to the meaningfulness and practical value of a finding. The two terms are virtually synonymous, and the one that gets used depends on whether the focus is on clinical interventions.

Finally, let me also remind you that not all systematic reviews and meta-analyses address EBP questions about effectiveness or causality. Some, for example, review assessment instruments. Some review qualitative studies. Table 8.2 lists various types of systematic review and meta-

Table 8.2   Types of Questions That Systematic Reviews and Meta-Analyses Seek to Answer

Types of Questions	Types of Designs Likely to Be Emphasized (Although Not Exclusively)	Illustrative Specific Questions
Effectiveness	Experiments and quasi-experiments	Does trauma-focused cognitive-behavioral therapy reduce trauma symptoms among children who have survived a hurricane?
Assessment	Tests of the reliability, validity, sensitivity, and cultural equivalence of measurement instruments for use in diagnosis or monitoring intervention progress and outcomes	Which instrument(s) are the most valid and sensitive for measuring trauma symptoms among African American and Latino children who have survived a hurricane?
Risk or protective factors	Cohort studies and case-control studies	What factors best predict whether children who have survived a hurricane will develop PTSD?
Prevalence	Surveys	What is the proportion of children in the United States in need of treatment for PTSD?
How interventions or other phenomena are experienced by people	Qualitative studies	What was it like for parents and children to stay at the Superdome after Hurricane Katrina? How were their lives changed by the hurricane?
Methodological questions	Surveys of published studies	What proportion of outcome studies published in psychotherapy journals use experimental designs? Are journals biased against publishing outcome studies with negative results?
Economic questions	Cost-effectiveness and cost-benefit analyses	Does exposure therapy or EMDR yield better long-term outcomes per dollar spent?

From *Systematic Reviews in the Social Sciences: A Practical Guide* (pp. 46–47), by M. Petticrew and H. Roberts, 2006, Malden, MA: Blackwell. Adapted with permission.

analysis questions, the designs they are likely to emphasize, and examples of some specific questions they may answer.

SYNOPSES OF RESEARCH STUDIES

The first of the following two synopses is completely fictional, including the names of the authors. Any connection to real people is purely accidental. The second synopsis summarizes parts (not all) of a real study, authored by Davidson and Parker (2001). I've modified it.

Study 1 Synopsis (Fictional)

"The Effectiveness of New Wave Parent Education Training: A Systematic Review"

Fictional Authors: Shirley Cruse and Tom McClain

The first three evaluations of the innovative "new wave" approach to parent education training (PET) suggested that it has the potential to be a historical breakthrough in dramatically improving on the effects of previous approaches to PET (Cruse, 1998; McClain, 1999; Cruse & McClain, 2000). For a description of the development of and theory underlying the new wave approach see McClain and Cruse (1997). The impressive findings of the early studies stimulated a great deal of excitement and enthusiasm for this new approach, and New Wave PET programs soon sprang up in localities around the world. To date, more than 30,000 practitioners have attended New Wave PET training workshops.

Were the findings of the early studies replicated in evaluations of subsequently developed New Wave PET programs? The purpose of this study was to conduct a systematic review to answer that question. We examined all the articles published in child welfare related journals since the first New Wave PET program was established in 1997. We also examined *Psychology Abstracts, Sociology Abstracts,* and *Social Work Abstracts* for each of those years, looking for articles on New Wave PET published in other journals.

In all, we found 30 published studies that evaluated a New Wave PET program. Ten of the studies used randomized experimental designs, 10 used quasi-experimental designs, and 10 used pilot studies without control groups. We decided to eliminate the 10 pilot studies from our analysis due to their weaker status on the EBP evidentiary hierarchy.

Of the 20 studies that were kept in our analysis, 13 supported the effectiveness of the New Wave PET program, 3 found it to be ineffective, and 4 had inconclusive results. We critically appraised the research methodology of all 20 studies. We found no serious flaws in 12 of the 13 studies supporting the effectiveness of the New Wave PET program. Each of the four randomized experiments with inconclusive results seemed particularly vulnerable to diffusion of treatment, in which the treatment as usual practitioners may have learned about and incorporated new wave techniques in their approach. In each of the three randomized experiments that found the New Wave PET program to be ineffective, the New Wave PET program practitioners did not implement the program properly based on our review of each article's description of how the parent training sessions were conducted.

Because we found 12 strong studies without serious flaws that supported the effectiveness of New Wave PET, no strong studies that found it to be ineffective, and four studies with inconclusive results that seem attributable to diffusion of treatment, our review supports the promising results of the early studies on New Wave PET and suggests that New Wave PET deserves the status of an evidence-based intervention.

Study 2 Synopsis

This meta-analysis aimed to answer three questions about EMDR. Is it an effective treatment? Is it more effective than exposure therapy? Are the eye movements a necessary component? Only published reports of randomized experiments were included. Articles presented only at conferences were excluded. Thirty-four such studies were found in searches of PsycINFO and Medline from 1988, when the first study of EMDR appeared, to April 2000. We analyzed our findings in May of 2000.

We organized our effect-size findings into different categories, based on the type of outcome measure reported. We found no significant differences in mean effect size across the different types of outcome measures of trauma symptoms, such as scores on validated self-report scales, behavioral measures, and physiological measures.

Regarding our first question, EMDR appears to be an effective treatment when compared to a no-treatment control condition, with a strong mean effect size (d-index = .98). It also appears to have strong effects when compared to nonspecific therapies (d-index = .87). However, when examining whether the eye movements are a necessary component of EMDR, we found the effect size to be very weak and not significantly different than 0. That is, there was no significant difference when comparing the outcome of EMDR with eye movements to EMDR with eyes not moving. Moreover, EMDR does not appear to be more effective than exposure therapy. Compared to imaginal exposure therapy, EMDR had a somewhat weak positive effect size (d-index = .39). Compared to in vivo exposure therapy, EMDR had a somewhat weak negative effect size of the same magnitude (d-index = −.39).

Because our study included only published studies, we decided to compare our results to the results of unpublished dissertations that met our other inclusion criteria. We searched *Dissertations Abstracts* for the years 1989 through 2000, using *EMDR* and *eye movement desensitization* as our search terms. We found nine dissertations that met our inclusion criteria. Three had been published and thus were already in our analysis. The other six found no difference between EMDR with eye movements and EMDR with eyes not moving, and thus had findings that were consistent with our findings.

In conclusion, EMDR appears to be better than no treatment and with strong effects. But our findings did not support claims that it is more effective than exposure therapy or that the eye movements are a necessary component.

KEY CHAPTER CONCEPTS

- Systematic reviews and meta-analyses attempt to synthesize and develop conclusions from diverse studies and their disparate findings.
- Some systematic reviews and meta-analyses are more trustworthy than others.
- When critically appraising systematic reviews and meta-analyses for potential bias, you should ask: Who sponsored, funded, or conducted the review? Were vested interests at stake?
- Relatively trustworthy reviews can be found at the web sites of the Cochrane and Campbell Collaborations.
- When critically appraising systematic reviews and meta-analyses, you should look for their inclusion/exclusion criteria and judge whether they are too narrow or too restrictive.
- An important issue is whether the review adequately critiqued the inclusion and exclusion criteria of the studies it reviewed. Did it clarify which studies were seriously flawed and which weren't, and sort the evidence accordingly? Likewise, did it sort the evidence according to client characteristics?
- Some reviews search for studies in a more comprehensive fashion than others. Some more comprehensive reviews look for unpublished studies, not just published ones.
- Instead of considering only one type of intervention, ideally a review should ask: Which interventions have the best evidence regarding their effectiveness with a target problem or population?
- An overarching issue in critically appraising systematic reviews is the review's transparency, which involves spelling out all the

details regarding inclusion and exclusion criteria, how studies were collected, source of funding, reviewer backgrounds, and whether different reviewers with different backgrounds agreed about the review conclusions. Transparency enables you to make a more informed appraisal and decision about the evidence supplied in a review. A review that lacks transparency in regard to anything relevant to your critical appraisal of it should be viewed warily.

- Effect-size statistics depict the average strength of the effects of an intervention across studies that use different types of outcome measures.

- Effect sizes come in two forms: correlations and z-scores. Correlations depict the strength of relationship between two variables in terms of a figure that can range from 0 (no correlation) to either +1.0 (a perfect positive correlation) or −1.0 (a perfect negative correlation).

- An effect size in the form of a z-score is called the d-index. It is calculated by dividing the difference between the experimental and control group means by the standard deviation.

- Meta-analyses can calculate the mean effect size for an intervention across a large number of studies.

- Benchmarks have been established for considering whether any study's effect size, or any mean effect size in a meta-analysis, is relatively strong, medium, or weak.

- A flawed meta-analysis might inappropriately lump together effect sizes from weakly controlled studies and well-controlled studies. If the better studies have effect sizes that are much stronger or much weaker than the effect sizes found in seriously flawed studies, then the meta-analysis will yield a misleading average effect size.

- A flawed meta-analysis also might inappropriately lump together effect sizes from clinically meaningful measures and effect sizes from clinically insignificant measures. This, too, can yield a misleading average effect size.

- The term *clinical significance* refers to the meaningfulness and practical value of a finding, and recognizes that statistically significant findings—even those with very strong effect sizes—can lack clinical significance. You can interpret clinical significance in terms of your clinical expertise and value judgments regarding the practical value and meaningfulness of a particular outcome indicator and its effect size.

- You should consider the issue of clinical significance not only when you appraise meta-analyses, but also when you appraise individual studies.

Review Exercises

1. *Use the Internet to find a systematic review and a literature review that does not claim to be systematic. Describe the key similarities and differences between the two reviews in terms of inclusion/exclusion criteria, comprehensiveness, potential bias, and transparency.*
2. *Critically appraise each of the reviews you found in Exercise 1.*
3. *Use the Internet to find a report of a meta-analysis. Critically appraise it in terms of the issues emphasized in this chapter.*
4. *Using Google, Yahoo, or some similar search engine, enter the search term* file-drawer effect. *Go to one or more of the links that come up and briefly summarize what you learn there.*
5. *Identify an outcome indicator that you would deem to be clinically insignificant for a problem of interest to you. Discuss your reasoning.*
6. *Identify an outcome indicator that you would deem to be clinically meaningful for a problem of interest to you. Describe how a statistically significant effect size on that indicator might be too weak to be clinically significant. Discuss your reasoning.*
7. *Two studies evaluate the effectiveness of different approaches for preventing school dropout. Study A evaluates Intervention A in terms of scores on a self-report measure of self-esteem (with higher scores indicating more self-esteem), and finds a mean of 80 in the experimental group and 50 in the control group, with a standard deviation of 10. Study B evaluates Intervention B according to two outcome indicators over the course of an entire academic year: (1) days truant, and (2) school grades (in percentage terms). For days truant, the experimental group's mean was 4, the control group's mean was 10, and the standard deviation was 3. For school grades, the experimental group's mean was 75, the control group's mean was 65, and the standard deviation was 10. Calculate the* d-index *effect sizes for each study. Which study's findings had more clinical significance? Discuss your reasoning.*

ADDITIONAL READINGS

Lipsey, M. W., & Wilson, D. B. (2000). *Practical meta-analysis.* Thousand Oaks, CA: Sage.

Petticrew, M., & Roberts, H. (2006). *Systematic reviews in the social sciences: A practical guide.* Malden, MA: Blackwell.

Rubin, A. (2007). *Statistics for evidence-based practice and evaluation.* Belmont, CA: Thompson Brooks/Cole.

PART III

CRITICALLY APPRAISING STUDIES FOR ALTERNATIVE EBP QUESTIONS

Chapter 9 ———————————————

CRITICALLY APPRAISING NONEXPERIMENTAL QUANTITATIVE STUDIES

As discussed in Chapter 3, not all evidence-based practice (EBP) questions pertain to making causal inferences about the effectiveness of interventions, programs, or policies. Some EBP questions have to do with improving practitioner understanding of the plight of clients, factors that predict desirable or undesirable outcomes among clients, or what it's like to have had a client's experiences. Such improved understanding can aid in choosing an intervention plan that best fits client circumstances and in delivering interventions in ways that are more sensitive to the plight of clients.

For these questions, nonexperimental designs are more appropriate than experimental or quasi-experimental ones. The designs pertinent to these questions can be quantitative, qualitative, or both. As discussed in Chapter 3, quantitative studies pertinent to this chapter put more emphasis on producing precise and objective statistical findings that can be generalized to populations, whereas qualitative studies put more emphasis on generating deeper, but more tentative insights that are riskier to generalize. We examine how to appraise various quantitative designs in this chapter and how to appraise qualitative studies in Chapter 10.

Although the types of studies to be discussed in this chapter and the next are more appropriate than experiments and quasi-experiments for answering EBP questions that do not pertain to making causal inferences about effectiveness, they often are used in connection with questions about effectiveness. When they are used that way, they reside below experiments and quasi-experiments on an evidentiary hierarchy for inferring causality, and their results have to be viewed with caution. Yet, they can be useful, especially when studies with more internal validity have not yet been conducted or when the nonexperimental studies shed light on the external validity of the experiments or quasi-experiments. Because nonexperimental studies can be used to address EBP questions about effectiveness as well as to answer other EBP questions, we examine their strengths and weaknesses in regard to both purposes. Let's begin with surveys.

SURVEYS

Surveys gather data by asking people questions or having them complete a scale (or several scales) that measure some phenomenon. For example, a survey of people who are caregivers for debilitated loved ones might ask questions about the degree of caregiver burden they experience and have them complete a self-report scale measuring their level of burden, depression, or anticipatory grief.

Surveys can be conducted in various ways: by mail using questionnaires and scales that respondents complete, by face-to-face interviews (which might involve the use of self-report scales administered orally), or online via e-mail or a web site. Each way has its advantages and disadvantages. For your purposes as a practitioner, the key questions will be the same regardless of which approach was used:

- Was the information collected in a valid, unbiased manner?
- Were the survey respondents representative of the target population?
- Were the conclusions warranted in light of the design logic, the type of data analysis employed, and the findings of that analysis?

Suppose, for example, you are appraising a survey of caregivers for loved ones suffering from Alzheimer's disease. Suppose the information collected included data on the following two variables: (1) whether the caregiver had participated in a caregiver support group sponsored by the

Alzheimer's Association, and (2) the degree of self-reported caregiver burden. Suppose further that although all members of the Alzheimer's Association were asked to participate in the survey, only 30% of them agreed to participate. Next, suppose that the survey was introduced with comments indicating that it was being conducted by the Alzheimer's Association and that its purpose was to document the effectiveness of the Association's support groups. Finally, suppose that it concluded that caregivers for loved ones suffering from Alzheimer's disease have an unexpectedly low degree of burden in general and that participating in a caregiver support group sponsored by the Alzheimer's Association significantly reduced their already low level of burden. Let's now answer the three questions for this example.

Measurement Issues: Was the Information Collected in a Valid, Unbiased Manner?

The description of this fictitious study should tell you that the answer to this question is no. By introducing the survey with comments indicating that it was being conducted by the Alzheimer's Association and that its purpose was to document the effectiveness of the Association's support groups, it could have predisposed respondents who participated in those groups to tell the researchers what they wanted to hear.

The same measurement issues that were discussed in Chapters 3 and 4 apply to surveys and other quantitative studies. A survey should provide evidence that its measurement procedures were reliable, valid, and sensitive to subtle differences. In addition, if the survey included respondents other than those in the majority culture, it should provide evidence supporting the cultural sensitivity of its measures. The ways such evidence can be supplied are examined in detail in Chapter 11, which will focus on criteria for selecting measurement instruments to assess clients and monitor their treatment progress. Now let's turn to the second question.

Sampling Issues: Were the Survey Respondents Representative of the Target Population?

There are several reasons to seriously doubt the representativeness of the survey respondents. To begin, the survey did not attempt to include caregivers who do not belong to the Alzheimer's Association. Conceivably, their degree of burden—along with various attributes such as socioeconomic status, ethnicity, and so on—might be unlike that of caregivers who belong to the Association. This would not be a problem if the study sought only to generalize to Association members, but it generalized to all caregivers for loved ones suffering from Alzheimer's disease. If your client is a member, then you would not have to worry about this particular issue, but if your client is not a member, then the applicability of the findings to your client is dubious.

Nonresponse Bias

Even if your client is a member of the Association, however, the fact that only 30% of those members responded should undermine your confidence that the findings would apply to your client. A response rate that low suggests a serious potential for **nonresponse bias.** Perhaps the caregivers experiencing the most severe levels of burden were much less likely to take the time to respond. Perhaps those who felt that participating in the support groups reduced their burden were much more likely to respond than those who felt otherwise.

Although some surveys with low response rates can have value, as will be discussed soon, those with less than a 50% response rate are generally considered to be highly suspect as to their vulnerability to nonresponse bias and whether they adequately represent the target population. However, exceeding a 50% response rate does not guarantee that a meaningful nonresponse bias has been avoided. Even with a 60% response rate, which is generally considered to be relatively good, the 40% who did not respond might differ in important ways from the 60% who did respond. No magic cutoff point well below 100% exists for ruling out the risk of a nonresponse bias. Nevertheless, we know that such a risk diminishes as response rates increase and that surveys with response rates that are well above 60% have much less risk of nonresponse bias than most surveys.

Even if it obtains an adequate response rate, a survey ideally should make a reasonable effort to compare the attributes of respondents to non-respondents. In the example we are discussing, if the Alzheimer's Association has demographic data (gender, ethnicity, age, educational level, occupation, and so on) for all of its members, the researchers could have compared the demographic attributes of its respondents to those of the population as a whole. If the differences are trivial, then doubt about the representativeness of the sample is not as severe as it would be if the differences are substantial. Regardless, however, if those attributes are unlike your client's characteristics, then the applicability of the findings to your client are nonetheless dubious. Perhaps, for example, your client is of a different ethnicity or is poorer and less educated than the average study participant.

Suppose the survey was conducted online and did not gather any demographic background data. That should make you especially wary of a nonresponse bias related to socioeconomic level. Poorer and less educated clients are less likely to have computers and Internet access. That's no problem if your client is not poor and often gets online. Otherwise, you should have serious misgivings as to whether respondents to an online survey experience caregiver burden in the way that your client experiences it.

Next we'll examine alternative sampling methods that increase or decrease the likelihood of obtaining a sample of respondents that is representative of the target population. You'll see that random sampling methods are preferred for maximizing the likelihood of attaining a representative sample. But even the best sampling methods don't preclude the possibility of nonresponse bias. No matter how a study selects members of the target population for inclusion in the study, those who refuse or somehow fail to participate might differ in key ways from the ones who do participate.

Nevertheless, some studies with poor response rates can have value, as noted earlier. Suppose, for example that half of the respondents to the Alzheimer's Association survey had indicated that they were so stressed out that on occasion they seriously considered doing something harmful to themselves or their relative with the disease. Even if none of the nonrespondents ever considered doing the same, the number of caregivers who so indicated would be large enough to concern planners and other practitioners and indicate the need to take this issue into account when planning service programs or treating clients. Thus, despite the importance of nonresponse bias, you should not automatically disregard a study that seems to have such a bias. It might still have findings that are useful to your EBP question.

Sampling Methods

Sampling refers to the way a study selects its participants, and a **sample** refers to that segment of a population that ends up participating in the study. There are two overarching types of sampling: **probability sampling** and **nonprobability sampling.** Probability sampling is generally deemed to be the safest way to try to achieve representativeness because it involves the use of random numbers (as mentioned in Chapter 4) to select study participants and thus is least vulnerable to researcher bias or judgment errors. Nonprobability sampling does not select participants randomly and consequently is riskier, but sometimes it is necessary. Let's look at the subtypes within each of these overarching types, beginning with probability sampling.

Probability Sampling   Suppose your EBP question inquires about the unmet needs of homeless people in New York City. You are asking the question because you are planning to develop a program that will attempt to meet those needs. You might find and appraise a study that surveyed a probability sample of homeless people that was already receiving some services from social service agencies in the city. Let's assume that there were 10,000 such people and the study could afford to interview no more than 500 of them. It would begin by numbering the people from 0 to 9999. Then it would examine a table of random numbers and select the cases with the first 500 numbers encountered on the list. For example, if the first three numbers on the list were: 5036, 7821, and 4952, then the people with those three case numbers would be selected for the sample.

The subtype of probability sample just described is a **simple random sample.** An equally valid subtype is called a **systematic sample.** Using a systematic sampling approach, the study would select one random number to identify a case to begin with, and then select every 20th case after that (not every 20th random number—every 20th case on the list of cases, beginning with the one case that was randomly chosen.) Why every 20th number? Because 500 is one-twentieth of 10,000. If they could afford to interview 1,000 people, then they would select every 10th number, because 1000 is one-tenth of 10,000.

Suppose the researchers wanted to ensure adequate representation of a small minority group in their sample—say, Native Americans. To do so, they would select a **stratified random sample.** To use this approach, they would need the agency case records to identify each homeless person's ethnicity. Then, instead of numbering all the cases from one to ten thousand, the researchers would number each ethnic group of concern separately—from one to however many cases shared that ethnicity. Then it would use simple random sampling or systematic sampling to select a specified number of prospective participants within each ethnic category. The specified number to be selected within each category could be based on the overall proportion of cases in that category in the population. Thus, if the study were selecting 500 names out of 10,000, which would be 5%, and there were 200 Native Americans on the larger list, then the study would select 10 Native Americans: 5% of the 200. Suppose, however, that there were only 10 Native Americans on the larger list. The researchers could then select a disproportionate number of them—probably all 10—and then weight their data in the overall analysis accordingly.

A third subtype of probability sampling is called **cluster sampling.** Using cluster sampling, the researchers would begin not with a list of individual people, but with a list of groupings—*clusters*—of people. Suppose, for example, that the survey was national in scope, and the researchers could not afford to travel to more than 20 locations to conduct their interviews. Moreover, they might not be able to obtain a list of homeless clients served by each social service agency in the nation. The researchers would number every geographic locality and then randomly select 20 of the locations. Then they would contact the relevant agencies in each location to obtain lists as described earlier regarding New York City. Then they would proceed to select a random sample from each list.

If you are appraising a study that used probability sampling, the foregoing descriptions will help you understand the relevant terminology. The important thing to remember, however, is that all of these subtypes of probability sampling are relatively safe ways to obtain a representative sample. Conversely, when a study reports using nonprobability sampling, warning signals should immediately pop into your mind, alerting you to be vigilant about the chances that the sample might be unrepresentative due to some form of bias or error in judgment. Before we examine nonprobability sampling, let's look at a couple of ways that probability samples can be biased.

Potential Bias in Probability Samples   Although selecting cases randomly prevents researcher bias or judgment errors regarding what specific cases to select, there are still two possible ways for a probability sample to be biased: (1) a relatively high nonresponse rate, and (2) using a biased list to begin with for selecting cases.

Regarding nonresponse bias, earlier I mentioned that people who refuse or somehow fail to participate in a study might differ in key ways from the ones who do participate and that even the best sampling methods don't preclude the possibility of nonresponse bias. Randomly selecting the names of people on a list does not ensure that those people will agree to participate in a study. Moreover, it doesn't guarantee that the people will be located to request their participation in the first place. Many homeless people, for example, might be hard to find, and the ones who are harder to find might differ in important ways from those who can be found. Their problems, for example, might be more severe, and they might have different service needs.

Regarding the possibility of a biased list for selecting cases, the people whose names are on that list might differ in important ways from the people not on the list. Recall that in the previous fictitious homelessness survey, for example, the list was provided by social service agencies and included only those homeless people who were already receiving some services from those agencies. The homeless people not receiving services, and who have no chance of being selected for the sample, might have very different levels of functioning and consequently very different needs than the homeless people already receiving services.

In this connection, whenever you read a study that uses probability sampling, you should appraise whether the list used to do the random selection was comprised of the entire population of names versus a perhaps skewed segment of that population. Recall the fictitious Alzheimer's Association survey example discussed earlier in this chapter. The survey included only those caregivers who belonged to the Association. Even using the most sophisticated probability sampling techniques, therefore, the survey should not claim to represent all caregivers—only those who are Association members.

This leads us to the distinction between the terms *population* and *sampling frame*. A sampling frame is a list of names that may include the entire population or only some segment of the population. Whether a sampling frame includes the entire population depends on how the population is defined. If a study is interested only in assessing the consumer satisfaction level of homeless people who received services, then the population of interest includes only those homeless people who received services, not those who never received services with which to be satisfied or dissatisfied. Therefore, excluding homeless people who received no services would not bias the sample or mean that the sampling frame (the list) was incomplete. Likewise, if the Alzheimer's Association survey only wants to find out how satisfied Association members are with the services provided by the Association, then the population of interest includes only Alzheimer's Association members. Excluding caregivers who are nonmembers would not bias the sample. Nevertheless, some study reports using limited sampling frames inappropriately generalize beyond their frame to a larger population. If the reports of these fictitious studies were to generalize to *all* Alzheimer's disease caregivers or *all* homeless people, that would be misleading. When you appraise a study that used probability sampling, you should keep the problem of potential overgeneralization in mind. Of course, the same caveat applies when you appraise studies that use nonprobability sampling, which we'll examine next.

Nonprobability Sampling   Nonprobability samples are not selected randomly. The specific basis for selection will vary. Some studies will merely select those cases that are most immediately available and convenient to sample and are thus termed **availability samples, convenience samples,** or **accidental samples.** An example would be assessing consumer satisfaction only among those clients who happen to show up for appointments during a given week, or interviewing those homeless people who happen to be hanging out at a nearby park on a warm afternoon. Availability sampling is the most vulnerable to bias. The people who are most convenient to select can be quite unlike those who are not so available. When you appraise a study using availability sampling, you should be vigilant as to that vulnerability. But not all studies using such methods are fatally flawed. Clinical outcome experiments, for example, typically use availability sampling. It's silly to suppose that researchers could randomly select people from the population and ask them to take part in an experiment that might treat them for trauma, depression, or some other problem. Typically, such studies must rely on using people who make themselves known as seeking treatment. That's why experiments and quasi-experiments are said to put less emphasis on external validity than on internal validity.

Another form of availability sampling that might have some value would be when service recipients at a particular agency are sampled because that agency is accessible to researchers. Suppose a study finds that a large proportion of the parents of Mexican American teens being treated by a substance-drug abuse program in a border town are themselves substance abusers or perhaps selling drugs. Practitioners providing drug abuse treatment to Mexican American teens in other programs and in other border towns might find that knowledge useful and worth looking into among their clients despite the possibility that the availability sample in the reported study might be unlike their clients.

Another form of nonprobability sampling relies on the researcher's judgment about how to maximize a sample's representativeness and is thus called **judgment sampling** or **purposive sampling.** (The latter term refers to the researcher's purpose of maximizing representativeness instead of just sampling those cases that happen to be the most convenient to sample.) Rather than merely interview the homeless people who happen to be in a nearby park on a warm afternoon, for example, the researchers could use their knowledge of where homeless people hang out at various times and various spots all over a city and then develop a sampling plan that—in the researcher's judgment—seems to offer the best chance of obtaining a representative sample of homeless people in that city. Rather than interview the parents of Mexican American teens being treated in one substance-abuse program in one border town, the researchers might identify all such programs in all border towns and then handpick several programs that in their judgment seem to represent the various ways such programs differ. Thus, they might select one program in a small town and a large city along the Texas-Mexico border and the same along the Mexican border in New Mexico, Arizona, and California. There is no guarantee that their judgment is accurate, and that their sample is as representative as they think it is, but if you read such a study, you can make your own assessment about their judgment. At least they made an effort to obtain a representative sample instead of just selecting cases that happened to be the most convenient.

Some studies might say they used *quota sampling*. That just means that their nonprobability sampling used preestablished quotas as to how many people would be included with specific characteristics. Thus, if they intend to survey 1,000 people, they might stipulate that once 500 of either gender were interviewed, they would only interview people of the other gender until they completed interviews of 500 males and 500 females. Quotas also could be specified regarding ethnicity or other background characteristics. Using quotas might be a nice touch, but it is far from a guarantee that a convenience sample will be representative. Interviewing an equal number of males and females hanging out at 2:00 P.M. in a nearby park where homeless people congregate does not make that park or that time of day any more representative of all homeless people in a city.

A more acceptable form of nonprobability sampling for hard-to-find populations like the homeless is called **snowball sampling.** Using this method, researchers begin where they know they can find some homeless people, interview them, and then ask them for help in locating other homeless people they know or other places where homeless people hang out. As each additional person included in the sample helps the researcher find more people, the sample accumulates like an ever-growing snowball. Despite not being random, and its consequent inescapable vulnerability to bias, snowball sampling is considered to be an acceptable method when attempting to survey hidden or stigmatized people who are hard to locate. When appraising a study that used snowball sampling, you should ask yourself whether the population really was hard to locate and, if so, view its vulnerability to sampling bias as a reasonable limitation, not a fatal flaw.

Appropriateness of Data Analysis and Conclusions

Recall that the third question to ask when critically appraising a survey is: Were the conclusions warranted in light of the design logic, the type of data analysis employed, and the findings of that analysis? For that question, let's return to our fictitious survey which concluded that caregivers for loved ones suffering from Alzheimer's disease have an unexpectedly low degree of burden in general and that participating in a caregiver support group sponsored by the Alzheimer's Association significantly reduced their already low level of burden. The former conclusion was not warranted in light of problematic representativeness of the respondents. The latter conclusion was not warranted in light of the study's nonexperimental design and consequent low degree of internal validity. Perhaps, for example, the caregivers who already had lower levels of burden simply were more able to participate in the support groups to begin with.

Surveys can offset problems connected to representativeness (external validity) and internal validity by using multivariate data analysis procedures. The logic and use of these multivariate procedures are the same as was discussed in Chapter 6, in connection with statistically controlling for potential selectivity biases in quasi-experiments.

Regarding external validity, suppose that the Alzheimer's Association quasi-experiment discussed in Chapter 6 had controlled for various demographic variables and found that level of caregiver burden among its members did not vary according to those variables. That would give you more reason to suppose that maybe its results applied to your client who is poorer or less educated or of a different ethnicity than most of the members of the Association.

With respect to internal validity, suppose the study found that the differences in burden level change between participants and nonparticipants in the Association's support groups were the same regardless of socioeconomic status or initial level of burden at pretest. Although you should still view the study as having had a low level of internal validity—much lower than rigorous studies using experimental or quasi-experimental designs—if no stronger studies exist, then that multivariate finding would give you more grounds to suppose that the support groups might be effective in reducing burden than if the data analysis failed to include multivariate controls.

Common forms of multivariate analysis that you'll encounter in studies have the following labels: *multiple regression analysis, logistical regression,* and *structural equation modeling.* There are additional forms that you'll encounter less often. Regardless, you don't need to take statistics courses on these procedures to be guided by their findings. Each tells you which variables are and which are not related when the other variables are controlled. They also tell you which variables are most strongly predictive of another variable when the other variables are controlled. Thus, a multiple regression analysis might report that when all other variables are controlled, the strongest predictor of level of caregiver burden is whether the caregiver participated in a support group.

The circles in Figure 9.1 illustrate the logic of that conclusion. The shaded area shows a fictitious partial correlation between support group participation and burden level after the three-way overlap between those two variables and socioeconomic status is removed. The circles show that although support group participation correlates with socioeconomic status, and although socioeconomic status correlates with burden level, even after the three-way overlap is removed, participation still correlates rather strongly with burden level in the imaginary results.

Conversely, a multiple regression analysis might tell you that the correlation between support group participation and level of burden weakens or disappears when socioeconomic variables are controlled. The circles in Figure 9.2 illustrate the logic underlying that conclusion. As in Figure 9.1, the shaded area shows the partial correlation between support group participation and burden level after the three-way overlap between those two variables and socioeconomic status is removed. However, this time the circles show that almost all of the correlation between support group participation and burden level can be attributed to the strong correlation between participation and socioeconomic status. After the influence of socioeconomic status is removed, the correlation (in the shaded area) between participation and burden level is tiny. In contrast, the partial correlation between socioeconomic status and burden level is strong after the three-way overlap is removed.

Figure 9.1   Circles Depicting the Results of a fictitious Multiple Regression Analysis That Implies a Strong Partial Correlation between Support Group Participation and Caregiver Burden

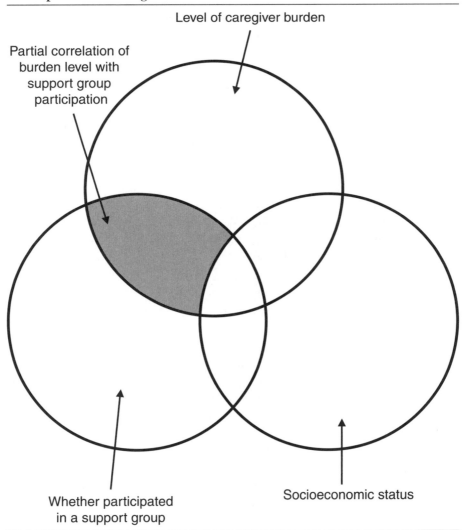

Although multivariate procedures do not provide sufficient grounds for making causal inferences, the plausibility of causality is stronger when alternative explanatory variables are controlled than when an analysis looks only at the relationship between two variables without controlling for any others. Moreover, putting aside the issue of causality, a multivariate analysis is more likely to indicate whether a particular finding seems applicable to your client than an analysis that fails to break down its findings by various client background characteristics. Thus, in critically appraising any quantitative study, whether multivariate procedures were

Figure 9.2   Circles Depicting the Results of a fictitious Multiple Regression Analysis That Implies a Weak Partial Correlation between Support Group Participation and Caregiver Burden

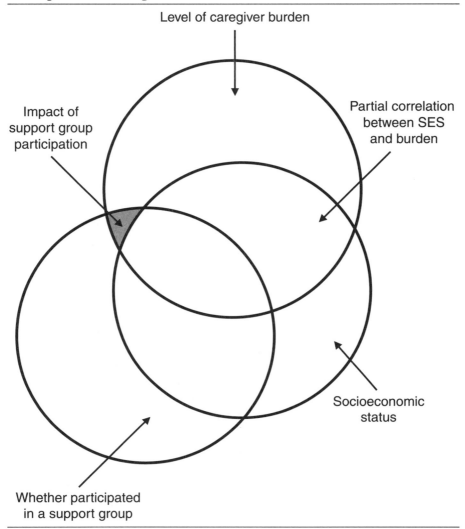

used is a key issue in considering the appropriateness of its conclusions and its applicability to your practice situation.

CROSS-SECTIONAL AND LONGITUDINAL STUDIES

Surveys, as well as other types of studies, can be conducted at one time or over a span of time. A **cross-sectional study** examines a phenomenon or relationships among variables at one point in time only. It does not assess changes over time. Thus, it is quite limited regarding the detection of causality or in merely describing the trajectory of phenomena. For example, a cross-sectional study would likely be less valuable in finding out how the nature and level of caregiver burden changes as the loved one becomes more and more incapacitated than would a study that assesses caregivers at different stages of their loved one's disease.

Nevertheless, cross-sectional studies can shed some tentative light on how things might change over time. For example, caregivers might be asked about the stage of their loved one's illness, how long they have been caring for him or her, and various other variables that could be controlled in a multivariate analysis.

To get a better handle on how phenomena change over time, **longitudinal studies** collect their data at different points over an extended period of time. Thus, a longitudinal study could assess caregiver burden among the same caregivers at different times to see how the nature and level of burden changes in connection to duration of caregiving and changes in the condition of the person being cared for. To illustrate how cross-sectional studies are weaker in that respect, suppose that a cross-sectional survey finds that caregivers who have been providing care longer report experiencing less burden than caregivers who have only recently begun caregiving. Does that mean that burden decreases over time? Or does it mean that the caregivers who perceive the least burden last longer as caregivers, whereas those who experience caregiving as more burdensome are more likely to place their loved one in a long-term care facility and thus not be among the respondents who have lasted very long as caregivers? A longitudinal study would be better able to answer these questions than a cross-sectional study.

Cohort Studies and Panel Studies

Some longitudinal studies assess different people at different times, while other longitudinal studies follow the same set of people over time. The studies that assess the same set of people over time offer better evidence as to the trajectory of change and possible causality, and thus are the most relevant to EBP questions. Some label these studies as *cohort studies.* Others call them *panel studies.* Regardless of which label is used, by examining the same set of people each time, these studies can show the time sequence of various changes and provide better clues as to what factors might cause these changes. These studies could show whether individual caregivers' level of burden changes as the duration of care increases or as other changes transpire—such as participating in a support group.

It is difficult to track the same people over time, however, and therefore these studies can experience high rates of attrition as some participants die, change their residence, or lose interest in the study and consequently drop out of it. Because those who drop out might be unlike the others—in ways that might be related to the variables of interest—a high rate of attrition can distort a study's findings and is something to keep in mind when you appraise these studies. As with cross-sectional studies, to help you judge whether the findings apply to your clients or practice situation, you should also consider the representativeness of the sample, the quality of the measurement, and whether multivariate data analysis procedures were used to improve control for alternative explanations for observed changes.

CASE-CONTROL STUDIES

Another set of studies that offer useful clues regarding possible causality use a **case-control design.** Studies using this design are called **case-control studies**—they collect data at just one point in time and in that sense resemble cross-sectional studies. However, they also can be seen as retrospective longitudinal studies because they ask people about past events.

A key feature of case-control studies is the use of matched groups of people who appear to be comparable except for some contrasting outcome. By using multivariate data analysis techniques, case-control studies attempt to determine what personal attributes and past experiences best distinguish the two groups. Past experiences can include anything that seems pertinent throughout their lives, including the receipt of a particular intervention.

Suppose we want to improve our understanding of the causes and prevention of posttraumatic stress disorder (PTSD) among military veterans who served in Iraq. We could interview a sample of such veterans who received treatment for PTSD at Veterans Administration hospitals and a matched group of Iraq war veterans who never were treated for PTSD but who resemble the PTSD group in other respects. We can ask each individual to recall his or her military experiences and earlier life experiences before contracting PTSD. With a multivariate analysis that includes all of these variables, we might be able to isolate some things that most strongly differentiate the two groups. This information might help identify military personnel most at risk for developing PTSD and things the military might do to try to reduce the incidence of PTSD. It might also enhance clinician understanding of key issues to focus on in treating PTSD.

If we seek clues as to what interventions might be the most effective in the treatment of PTSD among veterans, our entire sample could be comprised of veterans who had been treated for PTSD, but the matched groups would compare those who have and have not had their PTSD resolved. In addition to asking about military experiences and earlier life experiences before contracting PTSD, we would ask about experiences after contracting it, including information about the type of treatment they received, its duration, and so on. If our multivariate analysis finds that the variable that most strongly differentiates the two groups is whether they received 20 or more sessions of exposure therapy, then we would have credible evidence supporting the effectiveness of that intervention and that dosage level for it. The evidence would not be as strong as that coming from well-controlled, rigorous experiments and quasi-experiments, but it would still be useful. It might even be the best evidence available in the absence of studies with more internal validity.

While recognizing their potential utility, you should also be mindful of some limitations when appraising case-control studies. One key limitation is the possibility of **recall bias.** Knowing how things turned out can bias how people recall earlier events. Suppose, for example, our study finds that by far the most important factor distinguishing the two groups of veterans who have and have not had their PTSD resolved is their recollection of the quality of their relationship with their therapist. It would be tempting to conclude from this finding that the type of intervention provided matters much less than the quality of the therapist-client relationship. Although this conclusion would be quite plausible and consistent with some studies of psychotherapy in general, it is also plausible that perhaps the failure to resolve PTSD tainted the way the veterans recalled the quality of their relationship with their therapist. Perhaps the quality on average was the same for both groups, but the ones who had their PTSD resolved attributed it to their therapist and thus recalled the therapist in a much more favorable light than those whose PTSD is ongoing and who therefore perhaps resent their therapist for not curing them. If such recall bias is strong, it might eclipse the statistical impact of the type of intervention in the multivariate analysis.

In a study of the possible impact that adverse childhood experiences might have on adult homelessness, Herman, Susser, Struening, and Link (1997) illustrated one way to try to control for the impact of recall bias. They interviewed two groups of people. One group had been homeless at some time in their adult lives. The other group had attributes associated with a higher risk of homelessness (poverty, mental illness, and so on) but had never been homeless. They found that physical abuse and lack of parental care during childhood strongly distinguished the two groups even when a host of socioeconomic and other demographic variables were controlled in their multivariate analysis. To limit the influence of recall bias, they assessed the current emotional well-being of each respondent, reasoning that the worse the respondent's current emotional problems, the more likely they would be to recall—in a biased fashion—more adverse childhood experiences. By including that assessment in their multivariate analysis, their study could be appraised as having been less vulnerable to the influence of recall bias than studies that failed to control for current emotional state.

Case-control studies should also be appraised in light of other types of flaws that can also limit the value of studies using other types of designs. For example, Herman and his coauthors (1997) cautioned that their sample probably underrepresented people who had been homeless for a very long time.

SYNOPSES OF RESEARCH STUDIES

Study 1 Synopsis

A follow-up survey was conducted of dually diagnosed clients discharged from the [fictional] Schleboikyville Inpatient Chemical Dependency Treatment Program (SICDTP) located in the [fictional] city of Schleboikyville. All adult clients dually diagnosed with severe mental illness and chemical dependency and discharged during 2006 were to be interviewed by the SICDTP program evaluation staff 6 months after discharge. The purpose of the survey, and focus of the interviews, was to identify predictors of the clients': (a) frequency of prescribed attendance at self-help group meetings, and (b) postdischarge level of substance abuse as measured by administering the Addiction Severity Index.

A total of 200 dually diagnosed clients were discharged from the SICDTP program during 2006. Of these, 50 could not be located for the follow-up survey interviews. Another 50 clients refused to be interviewed. Thus, the ultimate sample was 100 discharged clients, 50% of the intended sample. The predictor variables assessed included various demographic, socioeconomic, and clinical history variables; compliance with prescribed psychotropic medication plans after discharge; and the number of contacts with their case manager after discharge.

Each of these predictor variables was analyzed descriptively and in separate correlations with each of the two outcome variables: (1) frequency of attendance at self-help group meetings and (2) postdischarge level of substance abuse. The two outcome variables also were examined descriptively. Another analysis assessed the correlation between frequency of attendance at self-help group meetings and postdischarge level of substance abuse.

Highlights of the findings follow. We found a surprisingly high degree of compliance with discharge plans, with 75% of the clients meeting regularly with their case managers and attending self-help group meetings as prescribed. The only significant predictors of attendance at postdischarge level of substance abuse were: (a) number of psychiatric inpatient admissions before entering SICDTP ($r = .60$, $p < .001$), (b) current compliance with prescribed psychotropic medication plans ($r = .70$, $p < .001$), and (c) number of contacts with case manager after discharge ($r = .65$, $p < .001$). The foregoing variables also were the only significant predictors of attendance at self-help group meetings, with correlations nearly as strong. Likewise, frequency of attendance at self-help group meetings was strongly correlated with postdischarge level of substance abuse ($r = .73$, $p < .001$).

Based on our findings, the following conclusions and recommendations were drawn:

- Contrary to conventional wisdom, dually diagnosed clients discharged from inpatient chemical dependency treatment programs have a high degree of compliance with discharge plans.
- Number of psychiatric inpatient admissions and compliance with prescribed psychotropic medication plans are significant predictors of postdischarge outcome.
- Case management is a very effective intervention in the aftercare of dually diagnosed clients discharged from inpatient chemical dependency treatment programs.
- Attendance at self-help group meetings after discharge is effective in preventing postdischarge level of substance abuse.

Consequently, inpatient chemical dependency treatment programs should be sure to: (a) offer case management after discharge, (b) educate clients predischarge about the importance of their attendance at self-help group meetings after discharge, and (c) instruct their case managers to continue to emphasize the importance of that attendance in their work with clients after discharge.

Study 2 Synopsis

The National Alliance on Mental Illness (NAMI) is a "grassroots mental health organization dedicated to improving the lives of persons living with serious mental illness and their families" (NAMI web site). In this fictitious study, NAMI research staff conducted a mailed survey of its members who are parents of adolescent or young adult persons living with psychotic disorders. The survey had three aims:

1. To assess the extent to which mental health professionals were being perceived by respondents as taking a supportive, psychoeducational approach in which they formulated an alliance with par-

ents instead of attributing their child's illness to faulty parenting or dysfunctional family dynamics.

2. To assess the degree of satisfaction respondents had with the mental health professionals with whom they interacted about their child's illness, and to examine the relationship between that level of satisfaction and the approaches assessed in aim 1.

3. To conduct a case-control analysis to identify risk factors distinguishing families that did and did not experience an onset of family emotional or relationship problems commencing after their adolescent or young adult child was first treated for a psychotic disorder.

The survey was conducted with a random sample. The sampling procedure began by randomly selecting 1,000 parents from the NAMI membership list who, according to NAMI data, had an adolescent or young adult child who had been treated for a psychotic disorder. The parent in each family who was identified as closest to the child was mailed a questionnaire that he or she could complete and return anonymously in a stamped, self-addressed envelope. Also enclosed was a separate postcard identifying his or her name, saying only that the person had responded anonymously in a separate envelope. Three follow-up mailings were made to those parents who had not returned a postcard. Each follow-up mailing contained another copy of the questionnaire, another postcard, and a letter urging him or her to participate in the survey.

The ultimate response rate was 50%. A randomly selected subsample of 50 of the 500 persons who had not returned postcards were then contacted by telephone, and 30 of them agreed to be interviewed by phone, answering the same questions as were on the mailed questionnaire. No differences were found between those 30 and the 500 mailed respondents regarding background characteristics or anything else asked in the survey.

One part of the questionnaire asked about demographic and socioeconomic background characteristics of the family. A second part asked about prior traumatic experiences affecting the family. Another part included items assessing the extent of family emotional or relationship problems that predated the entering of their child into treatment for a psychotic disorder. The next part asked about family emotional or relationship problems that commenced only after their child was first treated for a psychotic disorder. Next came items regarding whether mental health professionals were being perceived by respondents as taking a supportive, psychoeducational approach in which they formulated an alliance with parents versus attributing their child's illness to faulty parenting or dysfunctional family dynamics. The final part asked the following question to assess the degree of satisfaction respondents had with the mental health professionals with whom they interacted about their child's illness:

> Overall, to what extent have your expectations been met in dealing with the mental health professionals with whom you have interacted about your child's illness?
>
> ☐ Very much
> ☐ Somewhat
> ☐ Very little
> ☐ Not at all

The study's main findings were as follows:

- Respondents appear to be, for the most part, satisfied with their dealings with mental health professionals. One-third of them checked "Very much," and 50% of them checked "Somewhat" regarding having their expectations met. Only 17% checked "Very little" or "Not at all."
- Only 50% of the respondents indicated that they perceived mental health professionals as having taken a supportive, psychoeducational approach. The other 50% reported that the mental health professionals attributed their child's illness to faulty parenting or dysfunctional family dynamics.
- No correlation was found between parents' degree of satisfaction and their perception of whether mental health professionals interacted with them in a supportive or blaming manner.
- The case-control analysis found that the perception of whether mental health professionals interacted with parents in a supportive or blaming manner was the strongest risk factor distinguishing between those families who did and did not experience an onset of family emotional or relationship problems commencing after their adolescent or young adult child was first treated for a psychotic disorder. Even after controlling for all other background variables assessed in the survey, parents who perceived mental health professionals as implying that they were culpable in the causation of their child's disorder were three times more likely than other surveyed parents to subsequently divorce or enter therapy (usually for depression).

Because of these findings, the main recommendation of the study was as follows:

> Because previous research has shown the psychoeducational approach to be effective in forestalling relapse of psychotic episodes, and in light of the evidence in this and prior studies that making parents feel culpable is harmful, and because of the alarming proportion (50%) of mental health

professionals who are making parents feel culpable for their child's psychotic disorder: We recommend that efforts be taken by appropriate
training programs and professional organizations to decrease the proportion of mental health professionals who are making parents feel culpable
for their child's psychotic disorder and to increase the extent to which
these mental health professionals are taking an evidence-based, psychoeducational approach in their interactions with these parents.

KEY CHAPTER CONCEPTS

- Surveys gather data by asking people questions or having
  them complete a scale (or several scales) that measure some
  phenomenon.
- Surveys can be conducted in various ways: by mail using questionnaires and scales that respondents complete, in face-to-face
  interviews (which might involve the use of self-report scales administered orally), or online via e-mail or a web site.
- Each way has its advantages and disadvantages. The key questions will be the same regardless of which approach is used: Was
  the information collected in a valid, unbiased manner? Were the
  survey respondents representative of the target population?
  Were the conclusions warranted in light of the design logic, the
  type of data analysis employed, and the findings of that analysis?
- A key issue in appraising surveys is the potential for nonresponse
  bias.
- A response rate of less than 50% is generally considered to be inadequate in most surveys. To be good, the response rate should
  be 60% or more. But the risk of a meaningful nonresponse bias
  exists even with adequate response rates. Ideally, a survey should
  make a reasonable effort to compare the attributes of respondents to nonrespondents.
- Some studies with poor response rates can have value.
- Sampling refers to the way a study selects its participants, and a
  sample refers to that segment of a population that ends up participating in the study.
- Probability sampling is generally deemed to be the safest way to
  try to achieve representativeness because it involves the use of
  random numbers to select study participants and thus is least
  vulnerable to researcher bias or judgment errors.

(continued)

- There are two main ways for a probability sample to be biased: (1) a relatively high nonresponse rate, and (2) using a biased list to begin with for selecting cases.
- Whenever you read a study that uses probability sampling, you should appraise whether the list used to do the random selection was comprised of the entire population of names versus a skewed segment of that population.
- Four types of probability sampling are simple random sampling, systematic sampling, stratified random sampling, and cluster sampling.
- Nonprobability sampling does not select participants randomly and consequently is riskier, but sometimes it is necessary.
- Four types of nonprobability sampling are availability sampling, quota sampling, purposive (judgment) sampling, and cluster sampling.
- Surveys can offset problems connected to representativeness (external validity) and internal validity by using multivariate data analysis procedures.
- A cross-sectional study examines a phenomenon or relationships among variables at one point in time, only. It does not assess changes over time. Thus, it is quite limited regarding the detection of causality or in merely describing the trajectory of phenomena.
- To get a better handle on how phenomena change over time, longitudinal studies collect their data at different points over an extended period.
- Some longitudinal studies assess different people at different times, while other longitudinal studies follow the same set of people over time. The studies that assess the same set of people over time offer better evidence as to the trajectory of change and possible causality, and thus are the most relevant to EBP questions. Some label these studies as *cohort studies*. Others call them *panel studies*. Regardless of which label is used, by examining the same set of people each time, these studies can show the time sequence of various changes and provide better clues as to what factors might cause these changes.
- Case-control studies use matched groups of people who appear to be comparable except for some contrasting outcome. By using multivariate data analysis techniques, case-control studies attempt to determine what personal attributes and past experiences best distinguish the two groups.
- A key limitation in case-control studies is the possibility of recall bias. Knowing how things turned out can bias how people recall earlier events.

Review Exercises

1. *Use a database on the Internet (such as Google Scholar, PsycINFO, or Medline) to find a report of a survey that piques your interest. Critically appraise it in terms of the issues emphasized in this chapter: Was the information collected in a valid, unbiased manner? Were the survey respondents representative of the target population? Were the conclusions warranted in light of the design logic, the type of data analysis employed, and the findings of that analysis?*

2. *Use a database on the Internet (such as Google Scholar, PsycINFO, or Medline) to find a report of a study that used a case-control design and that piques your interest. (Hint: Enter case-control as your search term for titles. If using Google Scholar, use its Advanced Scholar Search option and check the circle for limiting your search to the social sciences.) Critically appraise the study in terms of the issues emphasized in this chapter.*

ADDITIONAL READINGS

Babbie, E. (1990). *Survey research methods.* Belmont, CA: Wadsworth.

Rubin, A., & Babbie, E. (2008). *Research methods for social work* (6th ed.). Belmont, CA: Brooks/Cole.

Chapter 10 ————————————

CRITICALLY APPRAISING QUALITATIVE STUDIES

Unlike quantitative studies, qualitative studies tend to employ flexible designs and subjective methods—often with small samples of research participants—in seeking to generate tentative new insights, deep understandings, and theoretically rich observations. As such, qualitative studies are less likely to pertain to evidence-based practice (EBP) questions about whether an intervention or some other explanation is really the cause of a particular outcome and more likely to pertain to EBP questions about how clients perceive the intervention process. Qualitative studies also are appropriate for delving into the deeper meanings of other experiences and perceptions clients (or prospective clients) might have and for helping practitioners get a deeper empathy for how they view their lives and the world.

Thus, as mentioned in Chapter 3, qualitative studies can help practitioners better understand what it's like to have had their clients' experiences. A homelessness shelter administrator, for example, might learn from a qualitative study that the reasons why so many homeless women refuse to use shelter services is their perception that the shelter is not safe for them. They may fear being raped or victimized in other ways. The authors of the qualitative study might have generated this finding by employing in-depth, open-ended interviews with homeless women or perhaps by living on the streets with them for a while as a way to observe and experience firsthand their experiences and how they perceive things.

The qualitative studies you read to guide your practice can use a variety of observational and interviewing techniques, as well as different techniques to analyze the open-ended qualitative data they collect. This chapter examines those techniques from the standpoint of what you need to know when critically appraising qualitative studies. Although you'll see some guidelines for appraising the rigor of qualitative studies, you should also keep in mind that qualitative research is less concerned with generating conclusive findings and more concerned with generating tentative new insights and helping you consider possibilities you may not have considered. Likewise, qualitative studies do not emphasize whether their findings can be generalized to populations. Instead, a good qualitative study provides ample information to help you, the consumer, judge whether its findings have a reasonable chance of being applicable to your client or practice situation. In this connection, qualitative methodologists prefer the term *transferability* to the term *generalizability*. This preference is based on the notion that, rather than implying that findings can be generalized to a population, a study should provide enough information to help the consumer judge whether its qualitative findings seem transferable to the consumer's specific concerns. Thus, a qualitative study that strikes you as being rather limited from the standpoint of quantitative research standards nevertheless can have significant value from an EBP perspective if it helps you consider and delve into issues with your clients that you might have previously overlooked—even if the qualitative findings apply to only some of your clients.

QUALITATIVE OBSERVATION

Many qualitative studies rely on the observation of behavior in the natural environment. Rather than merely ask homeless people about what goes on in a shelter for the homeless, a qualitative researcher might stay in a shelter and observe things directly. Rather than interview patients and staff about how patients are treated in a psychiatric hospital, a qualitative researcher might pose as a patient and experience that treatment firsthand. Qualitative observation often is referred to as *participant observation*. Studies will vary, however, in the extent to which an observer is really a participant.

At one extreme, the researcher might be a *complete participant* in the activity being observed. To get a candid and in-depth understanding of how nursing home staff view and treat nursing home residents, for example, a researcher might get hired as a patient-care staff member and not reveal her identity as a researcher to the other staff members. Doing so will, in addition, help the researcher experience directly what it feels like to be a patient-care staff member in a nursing home.

The ethics of such deception can be debated, and you can examine a research text like Rubin and Babbie (2007, 2008) for that topic. However, not all researchers who are complete participants are just deceptively posing as such. For example, suppose you genuinely seek to learn a new therapy being touted as a miracle cure, pay for and attend its training workshops, and in the process perceive it to be cultish and pseudoscientific in the way it attempts to indoctrinate its trainees. You might start taking detailed and copious notes about your observations and experiences in the training workshops and then write a qualitative research report based on your observations.

As a consumer of such research as part of the EBP process, you probably will be less concerned with the ethics of conducting such research than with critically appraising the research regarding the possible implications of its findings for your practice. One strength of the complete participant mode of observation is that the people being observed are not being influenced to act unnaturally because they know a researcher is observing them. Also, the people are being observed in their natural environment, and it is what they actually say and do in that environment that is being observed directly—not some biased account of it they might provide in a survey interview to portray themselves in a more socially desirable light. Another strength is that the complete participant role enables the researcher to experience directly what it feels like to be in the role of the people being observed. Experiencing things directly is a subjective research process and can be influenced by the researcher's own predilections. The objectivity emphasized in quantitative research is traded off for a subjective approach that can yield deeper, albeit tentative, new insights.

But trading off an emphasis on objectivity does not mean eschewing any effort to be objective whatsoever. Ideally, the complete participant should try to balance subjective and objective perspectives. The terms for these two perspectives in qualitative research are the **emic perspective** and the **etic perspective.** Employing the *emic perspective,* the researcher subjectively tries to adopt the perspective of the people being observed. Employing the *etic perspective,* the researcher tries to maintain the ability to step outside of the emic perspective and think critically and objectively as an outsider about the phenomena being observed and experienced. Thus, if workshop trainees attribute their enthusiasm about the new therapy they are learning to their belief that it seems so theoretically sound, the qualitative researcher might at times try hard to see things the way they do (adopting the emic perspective), while at other times perhaps wondering (adopting the etic perspective) whether the real reasons for their enthusiasm might be: (a) to avoid the cognitive dissonance that they would feel if they realized that they had paid so much money for a training in mere snake oil, or (b) their expectation that being certified in the new therapy will enhance the marketability of their private practice.

In appraising a qualitative study using the complete participant mode of observation, you should look for indications that the researcher attempted to balance the emic and etic perspectives, as opposed, for example, to "going native"—a process in which researchers lose their sense of detachment and over-identify with the people being observed. In addition to the potential for going native, another downside of the complete participant role is that the researcher, by virtue of being part of the phenomenon being studied, can affect that phenomenon.

Two alternatives to the complete participant approach, both of which still engage the researcher as a participant, are the *participant-as-observer* approach and the *observer-as-participant* approach. In the former role, the researchers participate fully in the phenomenon being studied, but tell the people being observed about their roles as researchers. In the latter role, the researchers also make their research aim known. But instead of participating fully, they merely interview and otherwise interact with the people being observed during the natural social processes. Although these roles lessen the risks of going native, they do not guarantee that it will not occur. These roles also lessen the risk associated with the complete participant affecting the phenomenon being observed; however, the trade-off is that knowing a researcher is observing them might change what the people being observed would normally do or say.

Another, more extreme, alternative is the *complete observer* approach. Researchers taking this approach eschew any participation whatsoever in the processes being observed. Thus, a researcher might observe the activity at a homeless shelter without posing as a homeless person, sleeping at the shelter, or engaging in any of those activities. To the extent that the observation can be unobtrusive (including not alerting the people being observed to the observation process), the chances of the researcher affecting things or going native are minimized. The trade-off, however, is that the researcher might get a more superficial sense of what is being observed and not get the opportunity to ask about it or experience it in more (subjective) depth.

In appraising qualitative studies that use one or more of these observation approaches, you should not ask whether the correct approach was used. Each has its advantages and disadvantages. As in much research, the decision of which approach to use involves trade-offs. Pursuing deeper subjective insights typically requires trading off an emphasis on more objectivity. Pursuing more objectivity typically means less opportunity to develop deeper subjective insights. Rather than ask whether the correct approach was used, you should look for signs that perhaps the researchers went too far in either direction with the chosen approach and recognize the limitations and tentative nature of the findings regardless of which approach was used. As long as you keep those limitations in mind and remember that the new insights generated are merely tentative, then those new insights can have significant value to you in your practice regardless of the approach used and its inescapable limitations. The same advice applies to appraising and using the findings generated by studies that rely on qualitative interviewing techniques. Let's now examine those techniques and explore how to critically appraise them.

QUALITATIVE INTERVIEWING

Qualitative interviewing techniques reflect the same priorities as qualitative research in general, with their emphasis on asking open-ended questions, probing for greater depth, and recognizing the value of interviewer flexibility and subjectivity. Although all qualitative interviews emphasize open-ended questions, the degree of structure in qualitative interviews varies among the studies you read. At one extreme, some studies employ very *unstructured, informal conversational interviews.* At the other extreme are studies that use a *standardized interview approach,* in which interviewers ask a list of open-ended questions in the exact order and with the same wording each time. In between these two extremes are studies that use the *interview guide approach,* which lists topics in outline form that interviewers are expected to cover, but which gives interviewers leeway in how to sequence and word questions.

Each approach has its advantages and disadvantages. Like research in general, trade-offs are inescapable in deciding which approach to use. The highly structured, standardized approach reduces the chances that interviewer bias will affect what questions are asked and how they are asked. However, the highly structured approach offers less opportunity to delve into unanticipated areas. Also, interviewees might be more guarded in their answers or less receptive to being interviewed at all than they would be with a more informal, conversational approach. In contrast, with the most unstructured, informal conversational interviewing approach, the interviewees may not even feel like they are being interviewed. Interviewers are free to pursue whatever comes up and to do so in a normal conversational manner that will put interviewees more at ease than when being asked a standardized list of predetermined questions. The interview guide approach attempts to combine the advantages of the two extreme approaches, by ensuring that different interviewers will cover the same material while allowing them to take a conversational tack and giving them more flexibility than the standardized approach to probe into unanticipated material. The interview guide approach also combines the disadvantages of the two extreme approaches because it does not give as much assurance as the standardized approach in minimizing bias and inconsistency and is not as informal and conversational as the opposite approach.

When you appraise a study using the standardized approach, you'll be better able to judge the quality of the interviewing because you'll know the exact wording and order of the questions asked in each interview. Even with the most highly structured qualitative interviews, though, interviewers have the opportunity to probe for more clarity and depth as needed. Thus, regardless of which approach is used, the interviewers should be well trained in the use of neutral probes. If an interviewee answers an open-ended question about her experiences at a homeless shelter by saying, "Not so hot," the interviewer should probe by saying something like, "Can you tell me more about that?" rather than saying something like, "Oh, did it have good air conditioning?" or "Were the staff mean to you?" When you appraise studies using any of these approaches, you won't see the wording of every probe and you therefore should look for information as to the qualifications, training, and supervision of the interviewers.

Life History

One example of a relatively unstructured approach to qualitative interviewing is called the *life history* method. Also sometimes called the *life story* method or the *oral history* method, this approach asks open-ended questions about how interviewees subjectively remember and interpret the significance and meanings of key events in their own lives. Robinson (1994, p. 81), for example, used this method with delinquent girls by starting each interview with the same open-ended question, "Tell me about your family?" Robinson found that most of the girls had been sexually abused and recommended that services be provided for them that are geared specifically to sexual abuse. If you read Robinson's study, you might wonder whether her own expectation about the importance of sexual abuse going into the study might have biased the way she conducted the unstructured interviews and analyzed what the girls said. But even if you think Robinson was biased, had you not considered the potential importance of prior sexual abuse as a treatment focus for delinquent girls, her study would have value in getting you to at least look into that possibility.

Focus Groups

Qualitative interviews can be done with individuals or groups. When conducted with groups, the groups typically are called *focus groups.* Focus group participants usually are chosen because they share some commonality relevant to the purpose of the interview. For example, a group of service recipients could be convened to discuss their satisfactions and dissatisfactions with particular services. Likewise, a group of community residents could be convened to discuss community problems and needed services relevant to those problems. Studies using focus groups commonly will convene multiple groups. For example, in a study of community needs, perhaps one group will be comprised of community leaders, another of staff from service provider agencies, another of grassroots community residents, and perhaps some with combinations of the foregoing types of people. Each group should be relatively small, perhaps comprised of approximately 8 to 12 people. Focus group studies vary in the degree of structure used in the group interviews, from unstructured to highly structured or in between.

Focus group interviews can bring out information that might not emerge in individual interviews. For example, one resident might identify a community need or problem that might not have occurred to other residents in individual interviews. Hearing about it, the other residents then might provide useful information about that need or problem. Likewise, if one service recipient expresses dissatisfaction about some aspect of service delivery, that can make others feel more comfortable in expressing their dissatisfaction with the same thing or perhaps some other aspects.

The downside of focus group interviewing is that group dynamics can influence some participants to feel pressured to say things they don't really feel or not to say things they do. Hearing someone else say how satisfied he or she is with service delivery might make other service recipients very reluctant to sound negative in taking a contradictory position about their own dissatisfaction. If one or two outspoken residents express strong opinions as to the need to provide a particular service to address a particular community problem, other less outspoken residents—who perhaps are more representative of the community—might feel pressured to agree even if they are skeptical. Thus, focus group interviews are vulnerable to the phenomenon of *groupthink,* in which the group members conform to the opinions of the group's most outspoken members. A related downside is that the people who agree to participate in a focus group in the first place—rather than being representative of the target population—may be the folks with the most extreme views. They may have the biggest axes to grind regarding dissatisfactions with services or regarding particular community issues.

As you can see in the foregoing discussions of qualitative observational techniques and qualitative interviewing techniques, each approach has advantages and disadvantages. Whichever approach is used, the choice involves trade-offs. Thus, when you are reading qualitative studies to inform your practice, rather than wonder whether the right approach was used or look for some statistical assurance that the findings were valid and unbiased, you should consider whether the study generated *tentative* new insights that might enhance your practice effectiveness. I emphasize the word *tentative* because no study—qualitative or quantitative—is a fool-proof route to the truth. Your enthusiasm or degree of skepticism about new insights should nevertheless be influenced by some methodological issues. For example, you might feel particularly skeptical about insights generated by a study that made no mention of interviewer qualifications, training, and supervision. At the end of this chapter, we examine some additional things to look for when you appraise the rigor of qualitative studies, regardless of which qualitative approaches and techniques were used. But first let's examine some additional qualitative research methods, beginning with sampling.

QUALITATIVE SAMPLING

In keeping with their emphasis on flexibility, qualitative research studies typically employ nonprobability sampling techniques. *Snowball sampling,* for example, is often used in finding prospective interviewees among hidden and hard-to-locate populations such as the homeless. (Snowball sampling was discussed in Chapter 9.) *Deviant case sampling* is often used when a study needs to find cases that are unusual in some respect. For example, a study that seeks to generate tentative insights about factors that might influence people to utilize services might interview people who use services frequently or complete the treatment regimen and look for distinctions between them and people who seem to need those services but who refuse to use them or who drop out of them early on.

A similar approach is called *critical incidents sampling.* Like deviant case sampling, this approach can be used to try to generate hypotheses about key events—both positive and negative—that seem to have influenced desirable and undesirable outcomes. Thus, researchers who seek to generate hypotheses about how to intervene successfully with a heretofore intractable problem might interview practitioners about their most successful experiences in treating that problem and their worst failures with it, looking for critical incidents that seem to be common among the successes and critical incidents that seem to be common among the failures.

Other qualitative sampling approaches include *intensity sampling, maximum variation sampling, homogeneous sampling,* and *theoretical sampling.* Intensity sampling is a less extreme version of deviant case sampling, in which unusual cases are selected, but ones that are not so extremely unusual as to comprise aberrations that could supply misleading information. Maximum variation sampling emphasizes heterogeneity in selecting cases, such as by selecting people with high, medium, and low levels of participation in a program or people in urban, suburban, and rural areas, and so on. Conversely, homogeneous sampling restricts the focus to cases that all share the same characteristic, perhaps looking into something like why some recent immigrants from Mexico refuse to participate in the substance-abuse treatment for their adolescent children. Theoretical sampling combines elements of the previous sampling approaches. It begins by selecting cases with similarities regarding characteristics or outcomes and looks for patterns among them that might help explain the similarities. When researchers using this approach reach a point where no new insights are being generated, they look for different types of cases and repeat the process.

Regardless of which of the approaches was used in a study you are appraising, you should keep in mind that they all are variations of nonprobability purposive (judgment) sampling. As such, they are susceptible to researcher biases and errors in judgment. Even when the researchers do not intend their samples to represent an entire population, but instead perhaps some unusual segment of that population, the sample might not really be representative of that segment. Saying this, however, does not denigrate qualitative sampling techniques. Nonprobability sampling techniques typically are unavoidable in qualitative research and thus come with the territory when researchers seek to answer the kinds of research questions for which qualitative research is more suited than quantitative research. No one study—quantitative or qualitative—is irrefutable. You should maintain your critical thinking posture with both types of studies and remember that all knowledge is provisional. No matter how rigorous a study's sampling procedures may be, its findings might not apply to your particular client or practice situation, and no matter how dubious the representativeness of a sample might be, tentative insights might be generated that help you with a particular case or situation. Nevertheless, you should be more skeptical about the potential value of the tentative insights generated by some studies than by others. The tentative insights derived from brief interviews with the first 20 homeless people encountered in a nearby park are probably less trustworthy than those derived from much lengthier interviews and observations with a much more comprehensive nonprobability sample.

GROUNDED THEORY

The foregoing sampling concepts are an important aspect of an overarching framework for qualitative research called **grounded theory** that many studies claim to have used. A key feature of this approach is the use of constant comparisons. It begins with a search for patterns or commonalities among an initial sample of cases. Next comes the search for more cases and observations that might or might not fit the initial patterns or commonalities.

The search is guided by theoretical sampling (as discussed previously). First, new cases are sought that seem to be similar to the cases on which the previous patterns and commonalities were based. Next, different kinds of cases are selected to see if the same insights are generated. If the new cases stimulate new insights, then more cases like them are sought until no new insights are being generated. More iterations of this process are repeated until the analysis of different kinds of cases cease yielding new insights.

Grounded theory can be used with any of the qualitative data collection methods and frameworks that have been discussed previously. Not all studies that claim to have used grounded theory provide a detailed account of how they did so. A claim to have employed grounded theory is no guarantee that it was implemented thoroughly and appropriately or that bias and other problems were adequately minimized in the collection and interpretation of data. One key issue is whether an adequate search was conducted looking for different types of cases that might disconfirm preliminary interpretations. If a study provides a detailed account showing that the grounded theory approach was implemented in a thorough fashion, you might consider that to be an important plus regarding the trustworthiness of its findings. The concept of trustworthiness in appraising qualitative research is key, as will be evident in the final section of this chapter.

FRAMEWORKS FOR APPRAISING QUALITATIVE STUDIES

Different people who have different worldviews advocate disparate sets of criteria for appraising the quality and value of any given qualitative study. For example, sets of criteria can vary according to whether the emphasis is on the objectivity versus the subjectivity of the data collection and interpretation, whether the research increases social consciousness about injustice, and whether the research is artistic and poignant. Table 10.1 lists key criteria emphasized in four different frameworks for appraising qualitative studies. How a person views the degree of trustworthiness of qualitative studies and their findings will be influenced by his or her views of reality and the aims of research.

Regarding views of reality, the standards valued by contemporary positivists who believe in trying to maximize objectivity and minimize bias contrast with the standards valued by postmodernists and social constructivists who believe that all we have are multiple subjective realities and that trying to be objective is therefore futile and self-deceptive. Regarding

Table 10.1   Criteria Emphasized by Alternative Frameworks for Appraising Qualitative Studies

Empowerment Standards	Social Constructivist Standards	Contemporary Positivist Standards	Artistic and Evocative Standards
Increase consciousness about injustice among research participants and research consumers	Embrace the advantages of subjectivity	Maximize objectivity and minimize bias	Give reader a new perspective
	Report multiple subjective realities in enough detail to provide the reader with a deep empathic sense of what it's like to see the world as the participants see it	Prolonged engagement	Creativity
Report the views of the disadvantaged		Triangulation	Aesthetic quality
Expose the ways that the powerful maintain, exercise, and benefit from their power		Peer debriefing and support	Interpretive vitality
		Negative case analysis	Embedded in reported experiences
		Member checking	Stimulating
Engage the disadvantaged as partners in the research process	Understand and report the researcher's own values and worldview	Paper trail and audit	Provocative
		Reliability of coding	Poignant (moves readers)
Spur and empower research participants to take action	Obtain agreement from participants that their subjective realities are reflected adequately in the findings		Clear and expressive exposition
			Feels true, authentic, and real to the reader
Identify potential social change strategies	Interpret inconsistencies from different data sources as a reflection of multiple subjective realities, *not* as a reliability problem or a reflection of possible bias		Literary writing style

From *Quality in Qualitative Evaluation: A Framework for Assessing Research Evidence,* by L. Spencer, J. Ritchie, J. Lewis, and L. Dillon, 2003, Government Chief Social Researcher's Office, U.K. National Center for Social Research. Available online as PDF file [170p.] at http://policyhub.gov.uk/docs/qqe_rep.pdf. Adapted with permission.

research aims, the standards valued by contemporary positivists who emphasize the pursuit of objective truth contrast with the standards of those who believe that creating new knowledge is less important than whether the research findings, or merely participating in the research, empowers a disadvantaged or oppressed target population. Let's now look further at the standards applicable to the empowerment, social constructivist, and contemporary positivist frameworks.

Empowerment Standards

You will encounter different labels for research that emphasize empowerment as the prime aim of research. One such label is *critical social science* or *critical theory.* These terms apply to the emphasis on the aim of empowerment in research in general. Regardless of which disadvantaged or oppressed group is targeted, the main criterion when appraising research is whether evidence is supplied supporting the notion that the research spurred its participants or target population to take action to improve their lot and perhaps redistribute power, or at least to become more aware of the need for change and to become more optimistic about achieving change. Those emphasizing this framework will recognize that it is unrealistic to expect a qualitative study to prove that the research caused things to improve; instead, testimonials provided by participants after completion of the study (and included in the study report) to the effect that the research changed their attitudes will probably suffice.

Another common label within the empowerment framework is *feminist research*. Those employing this approach might additionally refer to their research as using *feminist research methods*. The studies you encounter within this framework apply empowerment standards to the plight of women in a historically male-dominated society. Often assuming that women view reality and seek knowledge in ways that are fundamentally different from the ways men do, researchers using this approach commonly say that rather than question the objectivity and validity of what the women they interview say, they merely want readers to hear what women say from the women's own point of view. With the empowerment aim overshadowing the aim of objectivity, some feminist researchers might even begin interviews by telling interviewees of the empowerment aims of the research. They do this to raise the consciousness of the interviewees regarding feminist concerns and to encourage them to address those concerns. Of course, empowerment-oriented researchers of all stripes often do the same in regard to the particular focus of their research, regardless of the social issue involved.

Feminist research and empowerment research in general sometimes is referred to as *participatory action research*. The main distinction between participatory action research and the other forms of empowerment research is the extent to which the disadvantaged groups being studied take the lead in defining the research problem to be studied, identifying the desired remedies for that problem, and designing the research methods to be used in helping to achieve those remedies. Supporters of participatory action research like the way in which it—unlike traditional research approaches—does not reduce research participants to "subjects" or "objects" of research. By reducing the distinction between the researcher and the researched, those taking this approach view the mere act of participation as empowering the participants.

Social Constructivist Standards

Many researchers who emphasize empowerment standards share a social constructivist view of reality. The two frameworks are compatible because rejecting the notion of objectivity is one way to justify employing biased research methods tilted toward getting desired results that fit one's empowerment aims. Social constructivist standards for appraising qualitative research—in keeping with the emphasis on multiple subjective realities as all there is—stress the importance of reporting in detail all the different subjective realities of research participants. This detail is valued more than is trying to minimize respondent bias (as is done using the contemporary positivist standards—to be discussed soon). Likewise, social constructivist standards don't see inconsistencies in the findings from different data sources or interviewers as a reliability problem or a reflection of possible bias. Instead, such inconsistencies are seen merely as a reflection of multiple realities.

Thus, one indicator of trustworthiness of qualitative findings would be whether inconsistencies in the findings or interpretations are explained in terms of multiple subjective realities. Another would be whether the research participants agree that their own subjective realities are included in the findings. Therefore, if you use this framework to appraise the trustworthiness of the findings of a qualitative study, you will want the report to show that the findings were shared with research participants and the extent to which the participants acknowledged that their subjective realities are reflected in the findings. Another indicator of trustworthiness would be whether the realities of the participants are reported in enough detail to provide the reader with a deep empathic sense of what it's like to see the world as the participants see it. Providing sufficient detail also can help the practitioners judge whether the findings seem to fit their own clients or practice situations. This latter criterion is a bit like the concept of external validity in quantitative research, but instead of expecting a study to be generalizable, it expects the study to provide enough detail to let readers decide for themselves if the findings seem applicable to their own concerns.

Contemporary Positivist Standards

If you believe in the value of trying to maximize objectivity in qualitative research and see the aim of research as creating valid new knowledge, then you'll want to go beyond the foregoing standards when appraising qualitative studies to inform your practice. But going beyond empowerment and social constructivist standards does not require that you reject all of those standards. For example, if in its search for truth a study also helps empower disadvantaged and oppressed people, all the better. Indeed, you might see truth seeking as the best way to empower the oppressed. As discussed in Chapter 3, if a study justifies using biased research methods on the grounds that there is no objective truth, then why should those in power take the findings seriously? They could just dismiss the findings as one subjective reality that doesn't fit their view of social reality. Consequently, conducting and justifying research in that manner actually can work against the aim of empowering the disenfranchised because advocates of social change could not credibly claim to be speaking speak *truth* to power.

Thus, hoping that research findings will empower people does not require using an empowerment framework in appraising research. It can be compatible with a contemporary positivist framework. Also, you can be guided by a contemporary positivist framework's emphasis on objectivity and still find value in some social constructivist standards, such as wanting studies to report the multiple realities of research participants in enough detail to provide you with a deep empathic sense of what it's like see the world as the participants see it and to judge whether the findings seem to fit your own clients or practice situation.

However, from a contemporary positivist standpoint, you'll consider additional standards to help you decide how seriously you should take the findings—whether you should view them as relatively trustworthy or view them with a great deal of skepticism. According to Padgett (1998) you should look for six indicators of a qualitative study's trustworthiness. One indicator is called **prolonged engagement.** Prolonged engagement means that researchers spend a great deal of time with the people they are observing or interviewing so that they can develop a trusting relationship that will reduce participant tendencies to project a misleading favorable impression of themselves by withholding or distorting socially undesirable information. In an interview context, prolonged engagement means having lengthy interviews and perhaps a series of follow-up interviews that, in addition to building trust, can help interviewers detect distortion. Thus, trying to justify just one brief interview per participant on the grounds that a study is taking a qualitative approach probably won't fly. Qualitative research does not mean: "Anything goes!"

A second indicator of trustworthiness is whether the study used **triangulation.** Using triangulation means seeking corroboration among different sources of data or different interpreters of the data. For example, did a study use observational indicators or perhaps available data to corroborate what was said in interviews? Did it use multiple observers to collect data and multiple coders to code the data, and if so, was there agreement among them? Was more than one person used to interpret the findings—doing so independent (unaware) of each other's interpretations, and if so, did they arrive at similar conclusions?

A third indicator is whether a research team conducting the study met regularly to share alternative perspectives about how best to continue collecting the data and what the data mean? This indicator, called **peer debriefing and support,** can help researchers detect and correct biases and other problems in the way they are collecting and interpreting data.

A fourth indicator is whether the researchers conducted an adequate **negative case analysis,** which involves searching thoroughly for deviant cases that might disconfirm initial interpretations (as discussed earlier in this chapter regarding grounded theory). A fifth indicator—one that is shared with the empowerment and social constructivist frameworks—is called **member checking.** Did the researchers share their interpretations with the research participants, and did the participants indicate whether the interpretations ring true to them? A sixth indicator is whether the researchers left a **paper trail** of observational notes, interview transcripts, and so on. Doing so would enable independent qualitative researchers to **audit** the paper trail and judge whether they would arrive at the same conclusions and whether the research procedures used to control for biases and minimize other problems were adequate.

A study need not contain all of the foregoing six criteria to be deemed trustworthy. Most studies will not have the resources to do so. If a study you read meets just a couple of these criteria, that's pretty good. In this connection, a point I made earlier bears repeating. Although you should be more skeptical about the findings of some studies than others, no one study—quantitative or qualitative—has irrefutable findings. As a critical thinker, you should remember that all knowledge is provisional. The findings of even the most rigorous studies might not apply to your particular client or practice situation. And even the least rigorous qualitative studies might generate tentative insights that might help you with a particular case or situation. In the EBP process, you should search for and be guided by the best evidence you can find. But weaker evidence sometimes might be more applicable to your idiosyncratic situation than stronger evidence and can offer ideas that may prove useful in informing your practice when used with caution.

SYNOPSES OF RESEARCH STUDIES

Study 1 Synopsis

This study conducted qualitative interviews with 20 individuals who completed treatment for posttraumatic stress disorder (PTSD) one or more years prior to the interview: 10 who received eye movement desensitization and reprocessing (EMDR) therapy and 10 who received exposure therapy. The two treatment approaches share some similarities, but differ in some important ways. For example, with EMDR the therapist induces rapid eye movements (or other forms of bilateral stimulation) while the client holds in mind images, emotions, and cognitions connected to the trauma. EMDR is also thought to require fewer treatment sessions than exposure therapy and to induce less emotional distress as clients recall and discuss their traumatic experience.

Study participants were recruited through newspaper ads and flyers sent to psychotherapists in private practice and to mental health agencies in Pittsburgh and its suburbs. The mean age of the 20 participants was 35. All 20 were Caucasian. There were 14 females and 6 males. All were college graduates, employed full-time, and had an annual income between $30,000 and $70,000. No differences in the foregoing variables existed between the participants who had received EMDR and those who had received exposure therapy. For all but two of the women, their PTSD was connected to prior sexual abuse or assault. For all of the men, it was connected to military combat.

The interviews were conducted by the lead author of this article, who is an experienced EMDR therapist and a board officer of the EMDR International Association. An interview guide approach was used, with an outline of topics dealing with the following types of participant perceptions: (1) Did the treatment help them? (2) Did it harm them? (3) If yes to either 1 or 2, in what ways and how long lasting do the effects seem to be? (4) What did you like or dislike most about the therapy?

Each interview lasted 20 minutes and was tape-recorded. Using the grounded theory method and triangulation, the lead author and his research assistant independently listened to each tape to detect patterns and commonalities among the interviews according to whether EMDR or exposure therapy had been provided. There was 100% agreement between them with regard to each of the main findings described next.

The recipients of EMDR expressed much more confidence that the therapy had helped them and had long-lasting effects. Even those recipients of exposure therapy who felt helped by their treatment conveyed that the effects were short lived. In addition, the EMDR recipients tended to perceive the effects as being much more powerful—typically resolving their PTSD completely—while the exposure therapy recipients who felt helped perceived the improvement as only alleviating some of their symptoms, not resolving their PTSD. For example, one EMDR recipient said, "The trauma is behind me completely; it's ancient history. I'm over it. I'm doing things I couldn't do before, and I have no more PTSD symptoms." One exposure therapy recipient said, "Things are better, I guess. They seemed a lot better at first, but now it seems my symptoms are returning."

Although none of the interviewees felt harmed by their treatment, all of the EMDR recipients recalled experiencing only a mild degree of emotional distress as they as recounted their traumatic experiences during therapy, whereas all of the exposure therapy recipients recalled moderate to severe degrees of distress. The EMDR recipients also seemed to perceive having a much better relationship with their therapists than did the exposure therapy recipients. For example, one EMDR recipient said, "Not making me recount the painful details over and over again made me feel that my therapist was more compassionate than the exposure therapists I've heard about." An exposure therapy participant said, "I began to feel like my therapist was cold and uncaring by asking me to repeatedly tell her more and more details about my trauma; it was as if I were reliving it."

The foregoing findings support the claims that EMDR is more effective than exposure therapy, has longer lasting and deeper effects on PTSD symptoms, induces less emotional distress in the treatment process, and improves the quality of the therapist-client relationship. Although the study sample was small, we feel that it was adequate in light of the in-depth emphasis of qualitative research. Small samples come with the territory in qualitative research. One of the key strengths of our study was its use of triangulation, with 100% agreement in the interpretations of the two coauthors. In addition to illuminating the ways in which EMDR is a better treatment for PTSD than exposure therapy, we hope that the participant comments we have cited will give therapists a deeper sense of the different ways clients experience the two treatment approaches.

Study 2 Synopsis

The synopsis paraphrases and somewhat modifies the following real study: "The Health-Care Environment on a Locked Psychiatric Ward: An Ethnographic Study" (I. M. Johansson, I. Skärsäter, & E. Danielson, 2006, *International Journal of Mental Health Nursing, 15*(4), pp. 242–250).

This study used 3.5 months of participant observation to describe the conditions of inpatient care on locked, acute psychiatric wards in Sweden in the wake of de-institutionalization and the consequent reductions in available hospital beds and in time spent in hospitals. Major depression was the most common diagnosis among patients on the ward observed in this study. [The report next described in detail the physical layout of the ward and the rooms, the décor, and so on. Then it described the staffing.]

In addition to participant observation, data were collected by means of informal interviews and the analysis of available documents. The observation was ongoing every day except for the hours between midnight and 6:30 A.M. The observation focused on health care related ward activities. Maximum variation sampling was used in the selection of participants for observation and informal interviews. Extensive field notes were recorded during the observation, and the interviews were audiotaped.

The principal investigator (PI), a nurse with many years of experience in similar settings, accompanied the ward nurses in their daily activities and, in addition, sat in places on the ward where patients and staff frequented. The PI was more of a complete observer than a participant—she communicated with patients only when they initiated the communication. She observed staff as they worked in the nurses' office and at staff meetings. She observed what happened in patients' rooms by accompanying the nurses. Brief field notes were entered in an empty office as soon as possible after each set of observations. Later, when the day ended, the notes were elaborated into more detailed descriptions of what was observed. The PI collected all the data and took all the notes, but peer debriefing sessions were held regularly with her two coauthors, who also were involved in the observations and analyses.

The report next goes into detail about the coding of data and the qualitative data analysis procedures employed, which had many features of grounded theory. All coding was checked by the coauthors, and all the researchers discussed the data analysis.

The results emphasized control issues. Staff were mainly concerned with whether they had control or lacked it, and patients were mainly concerned with being controlled. The staff attempted to "maintain control by means of rules, routines, coercion, and pressure, although they did not always succeed. On the contrary, staff members were sometimes controlled by the patients" (p. 245).

For example, before they could leave the confines of the ward, patients had to be assessed by staff as to whether they were in a fit condition to leave. The patients' intended destination had to be noted along with when they planned to return. Another example involved searching through

> patient belongings, clothes, and room for sharp objects and medicines. The staff tried in this way to protect the patients from harming themselves and others. Another way of mastering the situation was withholding information or bringing pressure to bear on the patient in order to compel him or her to act in the manner desired by staff. . . . The use of coercion was justified by staff members on the grounds that it was for the protection of the patient or society. (p. 246)

Control issues also were evident in threats to staff from patients. Patients also

> checked to ensure that staff administered the correct medication or that they did not miss an assessment and conducted close surveillance in a proper way. When one of the nurses had close supervision of one patient, other patients sometimes sat nearby and supervised the nurse, which by nurses was experienced as very trying. Threats to contact the local newspaper or the use of violence when dissatisfied with the care were also sometimes made. (p. 247)

The patients' feelings of being controlled often had to do with staff availability and willingness to grant permission to leave the ward and with the consequent feeling of "being shut in," as shown by the following example:

> The new patient Stina knocks on the door of the nurses' office. When the door is opened, Stina says: "I can't stand being here, I can't stand it. I want to sleep in my own bed." Maud [a member of staff] helps the patient to phone her live-in partner. He doesn't answer; the patient immediately wants to redial the number but is not allowed to. She will have to wait a while before trying again. (p. 247)

Nevertheless, patients did have opportunities to contact the outside world. They could go for walks, have short leave periods, use the telephone, watch TV, read newspapers, and have visitors.

Patients used various strategies to influence staff and thus gain some control. The strategies included silent protests like refusing to participate in the care, expressing as groups their dissatisfactions with care after having discussed the matter together themselves. They tried to influence their care by using both passive and active strategies.

Concerns about control impeded other patient-care tasks. For example, repeatedly opening the door interrupted other staff duties. Moreover, the staff were not able to exert control due in part to the reliance on many temporary staff nurses. The unpredictable nature of the work led to competing demands on nurses as well as less control in the ward. The nurses continuously had to be prepared to act in emergencies and cope with uncertainty, which was another reason for their wish for control. At the same time, the illusion that it is possible to have full control was yet another burden on the nurses. Additionally, the constant power struggles with patients were stressful for nurses, especially when accompanied by physically threatening and demanding patients.

Nurses attempted to alleviate the power struggle by sharing responsibility for care with patients and their next of kin. For example, they involved patients in the care planning. However, some involuntarily admitted patients were unable to recognize their needs, and thus were sometimes incapable or unwilling to cooperate in their care or its planning.

In conclusion, the findings of this study imply the need to assess the expectations of patient-care staff in locked, acute psychiatric wards regarding control. They also imply the need for in-service training and for professional mentoring and supervision to help the staff have more realistic expectations and to cope better with the challenges and pressure involved in being in control. The findings also suggest the need to find ways to strengthen patients' participation in care and to reduce their sense of being controlled.

KEY CHAPTER CONCEPTS

- Many qualitative studies rely on the observation of behavior in the natural environment.
- Qualitative observation often is referred to as *participant observation*. Studies will vary, however, in the extent to which an observer is really a participant.
- At one extreme, the researcher might be a *complete participant* in the activity being observed.
- Advantages of the complete participant mode of observation include: (a) the people being observed are not being influenced to act unnaturally; (b) the people are being observed in their natural environment, and it is what they actually say and do in that environment that is being observed directly—not some biased account of it; and (c) the researcher can experience directly what it feels like to be in the role of the people being observed.
- Two alternatives to the complete participant approach are the *participant-as-observer* approach and the *observer-as-participant* approach. These roles lessen the risks of going native and of affecting the phenomenon being observed; however, the trade-off is that knowing that a researcher is observing them might change what the people being observed would normally do or say.
- Another alternative is the *complete observer* approach. Researchers taking this approach eschew any participation whatsoever in the processes being observed. To the extent that the observation can be unobtrusive, the chances of the researcher affecting things or going native are minimized. The trade-off, however, is that the researcher might get a more superficial sense of what is being observed and not get the opportunity to ask about it or experience it in more (subjective) depth.
- Although all qualitative interviews emphasize open-ended questions, the degree of structure in qualitative interviews varies among studies. At one extreme, some studies employ very *unstructured, informal conversational interviews*. At the other extreme are studies that use a *standardized interview approach,* in which interviewers ask a list of open-ended questions in the exact order and with the same wording each time. Between these two extremes are studies that use the *interview guide approach,* which lists topics in outline form that interviewers are expected to cover, but which gives interviewers leeway in how to sequence and word questions.

(continued)

- Each interviewing approach has its advantages and disadvantages.
- The highly structured, standardized approach reduces the chances that interviewer bias will affect what questions are asked and how they are asked, but offers less opportunity to delve into unanticipated areas. Also, interviewees might be more guarded in their answers or less receptive to even being interviewed at all than they would be with a more informal, conversational approach.
- With the most unstructured, informal conversational interviewing approach, the interviewees may not even feel like they are being interviewed. Interviewers are free to pursue whatever comes up and to do so in a normal conversational manner that will put interviewees more at ease than when being asked a standardized list of predetermined questions.
- The interview guide approach attempts to combine the advantages of the two extreme approaches, by ensuring that different interviewers cover the same material while allowing them to take a conversational tack and giving them more flexibility than the standardized approach to probe into unanticipated material.
- Regardless of which approach is used, the interviewers should be well trained in the use of neutral probes.
- The life history method asks open-ended questions about how interviewees subjectively remember and interpret the significance and meanings of key events in their own lives.
- Qualitative interviews can be done with individuals or groups. When conducted with groups, the groups typically are called *focus groups.*
- Focus group participants typically are chosen because they share some commonality relevant to the purpose of the interview.
- Each focus group should be relatively small, perhaps comprised of approximately 8 to 12 people. Focus group studies vary in the degree of structure used in the group interviews, from unstructured to highly structured or somewhere in between.
- Focus group interviews can bring out information that might not emerge in individual interviews.
- The downside of focus group interviewing is that group dynamics can influence some participants to feel pressured to say things they don't really feel or not say things they do really feel. A related downside is that the people who agree to participate in a focus group in the first place—rather than being representative of the target population—may be the folks with the most extreme views.

- Qualitative research studies typically employ nonprobability sampling techniques.
- Snowball sampling is often used in finding prospective interviewees among hidden and hard-to-locate populations.
- Deviant case sampling is often used when a study needs to find cases that are unusual in some respect.
- Critical incidents sampling can be used to try to generate hypotheses about key events—both positive and negative—that seem to have influenced desirable and undesirable outcomes.
- Intensity sampling is a less extreme version of deviant case sampling in which unusual cases are selected, but ones that are not so extremely unusual as to comprise aberrations that could supply misleading information.
- Maximum variation sampling emphasizes heterogeneity in selecting cases, such as by selecting people with high, medium, and low levels of participation in a program or people in urban, suburban, and rural areas, and so on.
- Homogeneous sampling restricts the focus to cases that share the same characteristic.
- Theoretical sampling combines elements of the previous sampling approaches. It begins by selecting cases with similarities regarding characteristics or outcomes and looks for patterns among them that might help explain the similarities. When researchers using this approach reach a point where no new insights are being generated, they look for different types of cases and repeat the process.
- No matter how rigorous a study's sampling procedures may be, its findings might not apply to your particular client or practice situation, and no matter how dubious the representativeness of a sample might be, tentative insights might be generated that help you with a particular case or situation.
- The grounded theory approach uses a constant comparisons method that involves searching for patterns or commonalities through multiple iterations with an expanding number of similar cases and eventually different types of cases that might disconfirm preliminary interpretations.
- How you view the degree of trustworthiness of qualitative studies and their findings is influenced by your views of reality and the aims of research.
- Those taking an empowerment approach—an approach often labeled as critical social science or critical theory—view

(continued)

trustworthiness in terms of whether evidence is supplied that supports the notion that the research spurred its participants or target population to take action to improve their lot and perhaps redistribute power, or at least to become more aware of the need for change and to become more optimistic about achieving change.

- Another common label within the empowerment framework is feminist research. The studies you encounter within this framework apply empowerment standards to the plight of women in a historically male-dominated society.

- Feminist research and empowerment research in general sometimes is referred to as participatory action research. The main distinction between participatory action research and the other forms of empowerment research is the extent to which the disadvantaged groups being studied take the lead in defining the research problem to be studied, identifying the desired remedies for that problem, and designing the research methods to be used in helping to achieve those remedies.

- Social constructivist standards for appraising qualitative research stress the importance of reporting in detail all the different subjective realities of research participants. Likewise, inconsistencies in the findings from different data sources or interviewers are not seen as a reliability problem or a reflection of possible bias in some sources or interviewers; instead, they are seen as a reflection of multiple realities.

- Indicators of the trustworthiness of qualitative findings from the social constructivist perspective include: (a) whether inconsistencies in the findings or interpretations are explained in terms of multiple subjective realities, (b) whether the research participants agree that their own subjective realities are included in the findings, and (c) whether the realities of the participants are reported in enough detail to provide the reader with a deep empathic sense of what it's like see the world as the participants see it.

- Providing sufficient detail also can help practitioners judge whether the findings seem to fit their own clients or practice situations.

- Indicators of trustworthiness from a contemporary positivist standpoint include prolonged engagement, triangulation, peer debriefing and support, negative case analysis, member checking, and leaving a paper trail.

- Prolonged engagement means that researchers spend a lot of time with the people they are observing or interviewing so that they can develop a trusting relationship that will reduce participant tendencies to project a misleading favorable impression of themselves by withholding or distorting socially undesirable information. In an interview context, prolonged engagement means having lengthy interviews and perhaps a series of follow-up interviews that, in addition to building trust, can help interviewers detect distortion.

- Triangulation means seeking corroboration among different independent sources of data or different independent interpreters of the data.

- Member checking involves sharing interpretations with the research participants, asking them if the interpretations ring true to them.

- Negative case analysis involves searching thoroughly for deviant cases that might disconfirm initial interpretations.

- Leaving a paper trail of observational notes, interview transcripts, and so on would enable independent qualitative researchers to audit the paper trail and judge whether they would arrive at the same conclusions and whether the research procedures used to control for biases and minimize other problems were adequate.

Review Exercises

1. *Using an Internet database like Google Scholar, Medline, or PsycINFO, find two articles reporting qualitative studies that emphasize the use of interviewing. (Hint: You might try entering* qualitative interviews *as your search term for titles.) Describe and contrast the interviewing approach used in each study. Critically appraise each study based on the concepts discussed in this chapter. Discuss how the appraisal might differ depending on whether empowerment, social constructivist, or contemporary positivist standards guided the appraisal.*

2. *Using an Internet database like Google Scholar, Medline, or PsycINFO, find two articles reporting qualitative studies that mention employing participant observation. (Hint: You might try entering* participant observation *as your search term for titles.) Describe and contrast the degree to which the researcher/ observer was a participant. Critically appraise each study based*

(continued)

on the concepts discussed in this chapter. Discuss how the appraisal might differ depending on whether empowerment, social constructivist, or contemporary positivist standards guided the appraisal.

3. *Using an Internet database like Google Scholar, Medline, or PsycINFO, find two articles reporting qualitative studies that mention employing grounded theory. (Hint: You might try entering* grounded theory *as your search term for titles.) Describe and contrast the degree of detail they provide about their use of grounded theory. Critically appraise each study based on the concepts discussed in this chapter. Discuss how the appraisal might differ depending on whether empowerment, social constructivist, or contemporary positivist standards guided the appraisal.*

ADDITIONAL READINGS

Denzin, N. K., & Lincoln, Y. S. (2000). *Handbook of qualitative research.* Thousand Oaks, CA: Sage.

Padgett, D. K. (1998). *Qualitative methods in social work research.* Thousand Oaks, CA: Sage.

Padgett, D. K. (Ed.). (2004). *The qualitative research experience.* Belmont, CA: Brooks/Cole.

PART IV

ASSESSING CLIENTS AND MONITORING THEIR PROGRESS

Chapter 11 ————————————

CRITICALLY APPRAISING AND SELECTING ASSESSMENT INSTRUMENTS

In the final section of this book, we focus on assessment instruments and monitoring progress. This chapter covers the selection of assessment instruments, and Chapter 12 covers monitoring progress. These two chapters pertain to steps that come at the beginning (this chapter) and end (Chapter 12) of the evidence-based practice (EBP) process. Regarding the beginning of the EBP process, Chapter 2 discussed the need to formulate EBP questions that incorporate client background and diagnostic characteristics. In that connection, we discussed the need to enter key characteristics in your search terms when using electronic literature databases. To know which diagnostic terms to enter, you might need to select and administer assessment instruments.

One reason why you may want to appraise and select assessment instruments is to help you formulate the right EBP question. Another reason is that even before the advent of EBP, it was a good idea to be as accurate as possible in the assessment part of practice as a basis for guiding treatment planning. A third reason is that with the advent of EBP, managed care companies and other third-party payers may insist on your using a valid assessment instrument as part of your justification for a particular treatment approach and perhaps also to monitor client progress. The latter concern leads to the fourth reason: Even without pressure from a third party, a measurement instrument can help you monitor client progress in the final stage of the EBP process.

Chapter 3 briefly identified the key questions to ask when appraising a particular assessment instrument. Is the instrument reliable? Is it valid? Is it sensitive to relatively small, but important changes? Is it feasible? Is it culturally sensitive? We also briefly touched on some of the ways these questions can be answered. In this chapter, we'll cover this material in more depth as well as provide some tips for locating good instruments.

RELIABILITY

An instrument is reliable if responses to it are consistent. Just as a scale to measure your weight would be unreliable if from one moment to the next it was changing what you weigh by many pounds, an instrument to measure some social or psychological construct would be unreliable if from one day or week to the next or from one item to the next—it was changing substantially the degree to which a person seems to be depressed, anxious, satisfied, and so on. The three main forms of reliability that you are likely to encounter when appraising measurement instruments are **internal consistency reliability, test-retest reliability,** and **inter-rater reliability.**

Internal Consistency Reliability

Internal consistency reliability is based on the notion that repeated measurements of the same phenomenon are inherent in any instrument that contains multiple items about different aspects of that phenomenon. For example, if a boy strongly agrees that he loves his mother on item 3, but then strongly agrees that he hates her on item 12, that's not internally consistent. Likewise, respondents to a measure of depression should not be indicating that they always feel sad on item 2 while indicating that they always feel happy on item 16. However, inconsistency does not necessarily mean responding in ways that are polar opposites. For example, inconsistency would be indicated by a person saying that he always feels happy on one item and then saying that he has lost interest in things on another item.

Reliability is not depicted in all or nothing terms. Instead, it is depicted as a matter of degree in terms of correlation statistics. Previous chapters have discussed the concept of correlation. Chapter 8, for example, mentioned that correlation statistics depict the strength of relationship between two variables in terms of a figure that can range from 0 (no correlation) to either +1.0 (a perfect positive correlation) or −1.0 (a perfect negative correlation). Although negative correlations can be just as desirable (or undesirable) as positive correlations in other research contexts, when depicting the reliability of a measurement instrument, only a positive correlation is desirable. That's because it would be inconsistent if the people who scored high on the phenomenon in question on some items scored low on that phenomenon on others. Thus, the closer to 1.0 the correlation, the more reliable the instrument.

There are three common ways to assess internal consistency reliability correlations:

1. Calculate inter-item correlations between each item.
2. Calculate the correlation between each item and the total scale score.
3. Split the instrument in half and calculate the correlation between the subscores on each half.

The best, and most common, internal consistency correlation statistic that you are likely to encounter is based on the latter approach. It is called **coefficient alpha.** The calculation of coefficient alpha involves breaking an instrument down into every possible split-half, calculating the split-half correlations for every pair of halves, and then calculating the mean of all those split-half correlations. To keep things simple, you can just think of coefficient alpha as the extent to which subscores on each half of an instrument correlate with each other.

Excellent internal consistency reliability is indicated by a coefficient alpha of .90 or more. Good internal consistency reliability is indicated by a coefficient alpha of .80 to .89. Lower than that can be acceptable for monitoring progress, but is deemed quite risky for diagnostic purposes. If an instrument is quite brief—just a handful of items or so—above .60 can be barely acceptable for monitoring purposes.

Table 11.1 illustrates the concept of internal consistency reliability. Notice how in the upper part of the table with internally consistent results the two clients (Ann and Jan) who score relatively low on any item tend to have relatively low scores on the other items, while the two clients (Dan

Table 11.1   Internal Consistency Reliability

Strongly Agree	Agree	Disagree	Strongly Disagree	
1	2	3	4	I feel sad.
1	2	3	4	I cry.
1	2	3	4	Life seems hopeless.
1	2	3	4	I've lost interest in things that I used to enjoy.

Internally Consistent Results

Client	I feel sad	I cry	Life seems hopeless	I've lost interest . . .
Ann	1	1	2	1
Dan	4	4	3	3
Jan	2	1	2	1
Nan	4	3	4	4

Internally Inconsistent Results

Client	I feel sad	I cry	Life seems hopeless	I've lost interest . . .
Al	1	4	2	3
Cal	4	1	3	2
Hal	2	4	3	1
Sal	1	3	2	4

and Nan) who score relatively high on any item tend to have relatively high scores on the other items. Notice how in the lower part of the table with internally inconsistent results how the way any client responds to any given item is not at all predictive of how they respond to other items. For the upper table, coefficient alpha would be high. For example, the summed subscores for Ann and Jan on the first two items would be 2 and 3, and for the last two items they would be 3 and 3. The corresponding subscores for Dan and Nan would be 8 and 7 for the first two items, and 6 and 8 for the last two. The same pattern would be obtained regardless of which items were paired (i.e., for every way the scale could be split in half). Thus, the clients with relatively low subscores on one half have relatively low subscores on the other half, while clients with relatively high subscores on one half would have relatively high subscores on the other half.

Test-Retest Reliability

Test-retest reliability is another common indicator of reliability that you are likely to encounter. One of the reasons it is not as commonly reported as coefficient alpha is because it requires administering the instrument on two occasions to the same people, which is less expedient and more costly than just administering it once and calculating its internal consistency reliability. The reason for administering the instrument on two occasions (no more than 2 to 3 weeks apart) is to determine if scores on the instrument are stable over time when people don't change. Thus, test-retest reliability assesses the **stability** of an instrument.

Having stability is important if an instrument is to be used to monitor treatment progress. You would want changes in scores over time to indicate changes in the phenomenon you are measuring and not just reflect an unstable instrument (like a scale that changes your weight reading by 10 pounds or more from one day to the next, not counting Thanksgiving). Of course, some people might change over the course of a couple weeks. But if the stability is assessed over a sufficiently large sample of people, and over the course of only a couple weeks or so, it is safe to assume that not so many people would change so much as to cause a reliable instrument to get a low test-retest correlation. As with coefficient alpha, correlations of .90 and above would be considered excellent, .80 to .89 good, and so on. Table 11.2 illustrates test-retest reliability in the same manner that Table 11.1 illustrated internal consistency reliability.

Table 11.2   Test-Retest Reliability

Strongly Agree	Agree	Disagree	Strongly Disagree	
1	2	3	4	I feel sad.
1	2	3	4	I cry.
1	2	3	4	Life seems hopeless.
1	2	3	4	I've lost interest in things that I used to enjoy.

High Test-Retest Reliability

	Total Score	
Client	At Time 1	At Time 2
Ann	5	4
Dan	14	15
Jan	6	7
Nan	15	14

Low Test-Retest Reliability

	Total Score	
Client	At Time 1	At Time 2
Al	5	10
Cal	14	5
Hal	6	12
Sal	15	7

Table 11.3   Circle the Number That Best Describes the Child's Observed Behavior

	Never	Rarely	Sometimes	Often
Loses temper	0	1	2	3
Refuses to do chores, etc.	0	1	2	3

Inter-Rater Reliability

Some instruments are developed not for self-report purposes, but rather for use by others who rate behaviors of people they observe. Thus, if you are monitoring the progress being made by a boy with a conduct disorder who resides in a residential treatment center, you might want two or more center staff members to rate his behavior. How often, for example, is he fighting, doing chores, and so on? Such a scale might look something like Table 11.3.

You would want the ratings between the staff members to be consistent; that is, to have a high degree of *inter-rater reliability* (also called *inter-observer reliability*). Toward that end, it would be nice if you can find a relevant behavioral rating scale that has been found to generate highly correlated ratings between different observers.

VALIDITY

It's important for instruments to be reliable. If they are not, they have no value. If your scale showed you weighed 120 pounds at bedtime and 175 pounds the next morning, you wouldn't trust it. However, consistency in responses (i.e., reliability) does not assure that an instrument is accurately measuring what it intends to measure. Ask O.J. if he murdered Nicole and Ron, and you'll get a consistent answer every time (i.e., "No"). That consistency, however, probably won't assure most folks of his innocence. When we ask whether an instrument really measures what it is intended to measure, we enter the realm of **validity.**

Before turning to the different types of validity, it's worth noting that reliability is a necessary precondition for validity. For example, an instrument obviously is not a valid diagnostic tool if it indicates that a client only has a conduct disorder on January 10 but on January 17 the instrument indicates that the client instead has a bipolar disorder. Conversely, a self-report instrument that indicates that a client never abuses drugs every time it is completed may or may not be valid. The client might be telling the truth, or he might be distorting the truth to convey the same (although false) socially desirable impression every time. If an instrument lacks reliability, we know it lacks validity. But if it has good reliability, then it would be nice to know about its validity. Let's now examine the different types of validity that you are likely to encounter.

Face Validity

The weakest form of validity is called **face validity.** To have face validity, the items on an instrument merely must *seem* to measure the intended concept. Thus, if an instrument designed to measure drug abuse contains items asking how often the respondent uses various drugs, it probably would *seem* to have face validity. However, just looking at the items on an instrument and deeming them on the *face* of it to *seem* to be appropriate does not ensure that respondents will complete the instrument in a valid, accurate, unbiased manner. In other words, face validity requires no evidence that the instrument is really valid; it just means that in somebody's judgment the items seem to tap the concept in question.

In the history of the social sciences, instruments have come and gone with face validity but they did not prove to be valid when tested (Rubin & Babbie, 2008). Thus, when authors seem proud that their instrument has face validity, I wonder if they really understand what that means. Imagine, for example, authors saying that their instrument lacked face validity. That would mean that they constructed an instrument with items that they did not think really tapped the concept they intended to measure. Who would do such a thing? It's hard to imagine any authors ever saying that their instrument lacked face validity.

So, you might wonder, why am I even mentioning face validity? The answer is because some studies that you might read may actually mention it and seem proud of it. Don't be fooled by that. Other than perhaps reflecting on the authors' possibly limited expertise, it means virtually nothing—especially if the authors don't go further and report on the more meaningful forms of validity, which we'll examine next.

Content Validity

A form of validity that is more valuable than face validity, but still of quite limited value, is called **content validity.** To have content validity, a group of experts must agree that the items on an instrument adequately cover the full domain of the concept that the instrument intends to measure. Thus, if an instrument designed to diagnose posttraumatic stress disorder (PTSD) contains items about feelings of anxiety and depression, but contains no items on intrusive thoughts, nightmares, feeling numb, and so on, experts on PTSD would judge it to lack content validity. So would an instrument designed to test mathematical knowledge that contained only items about addition, and not subtraction, multiplication, and so on. However, even content validity is based on judgments only and not hard empirical evidence. For an instrument to have such evidence, it must have one or more of the next forms of validity.

Criterion Validity

One form of validity that requires hard evidence is called **criterion validity.** To have criterion validity, an instrument must be tested on a group of people to see if it correlates with some external, independent indicator of the same concept that the instrument intends to measure. Thus, if the clients scoring highest (worst) on a measure of PTSD also are diagnosed as having PTSD in an independent, diagnostic interview—and if clients with low scores on the instrument receive a different diagnosis in an independent, diagnostic interview—then the criterion validity of the instrument would be supported. Likewise, if scores on a new, brief scale to measure PTSD correlated highly with an existing, longer version that is already known to be valid, then that would support the criterion validity of the new, brief scale.

There are three subtypes of criterion validity that you are likely to encounter. One is called **predictive validity.** To have predictive validity, the instrument scores need to correlate to some future criterion. Thus, scores on a scale designed to measure family risk of child abuse should correlate highly with whether families are reported for child abuse in the *future*. A second form of criterion validity is called **concurrent validity.** To have concurrent validity, the instrument scores need to correlate to some *current* criterion. An example would be the previously mentioned PTSD measure correlating with another measure of PTSD administered concurrently with the new measure. A third form of criterion validity is called **known-groups validity.** Known-groups validity is a form of concurrent validity that assesses whether the instrument scores accurately differentiate between groups already known to differ in regard to the concept being measured. Thus, a group of clients in treatment for PTSD should—on average—have instrument scores much more indicative of PTSD than a group of people not in treatment for PTSD. A group of families who are in treatment for child abuse should—on average—score much more in the direction of family risk than a group of parents that have never been reported for child abuse.

It's important to remember that the indicator being correlated with instrument scores really must be *external* and *independent*. If the person conducting the diagnostic interview already knows the instrument score, then the diagnostic interview is not independent and is too vulnerable to being biased by that awareness. If the report of the instrument's validity does not assure you of such independence and lack of bias, you should not put too much stock in its impressive results. Neither should you be very impressed with an indicator that is merely an extension of the instrument as opposed to a truly independent indicator. For example, suppose an instrument contains items asking children about the quality of their relationship with one of their parents, perhaps containing items for them to agree or disagree with such as, "I love my mother," "I really can't stand my mother," and so on. Suppose that instrument is administered concurrently with a separate question that asks whether there are serious problems in their relationship with that parent. If a child is biased toward responding to the instrument in a socially desirable way, and refuses to admit to real problems in the relationship, they probably will be similarly averse to admitting to serious problems in the separate question. Therefore, any correlation between the instrument score and the separate question answer would be more in the realm of reliability (i.e., assessing consistency) than in the realm of validity (i.e., seeing if the score correlates with an *independent* indicator of the same concept).

A corollary here is that just like appraising other types of studies, don't just look at the results being reported about an instrument's reliability or validity. Critically appraise the methodology as well. This corollary applies to all of the forms of reliability and validity that have been discussed so far, as well as the ones that follow.

Construct Validity

Some instruments can have criterion validity without really measuring the concept they are designed to measure. For example, people in treatment for PTSD, on average, will have more symptoms of anxiety than people who have never been traumatized and who have never sought psychotherapy treatment. Thus, if a scale really just measures an anxiety disorder, the latter people will probably have significantly lower average scores (indicating less anxiety) than those in treatment for PTSD. If the scale developers really thought the scale measured the concept of PTSD, they would interpret that significant difference as support for the scale's known groups (criterion) validity. Although they would be correct in doing so, they could not be confident that the scale measured the actual construct of PTSD—and not some related construct (such as level of anxiety)—unless they took additional steps to assess the scale's **construct validity.**

To understand construct validity, it might help to define the term **construct.** A construct is simply an umbrella term that conveys a multifaceted abstract concept. Unlike a concrete concept like a chair, a rock, or the number of times someone has been arrested, a construct like PTSD (or depression, anxiety disorder, or many other abstract concepts) cannot be observed directly and consists of many different indicators. Some of those indicators are shared with other constructs. For example, items asking how often a person feels various forms of bad moods, out of control, and so forth could be part of a measure of PTSD as well as part of a measure of some other disorder. Consequently, it's possible for an instrument to contain items that measure indicators of more than one construct. For the same reason, it's possible that the items on an instrument measuring one or more alternative constructs will outweigh the ones unique to the construct the instrument is designed to measure.

Assessing construct validity is akin to ruling out alternative *DSM-IV* diagnoses. For example, if you are diagnosing a child and suspect a conduct disorder, you might want to test for ADHD to see if you could rule it out. In a similar vein, when assessing the construct validity of an instrument, you'd want to test for and rule out other constructs that the instrument could really be measuring and that would account for its criterion validity. To do that, you'd administer measures of the other constructs it might be measuring and then see if its correlation with the indicator of the construct you think it measures is stronger than its correlation with the indicators of the other constructs. For example, if the instrument focuses primarily on PTSD indicators that are also indicators of an anxiety disorder or depression, then its correlation with some independent measure of either of those disorders might be at least as strong as its correlation with an independent indicator of PTSD. If so, it would lack construct validity, despite its apparent criterion validity.

To rule out competing constructs, assessing construct validity involves assessing both an instrument's **convergent validity** and its **discriminant validity.** Assessing convergent validity resembles assessing criterion validity. It asks whether the instrument correlates significantly with an independent, external indicator of the same construct. Assessing discriminant validity goes a step further and asks whether the convergent validity correlation is much stronger than the instrument's correlation with other constructs. Thus, if we know only that a scale designed to measure PTSD has a statistically significant .50 correlation with another indicator of PTSD, then all we have is criterion validity. But if we also know that the foregoing .50 correlation is much stronger than the scale's weaker correlations with indicators of anxiety and depression, then we have construct validity. We would no longer call the .50 correlation an indicator of criterion validity because when it is coupled with the other (weaker) correlations it gets called *convergent validity* in the context of having established the scale's discriminant validity. In other words, when the competing constructs get ruled out, we would then say we have convergent and discriminant validity, and thus have construct validity.

Some studies attempt to establish an instrument's construct validity by conducting a complex statistical procedure called *factor analysis.* In simple terms, this procedure examines whether certain clusters of items on an instrument correlate with each other more than with other clusters of items on the instrument. For example, an instrument might contain different clusters of items, with each cluster designed to measure a different dimension of the construct. Thus, one cluster of items might be meant to assess somatic indicators of PTSD, another cluster might be intended to measure intrusive thoughts, and so on regarding other possible clusters. If the items on each cluster correlate with each other more than with the items on other clusters, then the scale has **factorial validity.** Some studies interpret factorial validity as an indicator of construct validity even without any assessment of convergent and discriminant validity. Other studies just call it factorial validity, without equating that with construct validity.

The latter terminology is probably more correct from a technical standpoint. But for your purposes as a practitioner, the semantics are of no major importance. What really matters is that when you encounter these terms you understand what they mean from a practical standpoint (as explained earlier). If an instrument has criterion validity and has had that validity assessed in an unbiased fashion, that's pretty good. In fact, that could be sufficient for your purposes. If another instrument has the additional features of discriminant validity and/or factorial validity, all the better. If you must choose between an instrument with good criterion validity, and another with good construct validity, chances are some practical considerations will be paramount in making your decision as to which instrument to use. We'll look at those considerations soon. But first we must examine the issues of an instrument's sensitivity to subtle differences and its applicability with clients from different cultures.

SENSITIVITY

As mentioned in Chapter 3, one question to ask when choosing an assessment instrument is whether the instrument is *sensitive* to relatively small, but important changes. The **sensitivity** of an instrument refers to its ability to detect subtle differences in the construct being measured. Those subtle differences can pertain to small changes over time by the same person or small differences between people at the same point in time.

Suppose that an instrument has known-groups validity in differentiating between people in treatment for major depression and people with no trace of depression whatsoever. That information would not assure us that the instrument can accurately differentiate between people suffering from moderate and mild forms of depression or between people with severe and moderate forms of depression. Instead, we would need a study to also show that the instrument accurately differentiated between groups known to have severe, moderate, or mild levels of depression. Likewise, just knowing that an instrument accurately differentiated people who are and are not depressed would not assure us that the instrument can detect a client's improvement from a severe level of depression to a moderate level of depression or from a moderate level to a mild level.

The only way to know if an instrument will detect modest degrees of change by a client is if it has been found to do so in prior studies. But even if it has detected small changes in prior studies, you should be sure to examine the time frame used in those studies. For example, some instruments ask about behaviors, emotions, or cognitions during the past 6 months. Suppose a study using such an instrument administered a posttest 1 year after administering the pretest (and after 1 year of treatment) and found that the instrument was sensitive to a modest degree of change. If you plan to use that instrument to detect change from one week to the next over a much shorter time span, that finding would not be applicable to your situation. Indeed, just knowing that the instrument items refer to a 6-month time span should be enough to tell you that the instrument won't work for your weekly time frame.

Cultural Sensitivity

You may recall the humorous scenario in Chapter 4 in which a researcher tried to get an English-speaking person to complete a scale that was written in Chinese. Although that scenario was intentionally ridiculous, analogous (albeit less extreme) examples actually take place when English-speaking researchers administer scales in English to members of minority cultures who have difficulty with English or who don't understand the idiomatic meaning of phrases in the same way that members of the dominant culture understand them. As mentioned in Chapter 3, for example, if a measure of depression contains an item asking how often the person feels blue, a recent immigrant from Mexico—even if they can read English—may think you are asking them about the color of their skin or their clothes. Likewise, if you ask them how often their parent or spouse gets on their nerves—even if they can read English—they might think you are asking about physical touch or about reading their mind.

An instrument developed in one culture is **culturally sensitive** for another particular culture if it avoids problems in language and interpretation so that it has the same meaning when administered to members of that other culture. Thus, attaining cultural sensitivity requires taking steps that achieve an instrument's **measurement equivalence** in another culture.

Measurement equivalence involves three components. The first is called **linguistic equivalence** (also called **translation equivalence**). Attaining linguistic equivalence involves a process of translation and back-translation. In that process, after an instrument is translated into another language by one bilingual person, another bilingual person back-translates the instrument to the original language (without having seen the original version). Next, the original version and the back-translated version get compared, and more iterations of the process are completed as needed until discrepancies between the two versions no longer exist.

The second component of measurement equivalence is called **conceptual equivalence.** Conceptual equivalence pertains to whether an instrument's items have the same meaning across cultures. To illustrate how an instrument can have linguistic equivalence but lack conceptual equivalence, let's return to the example of asking recent immigrants from Mexico if they feel blue. The linguistic equivalent of that question would be "Esta azule?" But in Mexico, that question would not have the same idiomatic meaning as in the United States. That is, recent immigrants would understand the perfectly translated words regarding feeling blue, but would not know they were being asked about feeling sad. Thus, in order to have conceptual equivalence, the Spanish words for feeling sad would have to be substituted for feeling blue.

When you are considering administering an instrument to a member of a culture other than the one that was used to assess the reliability and validity of the original version of the instrument, you should check whether the reliability and validity of the instrument were tested (after back-translation) in that other culture. If they were, using the same methods of testing reliability and validity discussed earlier in this chapter, and if the results were satisfactory, then you can be reassured as to the instrument's linguistic and conceptual equivalence for that other culture. Your next concern should be the third component of measurement equivalence—called **metric equivalence.**

The concept of metric equivalence recognizes that the same answers or scores in two cultures might not depict the same level of the construct being measured. Suppose, for example, a scale has been designed to assess children's attitudes toward their mothers and contains some negative items such as "My mother annoys me." In the dominant culture in the United States, it's possible for children to agree with that statement even if they have a relatively good relationship with their mother overall. However, it might be much harder for children to agree with statements like that in a culture that places a stronger emphasis on respect for parents and that has strong taboos against expressing disrespect for them. Consequently, the same degree of agreement in the latter culture might depict a much more negative relationship with or attitude about their mother than would the very same answers from children in the dominant culture in the United States.

To assess and achieve measurement equivalence, therefore, the two versions of the instrument would have to be administered to very large samples of people in the two cultures, and comparative norms would have to be developed. Suppose, for example, the average score on the instrument is 50 in the United States and 30 in the other culture (with higher scores indicating worse parent-child relationships). Suppose further that the average score among children in treatment for parent-child relationship problems is 70 in the United States and only 50 in the other culture. That would tell us that when administering the instrument to a client who is a member of that other culture, a score of about 20 points lower probably is depicting the same degree of the problem as a score of about 20 points higher would depict among members of the majority culture. In other words, a score of about 50 from a member of the majority culture would suggest that parent-child relationship problems probably need not be a main focus of treatment, whereas the same score of 50 from a member of the minority culture might indicate the need to address parent-child relationship problems as a key part of treatment.

FEASIBILITY

The measurement equivalence, or cultural sensitivity, of an instrument reflects on the instrument's feasibility. If your client doesn't understand the language or meanings in an instrument, that instrument won't work for you. Cultural differences aren't the only reasons why a client might not understand an instrument's language and meanings. Other factors involve such things as age and client impairment. For example, young children might not know what is meant by items using such terms as parents being too *authoritarian,* being *insensitive* to their needs, being too harsh in their *discipline,* and so on. Thus, if you are choosing a scale to administer to a particular age group, you would want to see if its reliability, validity, and sensitivity have been established for that particular age group. Likewise, clients with certain types or levels of impairment might not be able to respond validly—if at all—to instruments developed for and tested out with less impaired people. One relevant type of impairment would involve reading. If your client has poor literacy skills, you should look for an instrument that is geared for and has been validated with such clients. The same applies to clients with physical impairments that hinder or make impossible their ability to read and complete an instrument—particularly one that is relatively lengthy or complex.

The length and complexity of an instrument may make it unfeasible to use even with adult clients who read well and are not too impaired to complete it. The time you have to spend with a client might not permit administering an instrument that takes an hour or so to complete. Likewise, clients might not want to spend that much time completing an instrument, may find it boring, frustrating, or fatiguing, and consequently might complete it haphazardly or refuse to complete it. Length and complexity become even more problematic if you are administering the instrument on a regular basis (daily or weekly, for example) to monitor treatment progress over time. Some lengthy or complex instruments might also be impractical from the standpoint of the difficulties you'll encounter in scoring them. The scoring system might be so complicated and time-consuming that you won't have time to do the scoring—especially if you are doing so repeatedly as you monitor treatment progress over time.

Thus, when you appraise an instrument for use in your own practice, don't just automatically select the one that seems to be the most valid and sensitive. Look for information about length, scoring, and other feasibility issues. An instrument that has decent validity and that fits well with the practical realities of your practice situation should be chosen over one with excellent validity but that appears likely to be unfeasible for you.

SAMPLE CHARACTERISTICS

In a similar vein, always be sure to critically appraise the sample used to empirically test out an instrument. If the characteristics of that sample (i.e., age, ethnicity, gender, impairment) differ in meaningful ways from the characteristics of the people to whom you intend to administer the instrument, then even the most impressive reliability and validity results might be inapplicable to your practice. Likewise, the norms for that sample might not apply to your client. For example, the cutoff scores indicating severe, moderate, or mild forms of depression based on a sample of undergraduate psychology majors might not apply to frail elderly clients, poorly educated middle-aged clients, young children, and so on.

It's better to use an instrument with decent validity results derived from a sample of people like the ones in your practice than to use an instrument with more impressive validity results derived from a sample of people quite unlike the ones in your practice, especially if you spot instrument features (language, length, and so on) that strike you as inapplicable to the clients in your practice. Moreover, if you can find no instrument that has been tested with people like those in your practice—and can only find instruments with good validity but that seem problematic for your practice—it's better to modify and adapt the instruments and have unknown validity than to use the unaltered version with good validity knowing that without the alterations the instrument has virtually no chance of having that good validity generalize to your practice. Thus, you might use fewer of the instrument's items, change the wording of some of the problematic items, and so on. For example, for people with poor literacy, you might change an item asking if respondents agree that their spouse is too domineering, instead asking if they agree that their husband or wife is too bossy.

Remember, however, that once you make such changes you cannot claim that the instrument has the same validity attributes as in the study you appraised. Thus, you should not be cavalier about making such changes. That said, however, you should also remember that good validity results should not be generalized from one sample to another sample with very different characteristics such as age, ethnicity, literacy, language, degree of impairment, and so on. Whether to tinker with an instrument might be a judgment call. We'll return to this issue in the next chapter when we discuss the use of instruments in monitoring client progress. But, first let's end this chapter by examining how you can locate various assessment instruments that you might want to use in your practice.

LOCATING ASSESSMENT INSTRUMENTS

There are three main sources for locating assessment instruments that you might want to consider using in your practice. One source is publishing houses that will sell you copies of an instrument. Some are modestly priced and can be purchased more economically if your agency orders them in bulk. Corcoran and Fischer (2000a, pp. 53–54) provide a comprehensive list of such publishers (Psychological Assessment Resources, Inc., WALMYR Publishing Co., and many more). These sources typically provide information about the reliability and validity of the instruments, citations of studies that assessed the reliability and validity, and other useful information to help guide your appraisal and selection decision.

A second source is reference books that review and appraise various assessment instruments for different target problems. One of the best books is the Corcoran and Fischer (2000a) volume cited previously: *Measures for Clinical Practice.* It reviews over 30 instruments pertinent to practice with couples, over 50 instruments pertinent to practice with families, and 49 instruments pertinent to practice with children. Its companion volume (Corcoran & Fischer, 2000b) reviews more than 250 instruments pertinent to practice with adults. The problem areas covered by the instruments in the two volumes are extensive. For each instrument, Corcoran and Fischer provide information covering the instrument's purpose, description, norms, scoring, reliability, and validity—along with a primary reference that you can obtain for more details. In addition, they provide a copy of each instrument.

Corcoran and Fischer also provide a list of other reference volumes that describe various assessment instruments. Rubin and Babbie (2007, p. 93; 2008, p. 168) list additional sourcebooks, including the following:

Handbook of Psychiatric Measures (American Psychiatric Association, 2000)

Assessment of Personality and Behavior Problems: Infancy through Adolescence (Martin, 1988)

Psychological Testing in the Age of Managed Behavioral Health Care (Maruish, 2002)

Handbook of Psychological Assessment in Primary Care Settings (Maruish, 2000)

Outcomes Measurement in the Human Services (Mullen & Magnabosco, 1997)

A third way to locate assessment instruments is by searching the literature in the same way you would search for evidence pertaining to other types of EBP questions. For example, when I recently googled the search term "instruments to assess PTSD," the links that appeared included the following (among many others):

- Scholarly articles for instruments to assess PTSD
- Assessment instruments developed by the National Center for PTSD
- A survey of traumatic stress professionals about which instruments are most commonly used to assess traumatic event exposure and posttraumatic effects
- Current measures of PTSD for children and adolescents
- A brief screening instrument to detect posttraumatic stress

To find individual studies that tested out particular instruments, I went to Google Scholar and entered the same search term. Among the many links that appeared were the following:

- Reliability and validity of a brief instrument for assessing posttraumatic stress disorder
- Validation of the PTSD checklist—Civilian version in survivors of bone marrow transplantation
- Convergent validity of measures of PTSD in Vietnam combat veterans
- Psychometric evaluation of Horowitz's Impact of Events Scale: A review
- The development of a Clinician-Administered PTSD Scale (CAPS)
- Child stress disorders checklist: A measure of ASD and PTSD in children
- The Child PTSD Symptom Scale: A preliminary examination of its psychometric properties
- Psychometric properties of the civilian version of the Mississippi PTSD Scale

Which source you use to locate and appraise assessment instruments that you might want to consider using in your practice will probably be influenced by practical issues such as how much time you have, instrument costs, and access to Internet search engines and databases. I recommend that, if possible, you include an Internet search along with the other sources. With such a search, you are more likely to find the most recent instruments and studies and can be more confident in the comprehensiveness of your search. I also recommend that, time and access permitting, you read the individual studies whose findings suggested that the instrument you lean toward selecting has desirable features (reliability, validity, sensitivity, and so on). That way, you can critically appraise the sampling and other methodological features of the study and thus have a better basis for deciding whether the instrument really seems to be as good as it is claimed to be and whether it really seems applicable to your practice situation.

SYNOPSES OF RESEARCH STUDIES

Study 1 Synopsis

The Dork Assessment Corporation is proud to report the results of a study on the reliability, validity, and norms for its popular new scale: The Dork Child Behavior Rating Scale (DCBRS). The DCBRS is completed by parents to measure conduct disorder behaviors in their children.

In our study, the DCBRS was completed by parents on 1,000 children in treatment for conduct disorders. Reliability was assessed in two ways. To assess test-retest reliability, the scale was first completed on each child while the parent waited in the reception area during their child's therapy session. That parent was then given a second copy of the DCBRS to take home and complete and bring with them at the next therapy session. The correlation between the test-retest scale scores was statistically significant and quite high ($r = .90$, $p < .001$). To assess inter-rater reliability, we used that part of the sample in which both mother and father were present in the reception area, and had each complete the DCBRS on their child. This was possible for 100 children. The inter-rater reliability was quite high ($r = .93$, $p < .001$).

Each therapist treating the children in our sample was asked about the face and content validity of the DCBRS. All agreed that both forms of validity were excellent and had no suggestions for improving the DCBRS. To assess the criterion validity of the DCBRS, after completing the DCBRS each parent responded to a question that asked, "Overall, how would you rate the conduct of your child?" The response categories were: Very Good, Good, Mixed, Bad, Very Bad. The correlation between those ratings and their DCBRS scores was very high ($r = .96$, $p < .001$).

The scores on the DCBRS can range from 0 to 100, with higher scores indicating worse conduct disorders. The range of scores in our sample was

50 to 90, with a mean of 70. Thus, practitioners using this scale can view scores above 70 as indicative of serious conduct disorders.

Study 2 Synopsis

Criticisms of the original study of the DCBRS, conducted by the Dork Assessment Corporation, prompted this study, which was conducted by two independent researchers on the faculty of Smartmouth University. The DCBRS is completed by parents to measure conduct disorder behaviors in their children.

In our study, the DCBRS was completed by 1,000 parents of 500 children in treatment for conduct disorders and 500 children in treatment for other disorders. Each child treatment agency in the metropolitan area of Gotham City was included in the study, and 85% of the active cases agreed to participate. Parents for whom English was not their prime language were excluded from the study. Approximately 30% of the cases were Caucasian, 25% African American, 25% Hispanic, 15% Asian American, 3% Native American, and 1% of various other ethnicities. Sixty percent of the children in each diagnostic category were male. The ages of the children ranged from 8 to 12, with a mean of 10. For each child, only one parent completed the DCBRS—the parent identified by the child's therapist as the one who spends the most time taking care of the child.

Reliability was assessed in two ways. To assess test-retest reliability, the scale was completed on each child twice—while the parent waited in the reception area during two of their child's therapy sessions spaced 2 weeks apart. The correlation between the test-retest scale scores was statistically significant and high ($r = .85$, $p < .001$). Internal consistency reliability was assessed using coefficient alpha, which was good, at .84 for both the test and retest completions.

To test for the known-groups validity of the scale, we compared the mean scale scores for the 500 children in treatment for conduct disorders and the 500 children in treatment for other disorders. With higher scores indicating worse conduct disorders, the mean of 70 for the children in treatment for conduct disorders was significantly ($p < .001$) higher than the mean of 40 for the children in treatment for other disorders. The validity analysis included only those scales that were completed first by each parent, not the ones completed a second time for the retest part of the test-retest reliability analysis.

To test the construct validity of the scale, each therapist rated the extent of each child's conduct problems from 0 (no conduct problems) to 10 (severe conduct problems), and each parent completed a different scale— one measuring the child's trauma symptoms. The correlation between the therapist ratings and the DCBRS scores was quite high ($r = .76$,

$p < .001$)—indicating convergent validity—and much higher than the correlation between the therapist ratings and the trauma symptom scale scores ($r = .32$)—indicating discriminant validity. Thus, our results support the construct validity of the DCBRS.

We found no differences in our results between parents of boys and parents of girls or between the various categories of ethnicity. Each of the foregoing reliability and validity analyses was repeated separately for those categories of ethnicity for which we had a sufficient sample size (Caucasians, African Americans, and Hispanics). Virtually identical results were obtained for each group, supporting the cultural sensitivity and measurement equivalence of the DCBRS for English-speaking parents in those three categories of ethnicity.

KEY CHAPTER CONCEPTS

- An instrument is reliable if responses to it are consistent.
- The best, most common, internal consistency correlation statistic that you are likely to encounter is coefficient alpha, which reflects the extent to which subscores on each of all the possible halves of an instrument correlate with each other.
- Test-retest reliability assesses the stability of an instrument over time by administering it to the same people on two occasions (no more than 2 to 3 weeks apart).
- Inter-rater reliability is assessed for instruments that are developed not for self-report purposes, but rather for use by others who rate behaviors of people they observe.
- Reliability is a necessary, but not a sufficient precondition for validity.
- The weakest form of validity is called face validity, which merely asks whether the items on an instrument seem to measure the intended concept.
- Content validity is another limited form of validity and involves asking a group of experts if they agree that the items on an instrument adequately cover the full domain of the concept that the instrument intends to measure.
- Criterion validity requires hard evidence and involves testing an instrument on a group of people to see if it correlates with some external, independent indicator of the same concept that the instrument intends to measure.

- Criterion validity can be in three forms: (1) predictive validity, in which the instrument scores are correlated to some future criterion; (2) concurrent validity, in which the instrument scores are correlated to some current criterion; and (3) known-groups validity, which assesses whether the instrument scores accurately differentiate between groups already known to differ in regard to the concept being measured.
- Construct validity involves assessing both an instrument's convergent validity and its discriminant validity. Assessing convergent validity asks whether the instrument correlates significantly with an independent, external indicator of the same construct. Assessing discriminant validity goes a step further and asks whether the convergent validity correlation is much stronger than the instrument's correlation with measures of other constructs.
- Factorial validity refers to whether certain clusters of items on an instrument correlate with each other more than with other clusters of items on the instrument in the intended fashion.
- The sensitivity of an instrument refers to its ability to detect subtle differences in the construct being measured. Those subtle differences can pertain to small changes over time by the same person or small differences between people at the same point in time.
- An instrument developed in one culture is culturally sensitive for another particular culture if it can avoid problems in language and interpretation and have the same meaning when administered to members of that other culture.
- Attaining cultural sensitivity requires taking steps that achieve an instrument's measurement equivalence in another culture. Three forms of measurement equivalence are linguistic equivalence, conceptual equivalence, and metric equivalence.
- Whether a reliable and valid instrument will be suitable for your practice depends on feasibility issues, such as the instrument's length and complexity, and the similarities or differences between your clients and the ones with whom the instrument has been tested.
- Three key sources for locating instruments include publishing houses, reference books that review and appraise various assessment instruments for different target problems, and Internet searches.

Review Exercises

1. *Using an Internet search engine like Google or Yahoo, enter a search phrase to find links to help you locate assessment instruments for a topic pertinent to your practice. For example, you might try entering a search phrase like one of the following:*
   - *Instruments to assess depression*
   - *Instruments to assess anxiety disorders*
   - *Instruments to assess eating disorders*
   - *Instruments to assess conduct disorders*

   Then go to several of the links and briefly describe the instruments and other information you find there.
2. *Using an Internet database like Google Scholar, Medline, or PsycINFO, enter a search phrase like the one you entered in Exercise 1. (It may be the same search phrase or perhaps one involving a different area of assessment.) Find and critically appraise two articles reporting on the reliability and validity of one or more assessment instruments.*
3. *Repeat Exercise 2, but this time find and critically appraise an article reporting the adaptation of an instrument for use in another culture and its measurement equivalence for that culture.*

ADDITIONAL READINGS

American Psychiatric Association. (2000). *Handbook of psychiatric measures.* Washington, DC: Author.

Corcoran, K., & Fischer, J. (2000). *Measures for clinical practice: A sourcebook: Vol. 1. Couples, families and children* (3rd ed.). New York: Free Press.

Corcoran, K., & Fischer, J. (2000). *Measures for clinical practice: A sourcebook: Vol. 2. Adults* (3rd ed.). New York: Free Press.

Chapter 12 ———————————————

MONITORING CLIENT PROGRESS

For several decades, research scholars have been urging practitioners to employ single-case designs to evaluate the effectiveness of the interventions they provide to clients (Rubin & Parrish, 2007). As you may recall from Chapter 7, to derive causal inferences from these designs, the practitioners would need to have at least a handful (and preferably more) of multiple data points in each of at least two phases: a baseline (A) phase and an intervention (B) phase. You may also recall that the internal validity of these designs is strengthened through replication, such as by employing an ABAB design (which involves a second baseline phase and then a second intervention phase) or by employing a multiple baseline design (which involves staggering the onset of intervention across more than one target problem, situation, or client). In addition, you may recall that even if a meaningful level of client progress is detected in the graphed results of these designs, the overall data pattern can be ambiguous as to whether the intervention or some alternative explanation is the cause of the progress.

Because of the feasibility constraints that practitioners experience in attempting to employ these designs, it should not surprise you to hear that the scholars who have been imploring practitioners to use these designs have been quite disappointed in the findings of various studies that have consistently shown that very few practitioners use single-case designs

(Rubin & Parrish, 2007). One of the chief practical barriers practitioners face in using these designs is the limited time they have with most clients to obtain sufficient data points across multiple phases. Most problematic is the baseline phase. To get an adequate baseline, the introduction of an intervention might have to be delayed for weeks. That's hard to do in this era of managed care. Moreover, putting aside the issue of managed care pressures to limit the number of treatment sessions, practitioners and their clients might not want to wait that long before starting an intervention that they have the most hope for.

However, if practitioners follow the full five-step evidence-based practice (EBP) process, the use of single-case design techniques can be streamlined and thus made feasible for them to use. That's because when they reach Step 5—the phase in which they would employ single-case design techniques—they are not burdened with the need to derive internally valid causal inferences as to whether the intervention, as opposed to some alternative explanation, is the real cause of improvement. The point of Step 5 is not to ascertain the effectiveness of an intervention. That issue should already have been addressed in the previous four steps—steps that led the practitioner to conclude that the selected intervention *already* has been shown to have the best evidence supporting the probable effectiveness for the client or situation in question. Consequently, the practitioner's concern in Step 5 is simply to monitor whether the client achieves the desired outcome after the chosen intervention is implemented. In other words, monitoring treatment progress will show whether the client appears to be among those people who don't benefit from the intervention. (Recall from earlier chapters that even our most effective interventions don't help everybody. Even the best studies with the most impressive results only show that the most effective interventions are merely those that have the greatest *probability* of achieving a successful outcome.)

Likewise, if the client does not achieve the desired outcome, monitoring will indicate the possibility that perhaps there is something about the way you are providing the intervention—or something about your practice context—that is making the intervention less effective than it was in the research studies on it. As mentioned in Chapter 2, by monitoring client progress you'll be better equipped to determine, according to the degree of progress, whether you need to continue or alter the intervention. Another possible advantage is that clients might benefit and become more committed to treatment if you share with them on an ongoing basis the charted graphs of their treatment progress. Such sharing also provides a chance for them to inform you of concurrent events in their lives that coincide with blips up or down on the graph. This information might enhance your ability to help the client.

Let's now turn to a simplified and feasible design that you can use for Step 5 of the EBP process. After that, we'll consider various feasible rapid assessment techniques that you can use to monitor client progress with multiple measurement points.

A PRACTITIONER-FRIENDLY DESIGN

By limiting the aim of Step 5 of the EBP process to monitoring client progress—and thus removing the expectation that practitioners will maximize internal validity for the purpose of deriving causal inferences—practitioners are released from the burden of collecting multiple data points while establishing the baseline. If circumstances permit them to collect multiple baseline data points without delaying the introduction of the chosen intervention, they certainly can do so if they want to. Otherwise, they can limit the number of preintervention data points to as few as one. The purpose of that lone data point would *not* be to establish a baseline to control for things like history, passage of time, and so on. Controlling for such things would be needed only if the aim were to derive an internally valid causal inference. Instead, the single data point would merely serve as a starting point to see how things progressed during treatment. In fact, it could be collected at the beginning of the first session when the intervention is introduced, rather than delaying intervention to establish a baseline.

For example, at the start of the first treatment session, the client could retrospectively estimate how many times during the previous week a particular target behavior occurred. Or at the start of that session the client could complete a brief instrument that measures the target problem. If the client is having an atypically good day or has just had an atypically good week, that would likely be reflected in data points early enough during treatment to enable you and the client to detect as much and then use the early treatment data points as a basis for monitoring improvement. Moreover, the client might know that things have been going atypically well and tell you so, thus enabling you to recognize that the aim might not be to improve on the first data point so much as to sustain that level or eventually return to it and then sustain it.

You and the client could discuss a level that could become the aim of treatment. If that level is achieved and sustained, success! If it is not, a different intervention might be needed. And if you then introduce a new intervention (hopefully one that is based on evidence found in earlier steps of the EBP process), then the data points already collected for monitoring progress with the original (unsuccessful) intervention can comprise a baseline in an AB design for deriving causal inferences about the effectiveness of the next intervention. Let's label the design I'm proposing the B+ design.

The B+ Design

The B+ design is simply the B phase of an AB design with the possible addition of at least one preintervention data point and any subsequent phases needed in case the desired level of progress is not reached during the B phase. The B phase can be terminated at any point when you and the client agree that the desired level of progress has been achieved and sustained long enough so that continuing the intervention is no longer needed—in a manner no different than in usual practice.

For example, consider the four results graphed in Figure 12.1. Graph 1 depicts a result that would suggest that—whatever the reason—a desired reduction in the number of temper tantrums has been attained and sustained. With only one preintervention data point, we cannot rule out things like history or maturation as the real cause of the improvement. But if our aim is limited to monitoring progress, rather than deriving internally valid causal inferences, we can conclude that the desired progress was achieved and sustained during the course of treatment with an intervention that earlier steps of the EBP process had already shown to have the best evidence of likely effectiveness for this particular client. In other words, although we do not know if this particular intervention was the real cause of the improvement for this particular client, we would nonetheless have evidence showing that there is *no* reason to suppose that this intervention—already shown to be probably effective in prior studies—was not the appropriate one to use for our client.

Next, consider Graph 2. Although the number of temper tantrums in phase A was lower than at the start of B, the consistently high level at the start of B suggests that the A data point might have been an aberration—perhaps an atypically good week when the child was told that Santa was making his list of who's naughty and nice. In all likelihood, the child's parent could tell you as much and perhaps even provide an estimate of the usual number of temper tantrums on previous days or weeks. Thus, despite the aberrant A data point, again we can conclude that the desired progress was achieved and sustained during the course of treatment with an intervention that earlier steps of the EBP process have already shown to have the best evidence of likely effectiveness for this particular client.

Next, consider Graph 3. In this graph, it was not possible to collect a pretreatment data point. Perhaps the traumatized client was in a crisis and in no shape to provide retrospective information or to be assessed at all before commencing intervention. Nevertheless, comparing the data points early during intervention to the later ones shows that a desired level of progress was being achieved and sustained and that there is *no* reason to suppose

Figure 12.1   Various Possible Results Using the B+ Design

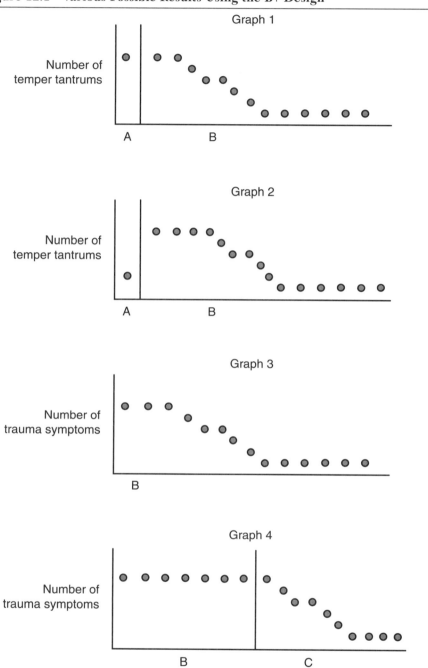

that the chosen intervention—already shown to be probably effective in prior studies—was not the appropriate one to select for this client.

Remember, however, that I am not saying that the data permit making a causal inference that rules out history or other threats to internal validity. All I am saying is that given the limited aim of monitoring progress during treatment to see if perhaps the chosen intervention is inappropriate for this client, we have evidence supporting the notion that the intervention we have selected was *not* inappropriate for this client. Moreover, we have evidence guiding decisions about whether a different intervention is needed or when it might be appropriate to terminate treatment.

Next, consider Graph 4. This is another graph in which it was not possible to collect a pretreatment data point. In this graph, however, the B phase data show that the client is not making the desired level of progress with the chosen intervention. Thus, despite the prior evidence supporting the *likelihood* that this intervention will be effective with this client, it appears that perhaps there is something about this client—or perhaps about the way we are implementing the intervention—that puts this among those cases that do not benefit from the intervention. Whatever the explanation, we would have evidence suggesting the need to try a different intervention. Based on what we found in our earlier steps of the EBP process, we would then turn to the next best intervention choice and implement it during the C phase. In Graph 4, the C phase data suggest that this second intervention may have been more appropriate for this client. In fact, because of the number of stable data points graphed in the (unsuccessful) B phase, we now can interpret the B data as an adequate baseline for making a tentative causal inference that the C phase intervention appears to be effective. (I say *tentative* because, as discussed in Chapter 7, without replication we have weaker grounds for ruling out history. Likewise, without replication we can't be sure that C would be effective had it not been preceded by the intervention in B.)

FEASIBLE ASSESSMENT TECHNIQUES

Before you can generate graphed data, you must formulate an assessment plan for monitoring progress. Formulating such a plan requires answering the following four questions:

1. What to measure?
2. Who should measure?
3. With what measurement instrument?
4. When and where to measure?

What to Measure?

The choice of what to measure requires that you translate the target problem or treatment goal into something that is observable, that is feasible to measure, and that has a reasonable chance of fluctuating from one data point to the next. For example, if the client is suffering from major depression with suicidal ideation, you'll need to translate the construct of depression into an observable indicator and to come up with a feasible way to monitor fluctuations in that indicator from week to week (or perhaps day to day) during the course of treatment. Obviously, the number of suicide attempts won't work as an indicator because (at least hopefully) such attempts won't occur often enough to have much chance of fluctuating from one data point to the next. Instead, you might choose a brief rating scale that the client can complete each day (perhaps at home) or each week (perhaps at the start of each treatment session) depicting their mood state for that day or week. If you can't find a scale that seems appropriate and feasible for a particular client, you can create a simple one yourself tailored to a particular client. For example, it can be as simple as the one displayed in Table 12.1. In fact, the individualized rating scale depicted in Table 12.1 can easily be modified to fit different clients with different target problems simply by changing the word *depressed* to *anxious, worried, angry, assertive, self-confident,* and so on.

Instead of measuring the magnitude of some overall approximation of mood or other emotion for the day or week, you might want to measure the frequency or duration of actual behaviors or cognitions. For a depressed client, that might mean recording the number of hours slept

Table 12.1   An Individualized Daily Rating Scale for Depressed Mood

Instructions: At the end of each day, enter the day's date and then circle a number to approximate how depressed you felt on average for that day.

Date	Average Level of Depression° for the Day						
	Not at all ⟶			Moderate		⟶	Severe
_____	0	1	2	3	4	5	6	7
_____	0	1	2	3	4	5	6	7
_____	0	1	2	3	4	5	6	7
_____	0	1	2	3	4	5	6	7
_____	0	1	2	3	4	5	6	7
_____	0	1	2	3	4	5	6	7
_____	0	1	2	3	4	5	6	7

°This scale can be adapted for other target problems or goals by substituting those problems (anxiety, anger, etc.) or goals (self-confidence, assertiveness, etc.) for depressed or depression.

The development of this scale was inspired by ideas in *Evaluating Practice: Guidelines for the Accountable Professional,* fifth edition, by M. Bloom, J. Fischer, and J. G. Orme, 2006, Boston: Pearson/Allyn and Bacon.

each night, the number of crying spells each day, the number of suicidal ideations each day, the number of positive or negative self-statements each day, and so on. For a child with an oppositional defiant disorder, it might be the number of tantrums per day or the duration of each tantrum. Or it might be the number of fights per week, the number of chores performed or refused, the number of minutes spent doing homework, and so on.

Who Should Measure?

There are four options regarding who should do the measuring: (1) you; (2) the client; (3) a significant other, like a parent, teacher, or cottage parent; and (4) using available records. Each option has advantages and disadvantages. The best choice—and perhaps the only feasible choice—will vary according to idiosyncratic client and practitioner circumstances. If you do the measuring, the main advantage is that you can be sure it is completed and performed appropriately.

You can do the measuring by having the client complete a brief assessment scale at the start of each appointment, or if you work in a residential setting, you can run spot checks on actual behavior (such as dropping by the cottage during study time for just a moment each day to check yes or no as to whether the client was engaged in an appropriate activity like studying or doing chores). The possible disadvantages of your doing the measuring are several. One is that the measurement can occur in your presence only. Thus, you'd have to wait for the next appointment to administer a scale. You couldn't record each morning how many hours the client slept the night before. Unless you work in a residential setting, your opportunity to observe behavior would probably have to be limited to observing parent-child or spousal/partner interactions in your office or viewing or listening to tapes of such interactions that they make at home. A second disadvantage is the chance that your observation would be obtrusive and bias clients to be on their best behavior. A third disadvantage is the time it will take you to do the measuring or observing.

Moreover, there are some things that only the client can observe and record, such as the number of positive or negative self-cognitions, suicidal ideations, cigarettes smoked, and so on. One advantage of having a client *self-monitor* his or her own cognitions or behaviors is that he or she may be the only one in a position to do the monitoring. But even when it's possible for you to do the measuring, having the client self-monitor will save you a great deal of time to attend to your other tasks. Perhaps the main advantage of self-monitoring, therefore, is feasibility. The main disadvantages of relying on a client to self-monitor are: (a) he or she might not follow through and do it in as consistent and appropriate manner as you would prefer; and (b) his or her desire to see him- or herself in a favorable light, or to have you see the client in a favorable light—might bias the measurement. What can be more obtrusive, for example, than to simultaneously act as both the observer and the person being observed?

Self-monitoring each time that a certain behavior or cognition occurs is not the only way that a client can do the measurement more feasibly than you can. The other is by completing a brief individualized rating scale like the one in Table 12.1 on a more frequent basis (perhaps daily) instead of only when he or she has an appointment with you. For example, each morning on awakening, the client might record how long or how well he or she slept during the night.

The third measurement option—using a significant other to observe and record behavior—has two key possible advantages. One, again, involves feasibility. It is more feasible for you to have a significant other perform this function for each client than for you to do it yourself. Moreover, with certain very young clients or severely impaired clients, a significant other might be the *only* feasible option. The second advantage is that the significant other might be able to conduct the observation much less obtrusively. It's a lot less obtrusive, for example, for a cottage parent to record the frequency of various desirable or undesirable target behaviors by a boy in residential treatment than for his therapist to show up and do so or for the boy to self-monitor his own behaviors. The two prime disadvantages of relying on significant others to do the measuring resemble the main disadvantages of relying on clients. One is that they might not follow through to conduct the observation and recording as consistently as you would prefer. The other disadvantage is that their measurement, too, can involve bias. They can be biased in the way they perceive client behaviors, such as when the parent or teacher who tends to scapegoat a child fails to notice the child's positive behaviors or when the parent wants the new therapy to be successful so he or she overlooks some negative behaviors. Significant others also can bias things if their observation and recording are particularly obtrusive, for example by reminding the child that they are keeping a list for the therapist of how many times the child misbehaves.

The fourth measurement option—using available records—can be particularly advantageous. Examining school records of how many times a child is tardy or absent, for example, is unobtrusive and a lot more feasible than any of the three foregoing options. Another example would be examining conduct incident reports that are part of the routine in a residential treatment center. Moreover, with available records you are not limited to just one pretreatment data point. You could go back in time and construct a baseline (A phase) graph like the ones discussed in Chapter 7—a graph that when compared to your intervention (B phase) graph can provide a basis for making causal inferences about the effects of your intervention. The prime disadvantage of relying on available records is that such records might not exist that correspond to the way you want to measure treatment progress. If they do exist, you might have trouble securing access to them. It's also conceivable that the data in them have not been gathered in as systematic and careful a manner as you would prefer.

Thus, each of the foregoing options has its advantages and disadvantages. Because there is no one best option or foolproof option, as a busy practitioner you should feel free to choose the one that works best for you in terms of feasibility and what source of data you prefer. It's hard enough for practitioners to implement the EBP process without burdening them with the expectation of trying to collect data in a scientifically pristine manner as if their prime role was to conduct research. Using any of the foregoing options in the context of the full EBP process is much better than less systematic ways of obtaining feedback about treatment progress without implementing EBP—ways that are at least as vulnerable to bias and inaccuracy as are any of the foregoing options. You should just select an option that enables you to feasibly implement Step 5 of the EBP process and avoid options that will be burdensome to the point of discouraging your ongoing engagement in EBP.

With What Measurement Instrument?

The type of instrument you choose or construct to collect or record data will be influenced by your decisions as to what gets measured and by whom. The three main instrument options are:

1. Behavioral recording forms
2. Individualized rating scales
3. Standardized scales

Behavioral Recording Forms

You will need an instrument to record actual behaviors if you choose to have those behaviors self-monitored or observed by you or a significant other. One option is to do *frequency recording,* which means recording the number of times the target behavior occurs. Another option is to do *duration recording,* which involves recording how long the target behavior lasts each time it occurs. Thus, as noted earlier, for a child with an oppositional defiant disorder, you could record the number of tantrums per day or the duration of how long each tantrum lasted.

The key priority in selecting or developing an instrument for behavioral recording is to keep it simple and nonaversive for the person doing the recording. Bloom, Fischer, and Orme (2006) provide extensive helpful details on how to do behavioral recording, as well as regarding the other measurement options discussed in this chapter. Most of the ideas in this chapter are based on their book, which I encourage you to obtain as a reference for additional helpful suggestions about any measurement options you select. For example, some simple techniques that clients can use to facilitate self-monitoring every time a particular behavior or cognition occurs include moving coins from one pocket to the other, clicking an inexpensive golf score counter worn on the wrist, or keeping a small 3 by 5 card for entering tic marks. Regardless of which technique is used, the frequencies should be entered on a form like the one in Table 12.2. For duration recording, a form can be used like the one in Table 12.3. You can use the exact forms in those two figures or construct a modified version that better suits your situation. Either form could be carried around in

Table 12.2   Frequency Recording Template

Client's Name: _____   Recorder's Name: _____

Behavior or Cognition Recorded: _____

Date	Number of Times Behavior or Cognition Occurred

Table 12.3   Duration Recording Template

Client's Name: _____ Recorder's Name: _____

Behavior or Cognition Recorded: _____

Date	Number of Minutes Behavior or Cognition Lasted

one's pocket for on-the-spot recording, entering slashes or minutes in the right hand column. If some other on-the-spot mechanism is used (such as transferring coins from one pocket to the other), the total count can be entered at the end of the day.

Bloom, Fischer, and Orme (2006) provide many other useful tips for behavioral observation and recording. Here are three of their suggestions that I think are key:

1. In keeping with the overarching principle of keeping things simple, limit the number of things being recorded to no more than one or two.

2. Establish clear guidelines as to when and where to record. (We'll examine the when and where question later in this chapter.)

3. Train the observer. Make sure the observer knows what to observe and how, when, where, and for how long to record it.

Individualized Rating Scales

When observing or recording the frequency or duration of behaviors is not feasible, or when the focus is on the *magnitude* of a target problem or treatment goal, you can construct an individualized rating scale like the one that appears in Table 12.1. Bloom, Fischer, and Orme (2006) provide some useful tips for constructing individualized rating scales. Here are four that I think are key:

1. In keeping with the overarching principle of keeping things simple, the number of scale points (response categories) should not exceed 11, and it may be best to keep the number between 5 and 7.

2. Fewer than 5 scale points will not be adequately sensitive to small, but meaningful changes.

3. The length of the blank spaces between the scale points should be equal.

4. Label at least the lowest, middle and highest scale points with terms like *none, moderate,* and *severe.* These terms serve as anchors that help the respondent judge which scale point is the most accurate one to circle. If possible, provide an anchor for every scale point, such as illustrated by the following:

Amount of Anxiety You Feel

1	2	3	4	5
Little or none	Some	Moderate amount	Strong	Intense

Bloom, Fischer, and Orme (2006) also provide helpful guidance for the completion of individualized rating scales. For example, they "should be completed often enough to detect significant changes in targets, but not so often that they become a burden for the respondent or intrude on intervention efforts" (p. 216). Nevertheless, they can be so easy to use that they can be completed up to several times per day. If completed more than once per day, a daily score can be the average of the day's scores. The scales should be completed at roughly the same, predesignated times each day. That's because the client's mood could be better or worse at certain times of every day than other times. For example, the client might feel lonelier and sadder at home alone in the evenings than while out and busy during the day. Thus, if the client completes the scale every evening at the start of treatment but then switches to completing it earlier every day later on, the scores can depict a misleading improvement in mood state even if no treatment progress is being made. In that connection, just in case the client does vary the time of day when the scale is completed, it's a good idea to include a space for the client to enter each time of day when they complete the scale. If you have arranged for the client to complete the scale at each treatment session, it's usually best to have that done before the treatment session begins so that the temporary effects of the treatment session don't influence clients to respond differently than they ordinarily would.

Standardized Scales

Whether measuring behaviors, cognitions, moods, or attitudes, a third instrument option is to use a standardized scale. Standardized scales differ from behavior recording forms and individualized rating scales in that they involve the uniform administration of the same scale items in the same way to different people.

Standardized scales vary in length. Some can be many pages long and are more suitable for a one-time administration at intake for preliminary assessment purposes. Shorter ones also exist, and they are more suitable for repeated administrations to monitor client progress over time.

The advantage of using brief standardized scales to monitor client progress is that they typically have had their reliability and/or their validity tested. A particular standardized scale might also have been found to be sensitive to relatively small, but important changes. Perhaps it has also been adapted and tested out for measurement equivalence with clients of a particular minority ethnicity that matches your client's ethnicity. From a feasibility standpoint, another advantage is that they might be easy to use and complete. Moreover, they save you the trouble of constructing your own recording form or individualized rating scale.

As with other options, standardized scales also have disadvantages. The general applicability means that they may not fit the unique target problems or goals of a particular client as well as a form or individualized rating scale that has been developed exclusively for that client. Some scales are copyrighted and expensive to purchase. Some require special psychometric training that a practitioner might lack. Also, even the briefer versions of standardized scales will probably be lengthier than individualized rating scales, and may not be suitable for administration more than once a week. Even weekly administrations might annoy or bore a client.

If you do opt to monitor progress with a standardized scale, your selection criteria should include the criteria discussed in Chapter 11. Is the scale reliable and valid? Is it sensitive? Is it applicable to your client's culture, age, level of impairment, and other characteristics? Is it feasible for both the client and you regarding length and complexity of scoring? Chapter 11 also identified useful sourcebooks for locating standardized scales that might be feasible for you to use in monitoring treatment progress. Perhaps the most helpful books for this purpose are Corcoran and Fischer (2000a, 2000b) and Bloom, Fischer, and Orme (2006, Ch. 7 and the appendix at the end of that chapter).

When and Where to Measure?

Your decision about when and where to measure will be influenced by your choices regarding what to measure, who should measure, and with what measurement instrument. For example, if you use a standardized scale, you'll probably have to administer it in your office and no more frequently than weekly. If the choice is to observe directly and record behaviors or cognitions, then it's best to do both at the precise time that the behavior or cognition occurs. Trusting memory to record later is risky, and recording with an unsure memory is more vulnerable to being influenced by bias. If it is not possible to record an occurrence immediately, then the sooner it is recorded the better.

As a general rule, measurement should occur as often as possible short of becoming an aversive burden to the people involved in the measuring. As mentioned earlier, the times of measurement should be predesignated and consistent so that variations accurately reflect the degree of progress being made and not the influences of differences in how the client tends to act or feel at different times of the day or different days of the week. The rationale for maximizing the frequency of measurement is that the more frequently you measure, and the more graphed data points you have, the easier it will be to pinpoint when changes in the target or treatment occur. With more accuracy in pinpointing when the changes occur comes a better basis for ascertaining what factors may have caused the change. If the change coincides with a change in treatment, there is reason to suppose that the treatment change might be having beneficial or undesirable effects. If it coincides with some other change in the client's environment, that information might be useful to address in treatment.

However, you should not feel pressured to measure so often that it saps your enthusiasm for doing the measurement or decreases the likelihood that clients or significant others will follow through with the measurement in an appropriate and consistent manner. As I've reiterated throughout this chapter, the key issue in Step 5 of the EBP process for practitioners is feasibility. History has shown that when practitioners feel that they have to monitor client progress in ways that are scientifically ideal but insensitive to the realities of practice, they are unlikely to employ scientific procedures at all. I hope this chapter has helped you see that if you are providing an intervention based on earlier steps in the EBP process, then the priority in implementing Step 5 is to do it in a way that will encourage you to keep doing it with all of your clients—not in a way that becomes burdensome.

SUMMARY

I've long believed that good teaching and good writing should end with a recap of the main points that have been learned. I'll do that now—in the context of the sequential things you should do as an evidence-based practitioner.

To begin, you should try to be a critical thinker. Rather than blindly accepting the testimonials from esteemed colleagues or prestigious authorities, you should be vigilant in trying to recognize the unfounded beliefs and assumptions implicit in those testimonials. Although you may respect the expertise of those whom you esteem as a starting point for contemplating what to do, you should want more. Specifically, you should seek the best scientific evidence available to guide your practice decisions. You should want such evidence not because being scientific is an end unto itself, but because it is a means to be more effective in helping your clients. Thus, you should recognize that seeking such evidence is a client-centered and compassionate endeavor. You should also recognize that doing so will make you a more ethical practitioner because using scientific evidence in trying to provide clients with the most effective treatments possible is part of what defines ethical practice.

Being an evidence-based practitioner also means engaging in the steps of the EBP process. That process starts by formulating an EBP question. Four common types of EBP questions are as follows:

1. What factors best predict desirable or undesirable outcomes?
2. What's it like to have had my client's experiences?
3. What assessment tool should be used?
4. What intervention, program, or policy has the best effects?

Next, you should search for evidence pertaining to your EBP question, perhaps relying heavily on electronic literature databases. You might have to narrow your question and use the word *and* as a connector to reduce the number of studies that result. If your search term is so narrow that you get too few useful references, you should restart your search with a broader term—one less *and,* perhaps—or by using the connecting word *or.* You need not read every study that comes up—the titles or abstracts alone can guide you as to which ones to read more fully.

When reading the relevant studies, you should critically appraise the quality of the evidence they provide, attempting to distinguish studies that have fatal flaws from those with less serious flaws and which merit guiding your practice. For example, when critically appraising studies that evaluate the effectiveness of an intervention, program, or policy, you should consider the following four questions:

1. From a logical standpoint, was the intervention, program, or policy the most plausible cause of the observed outcome or is some alternative explanation also quite plausible?

2. Was outcome measured in a valid and unbiased manner?

3. What is the probability that the apparent effectiveness, or lack thereof, can be attributed to statistical chance?

4. Do the study participants, intervention procedures, and results seem applicable to your practice context?

When critically appraising surveys that address alternative EBP questions, some of the key questions you might ask are as follows:

- Was the information collected in a valid, unbiased manner?
- Were the survey respondents representative of the target population?
- What was the potential for nonresponse bias?
- Were the conclusions warranted in light of the design logic, the type of data analysis employed, and the findings of that analysis?

When critically appraising qualitative studies, how you view their trustworthiness will be influenced by your views of reality, objectivity, and the aims of research. If your prime consideration involves the apparent potential for the study to have been biased, then key indicators of trustworthiness will be the study's use of prolonged engagement, triangulation, peer debriefing and support, negative case analysis, member checking, and leaving a paper trail.

When critically appraising studies on assessment instruments, you should ask the following key questions:

- Is the instrument reliable?
- Is it valid?
- Is it sensitive to relatively small, but important changes?
- Is it feasible for me or my clients to administer or complete?
- Is it culturally sensitive?
- Did the characteristics of the samples used to test out the instrument differ in important ways from the people with whom I intend to administer the instrument?

In conducting your search for and appraisal of evidence, systematic reviews and meta-analyses can save you time by synthesizing and developing conclusions from diverse studies and their disparate findings. However, you should remember that some systematic reviews and meta-analyses are more trustworthy than others. In considering their trustworthiness—and potential to have been biased—you should ask the following questions:

- Who sponsored, funded, or conducted the review? Were vested interests at stake?
- Were inclusion/exclusion criteria specified, and were they too narrow or too restrictive?
- Did the review clarify which studies were seriously flawed and which weren't, and sort the evidence accordingly?
- Did the review critique the inclusion and exclusion criteria of the studies it reviewed?
- Did it sort the evidence according to client characteristics?
- Was the review transparent; for example, did it spell out all the details regarding inclusion and exclusion criteria, how studies were collected, source of funding, reviewer backgrounds, and whether different reviewers with different backgrounds agreed about the review conclusions?

Based on your appraisal, you should decide how to proceed. However, your decision should not be based solely on which option has the best scientific evidence. You should integrate that evidence with your practice expertise and the unique realities of your practice situation, taking into account such factors as client characteristics and preferences and what is and is not feasible.

In the final stage of the EBP process, you should recognize that the interventions that have the best scientific evidence might not be effective with *every* client. To make this phase of the EBP process more feasible, you should understand that you do not need to use a complex (and probably unfeasible) design that controls for threats to internal validity. One possibility might be to employ the B+ design discussed earlier in this chapter. Because the previous steps of the EBP process led you to conclude that the option you are implementing already has been supported by the best scientific evidence, you merely need to monitor what happens *after* you implement your decision. If you are not satisfied with what happens, you should recognize the need to return to an earlier stage of the EBP process, in which you consider alternative options that might have had less supportive evidence, but which might yield a better outcome in your unique practice context.

LOOKING AHEAD

In this chapter and throughout this book, I have encouraged you to implement the entire EBP process in whatever manner works best for you and is consistent with the everyday real-world obstacles you might be facing that get in the way of perhaps a more ideal approach. As this book goes to press, various efforts are under way to try to alleviate those obstacles and promote a broader use of EBP among practitioners.

Some efforts are being undertaken by federal agencies such as the National Institute of Mental Health. Other efforts involve collaborative partnerships between universities and agencies, in which faculty experts in EBP are sensitized to agency realities and lend their expertise and other resources to help agencies implement the EBP process. University efforts also include initiatives to improve the teaching of EBP. For example, I recently spearheaded an international symposium on that topic. Some of the more significant recommendations that emerged from that symposium and that are currently being promoted by a task force comprised of symposium speakers are as follows:

- Integrate EBP content in all courses in the training of human service professionals.

- Inform students about the empirical support for every assessment and intervention practice taught in the standard curriculum.

- Provide far more extensive training in computerized bibliographic database searching and other information acquisition methods than have been offered thus far.

- Train internship instructors in EBP and provide supports to facilitate their capacity to provide EBP training to their student interns.

- Offer agency internship instructors and other agency staff free access to Internet bibliographic databases that are available to classroom faculty and students.

- Use active, problem-based learning that involves students in using the EBP process to formulate questions and make decisions related to their internship or their special interests.

- Use student interns to perform some of the tasks that would be useful for promoting EBP in agency practice, such as searching for and appraising evidence germane to agency practices.

Despite the foregoing efforts, the obstacles you might encounter in trying to implement the EBP process are unlikely to disappear soon. In the meantime, you should not feel that if you can't implement EBP in an ideal manner, it's not worth implementing it at all. Do the best you can, even if that means cutting some corners. I hope that what you have read in this book will help you do that and inspire you to persevere as an evidence-based practitioner no matter how daunting the obstacles you may encounter. Remember, the main reason to engage in EBP is the benefit it has for clients: you are trying to empower clients and enhance their well-being.

KEY CHAPTER CONCEPTS

- If you follow the full five-step EBP process, the use of single-case design techniques can be streamlined and thus made feasible for you to use.
- The point of Step 5 of the EBP process is not to ascertain the effectiveness of an intervention. The previous steps led you to conclude that the selected intervention *already* has been shown to have the best evidence supporting its probable effectiveness for your client or situation. Consequently, your concern in Step 5 is simply to monitor whether the client achieves the desired outcome after the chosen intervention is implemented. In other words, monitoring treatment progress will show whether the client appears to be among those people who don't benefit from the intervention.
- Also, by monitoring client progress, you'll be better equipped to determine whether you need to continue or alter the intervention in light of the degree of progress.
- By removing the expectation that you will maximize internal validity for the purpose of deriving causal inferences, you are unburdened by the need to collect multiple data points during baseline. You can limit the number of pre-intervention data points to as few as one. That one data point would merely serve as a starting point to see how things progress during treatment.
- The B+ design is simply the B phase of an AB design with the possible addition of at least one pre-intervention data point and any subsequent phases needed in case the desired level of progress is not reached during the B phase. The B phase can be terminated at any point when you and the client agree that the desired level of progress has been achieved and sustained long enough so that continuing the intervention is no longer needed—in a manner no different than in usual practice.
- The choice of what to measure for the purpose of monitoring client progress requires that you translate the target problem or treatment goal into something that is observable, that is feasible to measure, and that has a reasonable chance of fluctuating from one data point to the next.
- You can measure the target problem or treatment goal in terms of its frequency, duration, or magnitude.
- There are four options as to who should do the measuring: (1) you, (2) the client, (3) a significant other, and (4) using available

records. Each option has advantages and disadvantages. The best choice—and perhaps the only feasible choice—will vary according to idiosyncratic client and practitioner circumstances. Feasibility should be paramount in guiding your choice.

- There are three main options as to which measurement instrument to employ: behavioral recording forms, individualized rating scales, and standardized scales. Feasibility should be paramount in guiding this choice, as well.

- Your decision about when and where to measure will be influenced by your choices regarding what to measure, who should measure, and with what measurement instrument.

- As a general rule, measurement should occur as often as possible short of becoming an aversive burden to the people involved in the measuring. Again, feasibility is paramount.

Review Exercises

1. *Re-examine the four graphs in Figure 12.1. In your own words, explain what each of the four graphs would tell you as an evidence-based practitioner. Also explain why the first three graphs would have much less value had they not been based on an intervention that you selected based on the previous steps of the EBP process.*

2. *Think of a client or situation in your own practice. Develop a feasible measurement plan to monitor treatment progress for that client or situation. Describe what would be measured (in observable terms), who would measure, when and where they would measure, and with what measurement instrument.*

3. *Construct a behavioral rating form that would be feasible to use with a client or situation in your own practice. Discuss why it would be feasible to use.*

4. *Construct an individualized rating scale that would be feasible to use with a client or situation in your own practice. Discuss why it would be feasible to use.*

ADDITIONAL READING

Bloom, M., Fischer, J., & Orme, J. G. (2006). *Evaluating practice: Guidelines for the accountable professional* (5th ed.). Boston: Pearson/Allyn & Bacon.

Appendix A

CRITICAL APPRAISALS OF STUDY SYNOPSES AT THE END OF CHAPTER 4

The following critical appraisals for the two studies in Chapter 4 are based on each study's internal validity, measurement validity and bias, statistical conclusion validity, and external validity.

CRITICAL APPRAISAL OF SYNOPSIS 1

This study fails to control for a severe selectivity bias, and that bias seems severe enough to be a fatal flaw in the study's internal validity. The study lacked random assignment, and it is unlikely that the 1,000 inmates who volunteered to participate in the faith-based program were comparable to the 5,000 inmates who refused to participate. It seems quite plausible that those who volunteered to participate probably had more remorse, religiosity, and victim empathy to begin with than those who refused to participate. In fact, their greater beginning empathy is reflected in their higher average pretest score on the empathy scale. It follows that even without any intervention, they were much less likely to get re-arrested than those who declined participation. The selectivity bias in this study is so egregious that it overrides the fact that this study did control for passage of time and—to a lesser extent—for his-

tory. It controlled somewhat for history in that both groups experienced the same amount of elapsed time during which contemporaneous events could occur. However, it is conceivable that the Road to Redemption (RTR) participants, who probably were more remorseful and more religious than the nonparticipants to begin with, might have experienced more benign environments and influences after release than the nonparticipants.

From the standpoint of measurement, the study had several strengths. One was the use of official re-arrest records, which are unlikely to be invalid or biased. Another was the use of a validated, culturally sensitive empathy scale. Also commendable was having the inmates complete the scale outside of the RTR setting and in the office of someone who was not involved in providing RTR and who probably did not remember the treatment status of the inmates completing the scale. This strength, however, is offset by the likelihood that the more religious RTR participants may still have been biased in completing the scale, wanting to make a favorable impression on the chaplain, who apparently would be able to see how they answered the scale items.

As to the study's findings, the huge difference in re-arrest rates would be quite impressive had the study design been stronger. But that large difference appears to be more likely attributable to the study's severe selectivity bias than to treatment effects. The study's findings about the program's effectiveness in increasing victim empathy seem to have little value in guiding practice. The two groups clearly were not comparable to begin with regarding their empathy scores. Also, an increase from 40 to 46 does not seem to be very meaningful for a scale whose scores can range from 0 to 100. The statistical significance of the small difference between the groups regarding improvement in empathy should be considered in light of the study's very large sample, which made it possible to rule out the plausibility of attributing the small difference to chance.

Finally, from an external validity standpoint, this study leaves some important questions unanswered:

What were the characteristics of the RTR participants and nonparticipants regarding such things as ethnicity, religious affiliation, type of crime committed, and so on?

What were the characteristics of the victims who participated in the group sessions?

What were the characteristics the group leaders, and what kind of training and supervision did they receive?

In conclusion, despite this study's use of a quasi-experimental design, it was fatally flawed, and RTR certainly would not merit being deemed an evidence-based program based on studies like this. If, despite its flaws, this was the best or only study relevant to your evidence-based practice (EBP) question, you might consider testing out the RTR program's intervention approach if doing so is consistent with your practice judgment and if you can't think of a better idea.

CRITICAL APPRAISAL OF SYNOPSIS 2

By employing random assignment, this study controlled for history, passage of time, regression to the mean, and selectivity bias. Its control for selectivity bias is offset somewhat, however, by its small sample size. With only 10 inmates per group, a fluke plausibly could have occurred in the random assignment.

As to measurement, there was nothing wrong with finding re-arrest rates from the computerized records of the Arizona Department of Criminal Justice. However, despite the use of a validated scale, the measure of empathy was clearly vulnerable to problems of validity and bias. Having the chaplain translate the scale was commendable from the standpoint of cultural sensitivity, but he may have translated it in a manner that compromised its validity. The study did not check on that. The chaplain was unlikely to say anything that would bias the pretest scores, because the pretests were administered before the random assignment took place. However, with only 10 RTR participants, the chaplain probably knew who they were at posttest. It is therefore conceivable that he could have biased the way they answered at posttest—by making certain comments, how he responded verbally or nonverbally to answers, or in the way he translated the scale items.

In that connection, it is striking that the study found an insignificant difference in its unbiased measure of re-arrest rates while finding a huge difference in improvement of empathy scale scores. It seems quite plausible that the empathy score difference is too good to be true in light of the fact that it is not corroborated by a similar difference in re-arrest rates. Moreover, re-arrest rates are the more meaningful measure of outcome in terms of the value of this program to society.

Nevertheless, this synopsis might have understated the RTR program's actual effects on re-arrest rates. The 20% re-arrest rate for the RTR participants (2 out of 10) was lower than the 40% (4 out of 10) re-arrest rate for the control group. Although that difference easily could have been due to chance, it is possible that it was not due to chance. Given how small the sample size was in this study, the synopsis is incorrect in concluding that the RTR program is ineffective in preventing recidivism. A more appropriate conclusion would have been to call for further study with a larger sample. For example, the same difference in re-arrest rates with a sample of 100 inmates per group would have been statistically significant.

As to external validity, this study leaves unanswered most of the same questions that were unanswered in the first synopsis. However, it does report that all the participants were Spanish-speaking Mexican American male inmates in Arizona. That helps. If you are dealing with similar inmates in your practice setting, that's a plus in terms of the study's external validity for you. It also helps if you are dealing with a very different group of inmates outside of Arizona. That is, it helps you realize that this study's findings may not generalize to your setting.

Summing up, the conclusions in this synopsis are inappropriate and misleading. Deeming RTR as failing to reduce arrest rates is too negatively worded in light of the study's small sample size. Calling RTR a very effective and evidence-based intervention for increasing victim empathy is overstated and inadequately cautious in light of the potential problems of invalidity and bias in the way empathy was measured. The most appropriate conclusion would be to call for more research, using a larger sample and employing a measurement procedure less vulnerable to bias. Practitioners who read this study should neither conclude that its findings merit guiding their practice nor that RTR should be dismissed as ineffective in preventing recidivism. They should look for more rigorous studies and perhaps studies that might be more generalizable to their practice setting. Until they find better evidence, they should use their judgment as to how to proceed. If in their judgment they lean toward RTR as an intervention, the limited findings of this study should stir some doubt as to its likely impact on recidivism, but should not necessarily persuade them to choose a different intervention.

Appendix B ──────────────────

CRITICAL APPRAISALS OF STUDY SYNOPSES AT THE END OF CHAPTER 5

The following critical appraisals for the two studies in Chapter 5 are based on the experimental design concepts discussed in that chapter.

CRITICAL APPRAISAL OF SYNOPSIS 1

This study used the posttest-only control group design. One of its chief strengths was randomly assigning clients to treatment conditions. Another was its use of an unobtrusive, unbiased measure of outcome: agency records of future referrals for abuse or neglect.

One of the study's many limitations was that, with its small sample size, it is risky to assume that the groups would have been equivalent in their pretest scores or in various client characteristics, such as ethnicity, age (14-year-olds are less mature then 19-year-olds), educational level, and so on. Not comparing the two groups regarding those characteristics and not including pretest scores leaves the reader in doubt as to whether the results could be attributed to various differences in the characteristics of the groups.

The small sample size also made it difficult to get statistically significant results. Had the same sort of results been obtained with a larger sample, a statistically significant p value might have been obtained.

Another limitation pertains to the lack of equivalence between the practitioners in each group because Intervention X was provided by students whereas routine treatment was provided by experienced practitioners. It is therefore conceivable that Intervention X, if provided by experienced practitioners, would have had much better, statistically significant results.

Similarly, no information was provided on treatment fidelity. Even the most highly trained and experienced practitioners should have their treatment fidelity observed and rated. It is a serious flaw to assume that inexperienced students will deliver Intervention X in a skillful manner and to not bother assessing their fidelity. I would not call it a fatal flaw, however, in light of the study's results. Despite being provided by student practitioners, Intervention X obtained results that came close to being statistically significant. What's really egregious is the report's cavalier dismissal of the potential superior effectiveness of Intervention X and its recommendation that practitioners disregard it and seek other options.

That erroneous conclusion is even more unwarranted in light of the differential rate of attrition between the two groups. Because 6 of the 20 clients assigned to routine treatment dropped out, and none of the 20 Intervention X clients dropped out, it is conceivable that the 14 routine treatment clients for whom outcome data were obtained were the more highly motivated and more highly functioning clients. Had the other 6 clients been included in the outcome data, the results for the routine treatment group might have been worse, perhaps significantly worse than for the Intervention X clients.

Also perhaps masking the possible superior effectiveness of Intervention X was the potential occurrence of compensatory equalization, compensatory rivalry, and treatment diffusion. Perhaps the routine treatment practitioners went beyond the routine treatment regimen to compensate for their clients not being assigned to the exciting new intervention. Perhaps they did extra reading to bone up on new skills and treatment techniques so as not to be shown up by a bunch of students. Perhaps they learned about Intervention X in their reading or their discussions with the students and tried to incorporate aspects of it in their routine regimen. The report fails to address these possibilities.

Not all of the flaws in this study would necessarily result in an underestimation of the true effectiveness of Intervention X. Perhaps resentful demoralization had a deleterious impact on the results for routine treatment. Perhaps the students providing Intervention X were more biased than the routine treatment practitioners in completing the Family Risk Scale. (Of course, this concern is offset somewhat by the gathering of the unobtrusive case record data on future referrals for abuse or neglect.) Alternatively, it is possible that both groups of practitioners were determined to have their ratings reflect favorably on them and therefore so inflated the ratings that they failed to reflect true differences in risk and parental functioning between the two groups.

So, what's the bottom line if this were an actual study you had read in your search for evidence about how to intervene with teenage parents at high risk for abuse or neglect behavior? In light of the high position on the EBP research hierarchy regarding studies of intervention effectiveness, should the study's evidence be deemed strong because it used a randomized experimental design? Definitely not! Should Intervention X be disregarded solely because of the study's weaknesses and the lack of statistical significance in its findings? Again, the answer is no. The nature of this study's weaknesses and its potential for a Type II error do not provide a sufficient basis for disregarding the *potential* effectiveness of Intervention X. All things considered, the results of the study are inconclusive. We really don't know what to make of the possible effectiveness of Intervention X.

Of course, if a stronger study is available supporting the effectiveness of another intervention, then you should probably select that other intervention, assuming that it fits with your expertise and your client's state, characteristics, and preferences. If no stronger study exists, then you should continue to entertain the *possibility* that Intervention X might be effective. Perhaps you will find stronger studies in the future that evaluate it, and perhaps those studies will have more conclusive and consistent findings.

CRITICAL APPRAISAL OF SYNOPSIS 2

This was a very strong study that used an alternative treatment design with random assignment. It attempted to avoid measurement bias and the influence of experimental demand and experimenter expectancies by using an unobtrusive measure of one outcome variable (future referrals for abuse) and by using independent blind administrators of a validated self-report scale for the other outcome variable. Assessing the reliability of the perpetrator and victim responses on the latter measure and finding it to be high also was a strength. Another strength was the study's attempt to avoid treatment diffusion, compensatory equalization, compensatory rivalry, and resentful demoralization by locating the two types of treatment in two unconnected and distant agencies. Treatment fidelity was a strength in light of the amount of training and experience the practitioners had with the intervention they provided and in light of the objective way fidelity was assessed and found to be high, with inter-rater agreement in the fidelity ratings. The equivalence in practitioner characteristics, training, and experience in the two agencies was another important strength. One more strength pertained to attrition. The study had a low and equivalent rate of attrition in the two agencies, and further offset attrition concerns by including the treatment dropouts in the analysis of court records regarding future abuse.

The chief limitation of the study was the absence of a control group. Without it, the study's conclusion that "both inter-vention approaches are equally effective" is unwarranted. Because both groups improved to the same degree and had the same number of future referrals, threats to internal validity like history and maturation (or the passage of time) cannot be ruled out. This is not to say that the absence of a control group was a fatal flaw that made this a weak study. If one group had a significantly better outcome than the other, a control group would not have been required to conclude that the intervention approach with the better outcome was effective. Thus, the mistake is not in the design of the study, but in the report's conclusion. Rather than conclude that both interventions are equally effective, the report should have concluded that neither appears to be more effective than the other. The fact that both groups improved significantly in their scores from pretest to posttest is encouraging, but without another group that lacked such improvement, there are not sufficient grounds for ruling out history and maturation as plausible alternative explanations for the improvement. Rather than conclude that both interventions are equally effective, the researchers should have cautioned readers about the need for more research—preferably with the use of a control group—while acknowledging the encouraging aspects of the findings.

Appendix C

CRITICAL APPRAISALS OF STUDY SYNOPSES AT THE END OF CHAPTER 6

The following critical appraisals for the two studies in Chapter 6 are based on the quasi-experimental design concepts discussed in that chapter.

CRITICAL APPRAISAL OF SYNOPSIS 1

The main strength of this quasi-experimental study that used a nonequivalent comparison groups design is its presentation of data supporting the comparability of the two programs regarding staff-client ratios; services offered; educational degrees of staff members; and the age, gender, and ethnicity of their caseloads. Another strength is the unobtrusive nature of its outcome variable: arrest rates.

The main weakness of this study is a potential selectivity bias. The clients in the two programs might not be comparable on other key characteristics that the study failed to control. For example, it is conceivable that Program A is well known among the better-informed community residents for its culturally competent approach and not so well known among other community residents. Consequently, despite the similarities of the clients regarding age, gender, and ethnicity, families and clients in Program A might have more re-

sources, more motivation, and so on than clients in Program B. That is, perhaps the Program A families made sure that their teens entered the treatment program with the better reputation, whereas the Program B families—due perhaps to fewer resources, less motivation, and so on—had no preference and made no efforts to get in the culturally competent program.

The study should have made efforts to assess and perhaps control statistically for differences in things such as resources and motivation. Moreover, lacking such control, the study would have been strengthened had it employed multiple pretests or switching replications. For example, after the first year, it could have provided cultural competence training to the few bilingual, Mexican American practitioners in Program B and then assessed the arrest rates for the clients treated by those practitioners. To use multiple pretests, it could have added another outcome variable to measure, such as one of the existing validated scales measuring stage of change or motivation. Moreover, even just one pretest with such an instrument would have provided an indication of the comparability of the groups at the outset with regard to motivation to change.

Another important weakness of the study was in the way it interpreted its statistically significant results. The fact that its p value was less than .01 does not mean the results were "extremely" significant. The difference of only 6 percentage points in arrest rates is far less than extreme and not necessarily meaningful. That difference resulted in a less than .01 p value because the sample size was so large. This is not to imply that we shouldn't care about reducing arrest rates by 6 percentage points. Some reduction is better than none. But saying that the intervention is "much more" effective is incorrect and misleading because it ignores the influence of sample size and thus misconstrues the p value as a reflection of the strength of the program's effect.

CRITICAL APPRAISAL OF SYNOPSIS 2

The main strength of this quasi-experimental study that used a nonequivalent comparison groups design was its use of a switching replication. Doing so compensated for the possible differences between the two cohorts and ruled out a selectivity bias as a plausible explanation for the Dallas improvement on the first posttest because the Houston cohort improved comparably after it received the training.

Despite the importance of the switching replication feature of this study, the report reflects some weaknesses. First, the report should have assessed and reported possible differences in the background characteristics of the two cohorts, especially in light of the Houston cohort's lower mean pretest score. Not doing so could have been a fatal flaw without the switching replication, but with the switching replication we can deem that flaw to be minor.

Second, the report should have addressed the possible influence of the two

nonrespondents in each cohort after each received the training. Plausibly, the nonrespondents were much less favorable about evidence-based practice (EBP) after the training, and including their posttest scores would have lowered the mean. Again, however, this flaw was both reasonable and minor. It was *reasonable* in part because adequate follow-up efforts were made to obtain their responses. It was *minor* because there were only two nonrespondents in each cohort, and the mean improvement after the workshop was so great that even if the nonrespondents had much lower scores, the overall mean improvement probably would still have been significant.

Regarding the impressive degree of improvement, in which the mean posttest scores were above 90 on a scale where the highest possible score was 100, another flaw was the report's inattention to the meaningfulness of that degree of improvement. Just saying that the improvement was significant at $p < .05$ does not address the magnitude of the workshop's impact and its meaningfulness in practical terms. Remember, with a large sample, a small degree of improvement can be statistically significant. This study had a relatively small sample and probably would not have gotten statistically significant results had the workshop only had a modest impact.

At the same time, the very high posttest scores could have been due to a measurement bias. These were self-report scores, and the participants may not have wanted to disappoint the workshop providers by responding in ways that would depict their efforts as unsuccessful. In addition to that possible bias was the possibility that the practitioners wanted to portray their attitudes and behaviors in ways that reflected positively on themselves. Moreover, even if their responses were not biased, we should remember that the responses do not depict actual behavior. Even if the respondents had every intention of increasing their engagement in EBP, they might encounter practical barriers (such as limited time) to do so.

Indeed, the latter possibility might be the explanation for the decrease at second posttest of the mean score of the Dallas cohort. That is, perhaps the practitioners' attitudes about and propensity to engage in EBP eroded as they encountered real world barriers to engaging in EBP. Regardless of the reason for it, the decrease raises doubts about the longevity of the workshop's impact, and the report should have acknowledged that.

You might also be dubious about the measurement scale used in this study because the study synopsis said nothing about its sensitivity, reliability, or validity. The study should have addressed those issues. However, the study's results nevertheless support the sensitivity, reliability, and validity of the scale even though doing so was not the aim of the study. Recall the discussion of those issues in Chapter 3, which mentioned that if a treatment group's average scale scores improve sig-

nificantly more than the control group's, then that provides evidence that the scale is measuring what the treatment intends to affect and that the scale is sensitive enough to detect improvements.

The report should have acknowledged all of these limitations. Nevertheless, those limitations, and the failure of the report to acknowledge them, are not fatal flaws. They do not wreck the utility of the study in suggesting the workshop's potential effectiveness. If you were looking for evidence about which workshop approach to use to train practitioners in EBP, and this was the best or only evidence you could find, the nature of this study's results combined with its use of a switching replication would be grounds to try the workshop approach evaluated in this study. But you should do so in light of its measurement limitations and possible shortcomings regarding a long-term impact on actual behavior. Perhaps you could assess its impact over a longer term than this study did, perhaps using the measurement scale used in this study.

Appendix D

CRITICAL APPRAISALS OF STUDY SYNOPSES AT THE END OF CHAPTER 7

The following critical appraisals for the two studies in Chapter 7 are based on the time-series design concepts discussed in that chapter. The first focuses on a single-case multiple baseline design. The second focuses on a multiple time-series design.

CRITICAL APPRAISAL OF SYNOPSIS 1

This fictional study is egregiously flawed in three key respects. First, the measurement was fatally obtrusive and biased. It was obtrusive because the couple could try to be on their best behavior when making the videotapes for their therapist. Even worse, during the first baseline, Mr. and Mrs. T had no idea what the therapist would subsequently identify as undesirable behaviors. After that, they knew precisely what they had to do to make themselves look good to her. Thus, the obtrusiveness and bias were exacerbated by the fact that they didn't know what she was looking for during the first baseline, and then did know after that.

Second, although seven videotapes were made each week—one per day—the therapist graphed only one data point per week instead of seven. This violated a key principle of single-case design logic (and time-series design logic in general): the need to maximize data points to improve control for history, passage of time, and regression to the mean. For each data point on the graphs, there should have been seven—one per day. In this connection, you should keep in mind that no matter how much time is represented by a single data point, one data point is still just one data point. Even if it represents a whole year, if it is the only data point in the baseline graph, we have no way of seeing fluctuations or trends during that year that might show an improving trend, one or more aberrant days or weeks that regress to the mean, or other fluctuations suggesting the impact of extraneous events at different points during the year.

Third, the conclusion that history caused all of the three target problems to improve simultaneously ignores the plausibility of generalization of effects. History is only one plausible interpretation. At least equally plausible is the notion that once Mr. T became sensitized to his monopolizations and thus reduced them, Mrs. T no longer had as much need or as many opportunities to interrupt. And the drop in interruptions in turn automatically meant fewer "I pity the fool" outbursts. In fact, not only was generalization of effects a plausible rival explanation for the findings, it should have been obvious to the therapist at the outset that using these three behaviors for a multiple baseline design wouldn't work due to their the lack of independence and the consequent inevitability of the generalization of effects problem.

However, the problems of bias and obtrusiveness in this study, as discussed previously, were so egregious that even if generalization of effects was not relevant, and even if more data points had been graphed, it is hard to take the results of this (fictional) study seriously. I pity the fool who does so!

CRITICAL APPRAISAL OF SYNOPSIS 2

This fictional study is quite strong and provides a firm basis for implementing the program in other prisons. Step 5 of the evidence-based practice (EBP) process in those other prisons could examine whether re-arrest rates drop after the program's adoption. The adequate number of data points, the inclusion of re-arrest rates for all other medium-security state prisons in the same state, and the visually significant results provide a firm basis for ruling out history, passage of time, and regression to the mean as plausible rival explanations for the results. Instead, the most plausible inference is that the program caused the re-arrest rates to drop. There is no reason to suppose measurement bias could have affected the results because the data were collected unobtrusively from the state's computerized files. We could wonder whether history might have been a factor if all the prisoners in the program prison resided

after release in a part of the state that was different from where all the other prisoners resided. But if the prisoners in all the state prisons come from the same various parts of the state, there is no reason to suppose that things like different local economies and so on would have explained the lower re-arrest rates for the prisoners who received the prerelease intervention. Moreover, even if we ignore the re-arrest rates from the other prisons, and just examine the part of the graph that would represent a simple time-series design, the notion that history would have caused such a dramatic decline in re-arrest rates coinciding with the onset of the prerelease group program would seem far-fetched.

If you are the psychologist or social worker in another prison—even in another state—and no better evidence supporting a different program was available, it would make sense for you to try to have the evaluated program implemented. But you should remember that perhaps the prisoners in your prison or state are unlike the ones in the studied prison. You should be especially wary if yours is not a medium-security prison. Perhaps inmates in a maximum-security prison are much more hard-core and immune to the efforts to improve empathy for victims. And even if their empathy did increase, that might not translate into reduced crime among harder core criminals. You should also be wary if yours is a minimum-security prison. Perhaps the offenders in a minimum-security prison already have enough empathy for crime victims that their (perhaps relatively lower) propensity to re-offend would not be affected by participation in the program. Again, Step 5 of the EBP process is vital—to see if the program would be effective in your prison.

Appendix E ———————————————

CRITICAL APPRAISALS OF STUDY SYNOPSES AT THE END OF CHAPTER 8

The following critical appraisals for the two studies in Chapter 8 are based on the criteria discussed in that chapter for critically appraising systematic reviews and meta-analyses.

CRITICAL APPRAISAL OF SYNOPSIS 1

This synopsis was a real softball, and I hope you hit it out of the park. To begin, it reeks of egregious bias. By the citations in its first paragraph, you can tell that its authors probably invented the approach they are reviewing and are reaping significant monetary rewards through its training workshops. Not to mention the fame they are enjoying. Moreover, the report lacks transparency. The authors fail to mention their vested interests in the intervention approach they are reviewing.

It's nice that the authors articulated a narrow research question for their review, as well as a clear purpose for the review. But, again, they were less than fully transparent about their inclusion and exclusion criteria, and far less than comprehensive in their search for studies. Among other things, they made no effort to search more inclusive online lit-

erature databases, and no effort to find unpublished works (perhaps even some of their own) that did not get submitted due to obtaining negative findings.

Also quite noteworthy, they made no effort to find studies of alternative approaches to parent education training (PET). Rather than ask, "What intervention approaches are the most effective in promoting positive parenting and preventing child abuse and neglect?" they prematurely zeroed in on their favored program exclusively. Thus, even if their review had no other flaws, we would not know whether the studies evaluating their new wave intervention offer stronger evidence than studies evaluating other types of interventions for the same target population.

It is interesting that the decision to eliminate the 10 pilot studies they found came after the fact. That is, it was not part of any a priori exclusion criteria. Why did they include the pilot studies at first, and then decide to exclude them later? Did they not know going into the review that such studies have weak designs? If not, what does that say about their expertise in conducting this review? Assuming that they did understand the weaknesses of pilot studies at the outset, it is conceivable that perhaps those studies didn't find much improvement from pretest to posttest and thus would have questioned the effectiveness of their new wave approach even without a control group.

Thus, the issue of bias keeps cropping up, as it does again when they dismiss the studies with findings that they don't like due to the possible diffusion of treatment or unacceptable treatment fidelity. And what about those treatment fidelity ratings? Who made them? Were they made by unbiased, independent readers who were blind to the article's unwanted negative findings?

Interestingly, all 7 of the studies they dismiss used randomized experimental designs. Since they said that they found 10 randomized experiments in all, only 3 of the 13 studies that supported their approach were randomized experiments. Thus 7 of the 10 randomized experiments failed to support the effectiveness of their approach. All 10 of the quasi-experiments were among the 13 studies that supported their program. They say they found no serious flaws in 12 of those 13 studies. Easy for them to say. Did they examine the adequacy of techniques to make sure that nonequivalent comparison groups were really comparable? Did they assess potential measurement bias?

Finally, what about the effect sizes and clinical significance of the findings they like so much? They say nothing about that. Conceivably, all the studies with statistically significant findings supporting their approach may have had weak effect sizes—perhaps weaker than the effect sizes found in evaluations of other intervention approaches that they fail to include in their review altogether. Moreover, even if the effect sizes supporting their approach were strong, we don't know what was actually measured. Was it something meaningful like future incidents of abuse or unobtrusive obser-

vations of positive parenting? Or did they use obtrusive measures, just test parents on self-report measures of knowledge and attitudes, or perhaps merely assess client satisfaction?

In short, their conclusion that New Wave PET deserves the status of an evidence-based intervention is unwarranted in light of the egregious flaws in their review. Moreover, in light of some of those flaws—especially regarding comprehensiveness and bias—calling their review a *systematic* review is a misnomer.

CRITICAL APPRAISAL OF SYNOPSIS 2

This was a strong study, even stronger in its published form than in the way I shortened, simplified, and otherwise altered it a bit for the purposes of this book. It articulated clear and specific research questions and had a clear purpose. It was transparent about its inclusion criteria and comprehensive in its search for published studies. Excluding studies that did not use randomized experimental designs ensured that the findings of weakly controlled outcome studies did not cancel out those of well-controlled studies. It might nevertheless have been helpful to include reasonably well-controlled quasi-experiments, perhaps analyzing their results separately and seeing if they mirrored the results of the randomized experiments. Likewise, there is the possibility that perhaps some pilot studies failed to find pretest to posttest improvements, and perhaps some such studies went unpublished. Although only published reports of randomized experiments were included, the authors subsequently searched *Dissertations Abstracts* for unpublished works. The fact that they found some, and all had results that were consistent with their results, was another strength. Also commendable was the analysis of effect sizes according to different types of outcome measures, which partially addressed the clinical significance issue and did not just lump together dubious measures of outcome with meaningful ones. Although this study was not perfect (no study is), its limitations were reasonable and certainly very far from fatal, and the study deserves to guide decisions about evidence-based practice (EBP) practice questions concerning whether to use eye movement desensitization and reprocessing (EMDR) or exposure therapy in treating trauma symptoms.

Appendix F

CRITICAL APPRAISALS OF STUDY SYNOPSES AT THE END OF CHAPTER 9

The following critical appraisals for the two studies in Chapter 9 are based on the sampling, measurement, and multivariate data analysis concepts discussed in that chapter. The first focuses on a follow-up survey of dually diagnosed clients discharged from a fictitious chemical dependency treatment program. The second focuses on a fictitious survey of members of the National Alliance on Mental Illness (NAMI) regarding their experiences with mental health professionals treating their relatives.

CRITICAL APPRAISAL OF SYNOPSIS 1

This fictional study has some fatal flaws. Several involve sampling issues. The study generalizes to inpatient chemical dependency treatment programs across the board, despite being conducted in only one program in one obscure town. The study does not describe the characteristics of its participants. Perhaps the residents of that obscure town, and the patients treated in the program, are much less (or more) likely to be minorities, live in rural areas, or to have other characteristics that make them atypical.

The conclusions overlook the study's serious vulnerability to nonresponse bias

in that the 50% of discharged patients who could not be found or who refused to participate in the study very plausibly could have had a much lower compliance with discharge plans, and could have been functioning much worse than the ones who could be found and who agreed to participate. Moreover, the variables associated with their outcomes could have been quite different from the ones associated with the outcomes of the study participants.

Other fatal flaws involve the study's data analysis and unwarranted causal inferences. The cross-sectional survey design does not have the degree of internal validity that would justify the causal inferences it makes, and this problem is exacerbated by the study's failure to conduct a multivariate data analysis. Just reporting on a bunch of different variables does not make an analysis multivariate. To be multivariate, the analysis has to look at relationships among more than two variables simultaneously.

For example, does a correlation between two variables hold up when other variables are simultaneously controlled? Thus, the patients' history regarding severity and chronicity of psychiatric impairment (as indicated by number of prior psychiatric inpatient admissions) or their current compliance with prescribed psychotropic medication plans could be the real explanation for *both* their number of contacts with case managers after discharge and their behavior regarding the two outcome variables (frequency of attendance at self-help group meetings and postdischarge level of substance abuse).

A multivariate analysis should have looked at all of these variables simultaneously to see if the relationships between case management contacts and the two outcome variables diminished or disappeared when controlling for psychiatric impairment history and medication compliance. Likewise, differences in psychiatric impairment history and medication compliance could explain differences in self-help group meeting attendance, and therefore a multivariate analysis might have found that when those variables are controlled, the relationship between self-help group meeting attendance and postdischarge level of substance abuse diminishes or disappears.

A less egregious, but still noteworthy flaw pertains to the use of program staff to conduct the interviews. The staff could have been biased to ask questions or respond to answers in ways that influenced respondents to say things that the program staff wanted to hear. For example, depending on how respondents reported frequency of contacts with case managers, they could have asked leading questions indicating an expectation of positive or negative results regarding the outcome variables. Likewise, they could have had more positive facial expressions or had more reinforcing verbal reactions after hearing responses that fit the study's hypotheses. The study should have used more interviewers who did not have a stake in the study findings. If using such interviewers was not feasible, at least the study should have addressed the issue and perhaps made some efforts to assess the reliability and validity of the interviews.

Finally, the study reports use of the Addiction Severity Index (ASI) to measure postdischarge level of substance abuse. The ASI happens to be a highly regarded instrument whose validity has been supported in numerous studies. That's a strength of the study. However, the report does not mention anything about the validity of the ASI, such as through at least one sentence (with citations) about that. The study also should have addressed (and perhaps better controlled for) the possibility that if the interviewers administered the ASI orally, they could have biased the way the discharged patients responded, thus negating its validity.

CRITICAL APPRAISAL OF SYNOPSIS 2

This fictional study has some flaws that come with the territory of surveys and case-control designs, but the flaws are not sufficiently egregious to be deemed fatal or to prevent this study from guiding evidence-based practice (EBP). The study also has some important strengths. Let's consider the flaws first.

The report claims that the study had a random sample, but the only thing that was random was the sampling frame. The ultimate sample was comprised of only 50% of the parents randomly selected; thus, it is wrong to imply that only random numbers, and not other factors (such as how potential respondents felt about the questions being asked), influenced who got included in the data. Conceivably, the nonrespondents may have had different levels of satisfaction than the respondents, may have been more or less likely to have experienced being blamed by mental health professionals, and may have had different factors more strongly distinguishing between those families who did and did not experience an onset of family emotional or relationship problems commencing after their adolescent or young adult child was first treated for a psychotic disorder.

Moreover, even the sampling frame was comprised of NAMI members, only. Conceivably, parents who are not members would differ from NAMI members regarding the variables and relationships assessed in this study. Thus, even if the survey had gotten a 100% response rate, it would have comprised a random sample of parents belonging to NAMI only, and should not be deemed to be a random sample of all parents of an adolescent or young adult child who had been treated for a psychotic disorder.

Another flaw was in the way the survey measured the degree of satisfaction respondents had with the mental health professionals with whom they interacted about their child's illness. Asking, "To what extent have your expectations been met," is not the same as asking how satisfied you are. People with very low expectations can have those expectations met and—in light of the fact that they were treated as badly as they expected to be treated—still not be satisfied. Thus, the validity of this measure is debatable, and that might explain why it did not correlate with parents' perceptions of whether mental health professionals interacted with them in a supportive or blaming manner. It also raises doubt about the study's conclusion that respondents appear to be, for the most part, satisfied with their dealings with mental health professionals.

Another measurement issue pertains to the fact that the respondents were all NAMI members. NAMI is known for its endorsement of supportive, psychoeducational approaches and its criticism of mental health professionals who make parents feel culpable. Perhaps many respondents were familiar with NAMI's stance on these issues and therefore responded by telling NAMI what they thought NAMI wanted to hear.

Additional flaws worth noting pertain to the study's case-control analysis. Perhaps recall bias influenced many parents who experienced an onset of family emotional or relationship problems commencing after their adolescent or young adult child was first treated for a psychotic disorder. Perhaps those problems tainted the way they recalled their interactions with mental health professionals, making them more likely to perceive blame when it didn't really exist or to want to scapegoat the mental health professionals for the problems the rest of their family later experienced.

The recall bias possibility, however, is hard to avoid in case-control designs. It pretty much comes with the territory. Also, the fact that the study conducted a multivariate analysis—one that included variables regarding family demographic and socioeconomic background characteristics, prior traumatic family experiences that predated the child's treatment for a psychotic disorder, and the extent of family emotional or relationship problems that predated the entering of their child into treatment for a psychotic disorder—strengthened the plausibility of the notion that the perception of being blamed can contribute to the causation of family emotional or relationship problems. Thus, the multivariate analysis is a strength of the study. Moreover, if no other studies have investigated this phenomenon with more rigorous designs—such as experiments or well-controlled quasi-experiments—then this study's findings should have value in making practitioners aware of the extent of this problem and its possibly harmful implications. If nothing else, practitioners should then be mindful of this possibility in their own practice and should perhaps be stirred to investigate it further.

A measurement strength was the anonymity of the mailed questionnaires.

Because NAMI could not link respondent names to their questionnaires, it was easier for respondents to say things that might portray themselves or their families in an unfavorable light or to give answers that they suspected that NAMI did not want.

Another strength is the way the study dealt with the nonresponse bias issue. The three follow-up mailings to nonrespondents represent a good effort to maximize the response rate. Perhaps more impressive was the effort to conduct telephone interviews with a randomly selected group of the nonrespondents. Having found no difference in the data supplied by the respondents and the telephoned nonrespondents alleviates concerns that the study findings might not pertain to parents who did not respond.

While we should not dismiss the possibility of nonresponse bias as a nonissue, a couple of additional considerations bolster the potential value of the (fictitious) study despite the nonresponse limitation. One is the fact that a 50% return rate is generally considered acceptable for surveys of this type. The second consideration is the dramatic, alarming nature of the survey finding regarding the proportion of mental health professionals who are being perceived as interacting with families in ways that prior research has found to be harmful. If half of the 50% of respondents perceive being treated that way, then even if none of the nonrespondents have that perception, the respondents who do have that perception would comprise 25% of the questionnaire recipients. Unless NAMI members are much more likely than nonmembers to perceive being blamed for causing their child's psy-

chotic disorder, then at least 25% (and probably more than 25%) of mental health professionals interacting with these parents might be causing harm. Even though that's less than 50%, it's still far from acceptable, and the study's recommendation that efforts be taken to decrease the proportion of mental health professionals who are making parents feel culpable for their child's psychotic disorder would still be worth considering.

Evidence-based practitioners who administer mental health programs that employ practitioners who work with parents of adolescent or young adult children suffering from psychotic disorders would probably find this study to be valuable despite its flaws. If nothing else, the study should stir them to investigate how *their* practitioners view the notion of family culpability in the causation of psychotic disorders, whether the practitioners interact with parents in a manner that makes them feel culpable, and whether the practitioners are aware of the research suggesting that such an approach can be harmful. Depending on what they find in their program, they might also want to take actions to alleviate the problem—actions they may never had considered had they not read the (fictitious) NAMI survey report.

Please remember that I concocted the results of this fictitious study and that those results might have no connection whatsoever to the way mental health professionals really are interacting these days with parents of children with psychotic disorders. I am aware, however, of studies in the past whose results inspired me to concoct this synopsis!

Appendix G ───────────────

CRITICAL APPRAISALS OF STUDY SYNOPSES AT THE END OF CHAPTER 10

The following critical appraisals for the two studies in Chapter 10 are based on the empowerment, social constructivist, and contemporary positivist standards discussed in that chapter. The first synopsis emphasized the use of qualitative interviews; the second emphasized participant observation.

CRITICAL APPRAISAL OF SYNOPSIS 1

I created this synopsis as an over-the-top caricature to illustrate how some researchers seem to think that if they say their study is qualitative, then anything goes. Its flaws are many and severe, regardless of which framework is used to appraise it. From an empowerment standpoint, it is irrelevant in that it has no empowerment aims and makes no empowerment efforts.

From a contemporary positivist standpoint, it is virtually worthless and violates almost every standard imaginable. One interview lasting 20 minutes per interviewee, for example, falls woefully short of prolonged engagement. Its claim of having used "independent" triangulation is almost laughable. The lead author had an obvious bias, being an experienced eye

movement desensitization and reprocessing (EMDR) therapist and a board officer of the EMDR International Association, and no reason is provided to suppose that his assistant did not share his bias or was not influenced by it. No wonder there was 100% agreement between them! No mention was made of negative case analysis, member checking, or a paper trail. The authors apparently set out not to generate in-depth tentative new insights, but rather to grind their axes about why their favored therapy is better than an alternative and to merely reach foregone conclusions on behalf of preexisting claims about their favored therapy.

The authors claim to have used the grounded theory method, but provide no detail to support that claim. Furthermore, no information is provided to offset the aforementioned egregious bias that probably affected all phases of data collection, analysis, and interpretation. The brief interviewee quotes cited to support the authors' interpretations easily could have been selected for citation in a biased fashion—citing only those quotes that fit the authors' apparent predilections. Moreover, the brief quotes provide no in-depth insights—only superficial statements that the authors could have influenced interviewees to say in the first place.

From a social constructivist standpoint, you might be tempted to tolerate the apparently blatant degree of bias in this study based on the notion that there is no objective reality, that all we have are multiple subjective realities, and that efforts to be objective are merely futile acts of self-deception. You might laud the authors for at least being up-front about their affiliation with EMDR and the consequent implications that has for bias. Nevertheless, even using social constructivist standards, the synopsis has little value. It does not report the subjective realities of the research participants in detail. You do not get a deep empathic sense of what it's like to have had the interviewees' experiences—only some brief statements. In fact, the synopsis seems to suggest that instead of having multiple subjective realities, the interviewees all agree about the advantages of EMDR and the disadvantages of exposure therapy. In addition, there apparently was no member checking to assess whether the research participants agree that their own subjective realities are included in the findings.

About the only complimentary things to be said about this synopsis is that it was up-front about the authors' biases and provided some background data about interviewees bearing on the similarities between those who received EMDR versus exposure which could help you judge whether the findings seem to fit your own clients or practice situations.

CRITICAL APPRAISAL OF SYNOPSIS 2

This synopsis was based on an actual study. The published report was stronger than my abbreviated and modified version of it. By shortening the report and tinkering with some parts of it, I weakened it somewhat. Nevertheless, the synopsis still illustrates a useful qualitative study. No study is perfect, and the imperfections in this study tend to come with the territory of taking a qualitative approach and do not prevent the study's findings from having value to readers with evidence-based practice (EBP) questions about the care of patients on locked, acute psychiatric wards.

The study had several key strengths from a contemporary positivist standpoint. The most impressive strength was the study's prolonged engagement, in light of the observation occurring almost 18 hours per day for 3.5 months. Another strength was the use of peer debriefing and support. In addition, some triangulation apparently was used, in that the coding of data and the interpretations were corroborated by the three coauthors (although whether they were really independent in the process is unclear) and were based on interviews and documents in addition to the participant observation. The triangulation would be stronger, however, had the report shown how the different sources corroborated each other.

The use of maximum variation sampling somewhat supports the notion that the researchers were not just seeking cases in a biased manner to fit their predilections. Nevertheless, the report would be stronger if it added details about whether a negative case analysis was undertaken. Another strength was the authors' efforts to record extensive notes. Unlike the first synopsis, you get a sense of some serious efforts to get at deeper truths, as opposed to an inappropriate attempt to use the claim of qualitative inquiry to justify a superficial and biased inquiry. Also, the extensive field notes and audiotaped interviews conceivably could provide a paper trail for a future audit (although the authors do not address that point directly).

The study had both the advantages and disadvantages of taking an almost complete observer approach to participant observation. By minimizing her participation in events, the lead author tried to prevent influencing them. However, the observation was not unobtrusive. The staff and patients were aware of the observation and therefore could have been influenced by it. Had she been more of a nursing participant, her observation may have been less obtrusive, and she may have gotten a deeper empathic sense of the nursing experience on the observed ward. But participating has its downsides, too, and since the researcher herself was a nurse with many years of experience in similar settings, minimizing her participation was a reasonable option.

Another strength of the report was the detail it provided about the coding of data and the qualitative data analysis procedures employed, which had many features of grounded theory. (The synopsis does not provide that detail, but mentions that it exists in the published report of the actual study.) Detailed reporting was a strength in other areas, as well, such as regarding staff attributes, the physical layout of the ward, and the findings. Although the findings cannot be generalized to other wards (limited external validity usually comes with the territory of in-depth qualitative research like this), you get a good basis to judge whether the studied ward resembles the ward pertaining to your EBP question.

The extensive detail in the report is a strength from the social constructivist standpoint, as well. In addition to helping you decide for yourself if the findings seem applicable to your own practice situation, the detail gives you a deep empathic sense of what it's like to experience the ward as the staff and patients experience it. Social constructivists, however, probably would like more detail as to the *different* subjective realities of research participants. They might also want to see the results of member checking as to whether the staff and patients agree that their own subjective realities are included in the findings.

Although the study was not based on an empowerment framework, it has some value from that standpoint, as well. By focusing on the frustrations experienced by both staff and patients in regard to control issues, the report develops implications for empowering both staff and patients.

In conclusion, despite its imperfections, this study illustrates some of the key advantages of qualitative research. Although we cannot rule out the possibility that the study's observations and interpretations might have been heavily influenced by the researchers' predilections, and although we cannot safely generalize its findings to other settings, it will have substantial value if its findings give you tentative new or deeper insights that might enhance your practice in your own setting.

Appendix H

CRITICAL APPRAISALS OF STUDY SYNOPSES AT THE END OF CHAPTER 11

The following critical appraisals for the two studies in Chapter 11 are based on the concepts discussed in that chapter. Each synopsis focused on the same fictitious scale, developed by a fictitious assessment corporation, to assess conduct disorder behaviors in children. That fictitious corporation carried out the first (fictitious) study. Independent researchers on the faculty of a fictitious university carried out the second (fictitious) study.

CRITICAL APPRAISAL OF SYNOPSIS 1

This (fictitious) study has many severe and fatal problems. It is so flawed that you can't help but wonder whether the profit motive was all the Dork Corporation cared about.

The test-retest reliability was flawed because parents could have completed the retest so soon after the initial completion that they could have been biased by remembering how they answered the items on the initial completion. It's good that not so much time had elapsed that the children's conduct disorder behavior could have changed significantly, but in many or most cases the second completion could have been later on the same day or

the next day after the initial completion. The inter-rater reliability was egregiously flawed because the mother and father could have been discussing and comparing their responses to each item. Thus, the two ratings appear quite unlikely to have been independent and unbiased.

It's nice that each therapist treating the children in the sample agreed that the face and content validity of the Dork Child Behavior Rating Scale (DCBRS) were excellent, but so what! As discussed in Chapter 11, face validity provides no empirical assurance that the scale really measures what it intends to measure, and content validity doesn't go much further. Moreover, the synopsis tells us nothing about the way in which the therapists were asked about the face and content validity. Given the vested interest of the Dork Corporation in the DCBRS, they could have been asked in a very leading and biased fashion, making it hard for them to be critical of the scale's face and content validity.

A fatal flaw also is evident in the way that the criterion validity of the DCBRS was assessed. The so-called "independent" indicator of conduct was not really independent at all. The overall rating of conduct was provided by the same source (the parent) immediately after completing the DCBRS. This is fatally flawed in two ways. First, their rating could be biased by the ways in which they responded to the DCBRS items. Second, if they are biased toward portraying their child's behavior as more positive or more negative than it really is, then they would probably be biased in their overall rating in the same way.

The statement in the synopsis—that practitioners using this scale can view scores above 70 as indicative of serious conduct disorders—is erroneous and misleading. All the children in the sample were being treated for conduct disorders. No information is provided regarding norms for children without conduct disorders. Without the latter information, we have no basis for knowing what scores differentiate between those children who are and are not likely to need treatment for conduct disorders.

The foregoing flaws are errors of commission. The report also leaves much to be desired regarding errors of omission. For example, no information is provided about the background characteristics of the sample regarding such things as the children's ages, gender, and ethnicity. What about other diagnostic information? How many children, for example, had comorbid diagnoses? What about the length of the instrument and how long it takes parents to complete it? Apparently nothing has been done to assess the cultural sensitivity or measurement equivalence of the instrument for using it with members of cultures other than the dominant culture because that issue was not addressed in the report. Conceivably, every family in the study could have been Caucasian, affluent, and having their child treated by an expensive private practitioner (as opposed to more affordable child and family treatment agencies). Equally conceivable, most of the families could have been relatively poor, of minority ethnicity, and having their child in

treatment in an agency. We just don't know about any of these omitted issues, and thus have no basis for judging the feasibility or suitability of the scale for our own practice situations.

CRITICAL APPRAISAL OF SYNOPSIS 2

This (fictitious) study of the same DCBRS instrument as assessed in the first study was a much stronger study than the first study, perhaps in part because the investigators did not have an apparent vested interest in the scale, unlike the first study, in which the corporation conducting and reporting the study stood to profit from marketing the scale.

One strength of this study was in its sampling, which seemed reasonably diverse and representative. Moreover, we are given more information than in the first study to enable us to judge whether the characteristics of the study participants resemble the characteristics of our own clients. Excluding parents for whom English was not the prime language was both a strength and a limitation. It was a strength from the standpoint of not underestimating the reliability for English-speaking parents. It was a limitation in that the study results are not generalizable to parents for whom English is not the prime language. However, future studies can address that issue; therefore, excluding such parents was probably a wise decision.

The test-retest reliability assessment was strong because the test and retest were spaced 2 weeks apart. Augmenting that analysis with coefficient alpha provided corroborating evidence of the scale's reliability. The known-groups validity analysis was appropriate in that there is no reason to suppose a lack of independence between the scale scores and the focus of treatment. Another strength was the study's assessment of the scale's construct validity, which also was conducted in an appropriate, unbiased manner. Finally, analyzing the reliability and validity results separately according to gender and ethnicity appropriately helps readers judge whether the scale is reliable and valid for their clients and shows that the scale has measurement equivalence across the three categories of ethnicity.

Glossary

AB design   A simple time-series design applied to a single case, consisting of a baseline (A) phase and an intervention (B) phase.

ABAB design   A single-case design consisting of two baseline (A) phases and two intervention (B) phases. By adding the extra phases, this design controls for history (a threat to internal validity) better than does the AB design.

accidental samples   (See **availability samples.**)

and   A conjunction used in a search term to more narrowly target the number of studies that will come up when using an electronic literature database.

audit   (See **paper trail.**)

availability samples   (See also **convenience samples** or **accidental samples.**) Types of nonprobability samples in which cases are selected for a study simply because they are the ones most immediately available and convenient to sample.

baseline   The phase in a time-series design comprised of data points before a change in program, intervention, or policy is implemented.

Campbell Collaboration   A highly regarded source of rigorous, objective systematic reviews of research on interventions in the areas of social welfare, education, and criminal justice.

case-control design   A correlational design that uses matched groups of people who appear to be comparable except for some contrasting outcome. By using multivariate data analysis techniques, they attempt to determine what personal attributes and past experiences best distinguish the two groups.

case-control studies   Studies that employ the case-control design.

classic pretest-posttest control group design   An experimental design for evaluating treatment outcome in which clients are assigned randomly to treatment conditions and then pretested and posttested before and after the treatment condition has been provided.

clinical significance   The meaningfulness and practical value of a finding. Statistically significant findings—even those with very strong effect sizes—can lack clinical significance.

cluster sampling   A probability sampling approach in which researchers begin with a list of groupings (clusters) of people. Next, they number every cluster and then randomly select some of them. Then they select a random sample of individuals from each cluster.

Cochrane Collaboration   A highly regarded source of rigorous, objective systematic reviews of research on health care interventions.

coefficient alpha   A commonly used indicator of the internal consistency reliability of an instrument, calculated by breaking an instrument down into every possible split-half, calculating the split-half correlations for every pair of halves, and then calculating the mean of all those split-half correlations. To keep things simple, you can think of coefficient alpha as the extent to which subscores on each half of an instrument correlate with each other.

compensatory equalization   Efforts by practitioners or clients in treatment-as-usual control groups to offset a perceived inequality in service provision by exceeding the routine treatment regimen.

compensatory rivalry   Efforts by practitioners or clients in a treatment-as-usual control group to compete with their counterparts in the experimental group.

conceptual equivalence   A desired attribute of an instrument that pertains to whether an instrument's items have the same idiomatic meaning across cultures after translation.

concurrent validity   A form of criterion validity that assesses whether instrument scores correlate to some current criterion.

construct   A word we use as an umbrella term that conveys a multifaceted abstract concept.

construct validity   A form of validity that goes beyond criterion validity to see if an instrument really measures the intended construct and not some related construct. It consists of **convergent validity** and **discriminant validity.**

content validity   A relatively weak form of validity assessed by asking a group of experts whether they agree that the items on an instrument adequately cover the full domain of the concept that the instrument intends to measure.

convenience samples   (See **availability samples.**)

convergent validity   One part of construct validity, assessing whether an instrument correlates significantly with an independent, external indicator of the same construct.

correlation   One of the three criteria that are all necessary for inferring causality, in which the changes in outcomes must be associated with changes in the intervention condition.

correlational studies   Studies that—instead of manipulating logical arrangements—rely on statistical associations that can yield preliminary, but not conclusive, evidence about intervention effects.

criterion validity   A relatively strong form of validity, in which an instrument is tested out on a group of people to see if it correlates with some external, independent indicator of the same concept that the instrument intends to measure.

cross-sectional study   A design that examines a phenomenon or relationships among variables at one point in time, only. It does not assess changes over time. Thus, it is quite limited regarding the detection of causality or in merely describing the trajectory of phenomena.

culturally sensitive   A characteristic of a measurement instrument that refers to the ability of members of different cultures to understand its language and conceptual meanings and to complete it in a valid manner.

***d*-index**   An effect-size statistic in which the difference between the experimental and control group means is divided by the standard deviation.

differential attrition   An alternative explanation for outcome study findings that occurs when a much larger proportion of participants in one group drop out of treatment or out of the measurement than in the other group.

discriminant validity   One part of construct validity, assessing whether the convergent validity correlation is much stronger than the instrument's correlation with other constructs.

dismantling designs   Experimental designs that randomly assign clients to various groups that receive different combinations of the components of a multifaceted intervention, to see which components most account for the intervention's effects and which components might not even be needed.

effect size   A statistic that depicts the average strength of the effects of an intervention across studies that use different types of outcome measures.

emic perspective   An aspect of participant observation in qualitative research in which the researcher subjectively tries to adopt the perspective of the people being observed. This perspective needs to be balanced with the **etic perspective.**

etic perspective   An aspect of participant observation in qualitative research in which the researcher tries to maintain the ability to step outside of the emic perspective and think critically and objectively as an outsider about the phenomena being observed and experienced.

evidence-based practice (EBP)   A process for making practice decisions in which practitioners integrate the best research evidence available with their clinical expertise and with client attributes, values, preferences, and circumstances.

experimental demand or experimenter expectancies   Perceptions by clients that they are expected to report improvement and may therefore do so even if an intervention is ineffective.

experimental designs   The gold standard for evaluating whether a particular intervention—and not some alternative explanation—is the real cause of a particular outcome. The key feature involves random assignment to the groups being compared.

external validity   A desired attribute of a study pertinent to the extent to which its findings apply to settings and people outside of the study.

face validity   The weakest form of validity that refers to whether the items on an instrument merely seem to measure the intended concept.

factorial validity   A type of measurement validity that is achieved when the items on each intended cluster of items correlate with each other more than with the items on other intended clusters.

file drawer effect   A potential limitation of systematic reviews and meta-analyses, based on the notion that researchers whose findings fail to support the effectiveness of an intervention are less likely to submit their studies for publication than researchers with positive findings.

grounded theory   An overarching framework for much qualitative research. A key feature is the use of constant comparisons. It begins with a search for patterns or commonalities among an initial sample of cases. Next comes the search for more cases and observations that might or might not fit the initial patterns or commonalities.

The search is guided by theoretical sampling. First, new cases are sought that seem to be similar to the cases on which the previous patterns and commonalities were based. Next, different kinds of cases are selected to see if the same insights are generated. If the new cases stimulate new insights, then more cases like them are sought until no new insights are being generated. More iterations of this process are repeated until the analysis of different kinds of cases stops yielding new insights.

history   A threat to internal validity (i.e., an alternative explanation) that refers to the possibility that other events may have coincided with the provision of the intervention and may be the real cause of the observed outcome.

internal consistency reliability   High positive correlations among items on an instrument. There are three common ways to assess internal consistency reliability correlations: (1) Calculate inter-item correlations between each item, (2) calculate the correlation between each item and the total scale score, and (3) split the instrument in half and calculate the correlation between the subscores on each half.

internal validity   A desired attribute of an outcome study design in which logical arrangements permit causal inferences as to whether the observed outcome really reflects the effectiveness (or lack thereof) of an intervention versus some alternative explanation.

inter-rater reliability   The degree of consistency in the ratings of behaviors of the people they observe.

intervention   The phase in a time-series design comprised of data points after a change in program, intervention, or policy is implemented.

judgment sampling   A form of nonprobability sampling that relies on the researcher's judgment about how to maximize a sample's representativeness.

known-groups validity   A form of concurrent validity that assesses whether the instrument scores accurately differentiate between groups already known to differ in regard to the concept being measured.

linguistic equivalence (also called translation equivalence)   An attribute of an instrument that is achieved after a successful process of translation and back-translation so that members speaking the translation language understand the wording.

longitudinal studies   Studies that attempt to get a better handle on how phenomena change over time by collecting data at different points over an extended period of time.

measurement bias   An undesirable aspect of measurement that occurs when something influences the research data to incorrectly depict a phenomenon as being better or worse than it really is.

measurement equivalence   A characteristic of a measurement instrument that refers to the ability of members of different cultures to understand its language and conceptual meanings and to have comparable scores on it.

measurement validity   A desirable attribute of measurement that occurs when a measure accurately depicts the concept that it intends to measure.

member checking   A strategy for improving the trustworthiness of qualitative research in which the researchers share their interpretations with the research participants to see if the participants indicate whether the interpretations ring true to them.

meta-analyses   Systematic reviews that apply statistical techniques that merge the findings of many different studies.

metric equivalence   A form of cross-cultural measurement equivalence that recognizes that the same answers or scores in two cultures might not depict the same level of the construct being measured. In order to assess and achieve measurement equivalence, therefore, the two versions of the instrument would have to be administered to very large samples of people in the two cultures, and comparative norms would have to be developed.

multiple baseline design   A single-case design that improves control for history by introducing the intervention to different target problems, different situations, or different clients at different time points. If improvement consistently coincides with the introduction of the B phase, then history becomes far-fetched as a rival explanation for the improvement.

multiple component design   A single-case design that attempts to ascertain whether any part of an intervention is unnecessary and whether any part is most responsible for the intervention's effects.

multiple pretests   A feature that can be added to the nonequivalent comparison groups design for the purpose of detecting the possibility of a selectivity bias.

multiple time-series designs   Time-series designs that increase internal validity by collecting multiple data points over time from both an experimental group and a comparison group before and after an intervention is introduced to the experimental group.

negative case analysis   A strategy for improving the trustworthiness of qualitative research that involves searching thoroughly for deviant cases that might disconfirm initial interpretations.

nonequivalent comparison groups designs   Quasi-experimental designs that mirror experimental designs, but without the random assignment. That is, different treatment conditions (including perhaps a no treatment condition) are compared, but the clients are not assigned to each condition randomly.

nonequivalent dependent variable   A variable that can be used to try to improve the control for a selectivity bias in a nonequivalent comparison groups design. It has two key features: (1) it represents a possible change that is not targeted by the intervention being evaluated, and that therefore should not change as a result of that intervention; and (2) it should be something that is likely to change if the reason for the change in the targeted variable is merely an ongoing change process of self-betterment.

nonprobability sampling   A sampling approach that does not select participants randomly and consequently is riskier than probability sampling, but is sometimes necessary.

nonresponse bias   A threat to the generalizability of survey findings stemming from the likelihood that those who refuse or somehow fail to participate in the survey might differ in key ways from those who do participate.

novelty and disruption effects   A form of research reactivity that occurs when the improvement in outcome is not due to the intervention, but to the excitement, energy, and enthusiasm in a setting that is unused to innovation.

obtrusive observation   A form of observation in which clients are aware that they are being observed and why. Obtrusive observation thus can influence clients to behave in socially desirable ways that misrepresent their typical behavior patterns.

paper trail   A feature of qualitative research that can strengthen the trustworthiness of a study. It consists of observational notes, interview transcripts, and so on. Leaving a paper trail of these things enables independent qualitative researchers to audit the paper trail and judge whether they would arrive at the same conclusions and whether the research procedures used to control for biases and minimize other problems were adequate.

passage of time   A threat to internal validity (i.e., an alternative explanation) that refers to the possibility that the mere passage of time may be the real cause of observed client improvement after the onset of treatment.

peer debriefing and support   A strategy for improving the trustworthiness of qualitative research in which the members of a research team conducting the study meet regularly to share alternative perspectives about how best to continue collecting the data and what the data mean.

This can help researchers detect and correct biases and other problems in the way they are collecting and interpreting data.

placebo effects   A form of research reactivity that occurs when the desired improvement in a dependent variable results from client perceptions that they are getting special attention or a special treatment. In other words, the desired improvement might be attributed in part—or in total—to the power of suggestion, as opposed to the intervention being evaluated.

plausible alternative explanations   Things that must be ruled out as part of the three criteria for inferring causality. (See also **threats to internal validity.**)

posttest-only control group design   An experimental design for evaluating treatment outcome in which clients are assigned randomly to treatment conditions and then posttested after the treatment condition has been provided.

predictive validity   A form of criterion validity that assesses whether instrument scores correlate to some future criterion.

probability sampling   The safest way to try to achieve representativeness, because it involves the use of random numbers to select study participants and thus is least vulnerable to researcher biases or judgment errors.

prolonged engagement   A way to improve the trustworthiness of qualitative research by spending a lot of time with the people being observed or interviewed so that a trusting relationship can be built that will reduce participant tendencies to project a misleading favorable impression of themselves.

purposive sampling   (See **judgment sampling.**)

quasi-experimental designs   Designs that attempt to control for threats to internal validity without using random assignment to treatment conditions. They come in two major forms: nonequivalent comparison groups design and time-series designs.

quasi-experiments   Studies that have the features of experimental designs, but without the random assignment, for evaluating the effectiveness of a particular intervention.

random assignment   The best way to avoid a selectivity bias, achieved by using random processes to assign clients to the different treatment conditions being compared. It does not mean *haphazard* assignment. It is a controlled process in which every study participant has the same chance of being assigned to either treatment condition, such as by tossing a coin for each participant or using a table of random numbers.

recall bias   A potential limitation in case-control studies because knowing how things turned out can bias how people recall earlier events.

reliability   Consistency in measurement.

research reactivity   A result of research procedures—as opposed to the tested intervention—influencing the dependent variable and thus confounding the results of outcome studies.

resentful demoralization   An undesirable reaction that occurs among clients when their confidence or motivation declines because they got excluded from the special treatment, and that diminished confidence or motivation becomes the real cause of poorer outcomes among the control group. Resentful demoralization can also affect treatment as usual practitioners. Their enthusiasm, confidence, or efforts might wane because they feel less valued or feel stuck providing a treatment that seems less promising than the one being evaluated.

sample   That segment of a population that ends up participating in a study.

sampling   The way a study selects its participants. There are two overarching types of sampling: probability sampling and nonprobability sampling.

selectivity bias   A threat to internal validity (i.e., an alternative explanation) that refers to the possibility that one group might improve more than another group not because of treatment effects but because the two groups were not really equivalent (comparable) to begin with.

sensitivity   The attribute of an instrument that refers to its ability to detect subtle differences in the construct being measured. Those subtle differences can pertain to small changes over time by the same person or small differences between people at the same point in time.

simple random sample   A probability sample selected by numbering each case and then selecting numbers from a table of random numbers.

simple time-series designs   Quasi-experimental designs that supplant the need for a control or comparison group by graphing multiple data points both before and after a new intervention, program, or policy is introduced.

single-case designs   Design in which a single client or group is assessed repeatedly at regular intervals before and after treatment commences for the purpose of evaluating treatment effectiveness or monitoring treatment progress.

snowball sampling   A form of nonprobability sampling for hard-to-find populations. Using this method, researchers begin where they know they can find some members of the hard-to-find population, interview them, and then ask them for help in locating other members they know or other places where members hang out. As each additional person included in the sample helps the researcher find more people, the sample accumulates like the rolling of an ever-growing snowball.

stability   (See **test-retest reliability.**)

statistical conclusion validity   A desirable quality of quantitative research findings that occurs when statistical tests of significance rule out chance as a plausible explanation for those findings.

statistical regression to the mean   A threat to internal validity (i.e., an alternative explanation) that refers to the possibility that one group might improve more than another group not because of treatment effects but because their scores were extreme at pretest and therefore perhaps not really reflective of their typical level of functioning.

statistically significant   The term to indicate that the probability that a finding can be attributed to chance (such as a fluke in random assignment) is so small (usually .05 or less) that chance can be ruled out as a plausible explanation for that finding.

stratified random sample   A probability sample chosen to ensure adequate representation of small minority groups. Researchers number each ethnic group of concern separately—from one to however many cases shared that ethnicity. Then they use simple random sampling or systematic sampling to select a specified number of prospective participants within each category of ethnicity.

substantive significance   The meaningfulness and practical value of a finding. Statistically significant findings—even those with very strong effect sizes—can lack clinical significance.

switching replications   A way to improve control for a selectivity bias in a nonequivalent comparisons groups design by providing the tested intervention to the comparison group after the posttest has been completed and then—following that intervention—administering a second posttest.

systematic sample   A probability sample chosen by selecting one random number to identify a case to begin with, and then selecting every *n*th case after that.

test-retest reliability   A form of reliability that assesses the stability of an instrument by administering the instrument on two occasions to the same people.

threats to internal validity   Alternative explanations that must be ruled out as part of the three criteria for inferring causality.

time order   One of the three criteria that are all necessary for inferring causality, in which the provision of the intervention must precede or co-incide with the change in the outcome being measured.

translation equivalence   (See **linguistic equivalence.**)

transparency   A desired feature of systematic reviews and meta-analyses, in which researchers should spell out all the details regarding inclusion and exclusion criteria, how studies were collected, source of funding, reviewer backgrounds, whether different reviewers with different backgrounds (and perhaps different orientations) agreed about the review conclusions, and so on.

treatment diffusion   A phenomenon that occurs when practitioners in the treatment-as-usual control condition happen to learn about and incorporate aspects of the intervention being provided to the experimental group. When that happens, the planned difference in treatment between the two groups will be compromised. The unanticipated similarity in treatment will thus threaten to yield outcomes between the two groups that are more similar than they should be if the tested intervention truly is more effective than routine treatment without the aspects of the tested intervention.

treatment fidelity   Providing the tested intervention in a skillful manner. When this is not done, then findings can underestimate an intervention's true degree of effectiveness.

triangulation   A strategy for improving the trustworthiness of qualitative research by seeking corroboration among different sources of data or different interpreters of the data.

unobtrusive observation   The opposite of obtrusive observation. Clients are unaware that they are being observed. Thus, they are less likely than with obtrusive observation to behave in socially desirable ways that misrepresent their typical behavior patterns.

validity   A term referring to whether a measurement instrument that refers to really measuring what it intends to measure. If it does, then it has validity.

visual significance   The characteristic of a time-series graph that implies ruling out the plausibility of rival explanations (threats to internal validity) for the improvement merely by eyeballing the graph.

z-score   An approach to calculating an effect size in which the difference between the experimental and control group means is divided by the standard deviation. The dividend is called the **d-index.**

References

American Psychiatric Association. (2000). *Handbook of psychiatric measures.* Washington, DC: Author.

Anderson, C. M., Reiss, D. J., & Hogarty, G. E. (1986). *Schizophrenia and the family: A practitioner's guide to psychoeducation and management.* New York: Guilford Press.

Barber, J. G. (in press). Putting evidence-based practice into practice. In K. M. Sowers & C. N. Dulmus (Eds.), *Comprehensive handbook of social work and social welfare: Vol. 1. The profession of social work.* Hoboken, NJ: Wiley.

Bilsker, D., & Goldner, E. (2004). Teaching evidence-based practice: Overcoming barriers. *Brief Treatment and Crisis Intervention, 4,* 271–275.

Bloom, M., Fischer, J., & Orme, J. G. (2006). *Evaluating practice: Guidelines for the accountable professional* (5th ed.). Boston: Pearson Allyn & Bacon.

Botkin, A. L. (2000). The induction of after-death communications utilizing eye-movement desensitization and reprocessing: A new discovery. *Journal of Near-Death Studies, 18,* 181–209.

Bourgois, P., Lettiere, M., & Quesada, J. (2003). Social misery and the sanctions of substance abuse: Confronting HIV risk among homeless heroin addicts in San Francisco. In J. D. Orcutt & D. R. Rudy (Eds.), *Drugs, alcohol, and social problems* (pp. 257–278). New York: Oxford University Press.

Brannen, S. E., & Rubin, A. (1996). Comparing the effectiveness of gender-specific and couples groups in a court mandated spouse abuse treatment program. *Research on Social Work Practice, 6,* 405–424.

Bush, C. T., Langford, M. W., Rosen, P., & Gott, W. (1990). Operation outreach: Intensive case management for severely psychiatrically disabled adults. *Hospital and Community Psychiatry, 41,* 647–649.

Chisholm, D., Sanderson, K., Ayuso-Mateos, J. L., & Saxena, S. (2004). Reducing the global burden of depression: Population-level analysis of intervention cost-effectiveness in 14 world regions. *British Journal of Psychiatry, 184*(5), 393–403.

Chwalisz, K. (2003). Evidence-based practice: A framework for twenty-first-century scientific-practitioner training. *Counseling Psychologist, 31,* 497–528.

Corcoran, K., & Fischer, J. (2000a). *Measures for clinical practice: A sourcebook: Vol. 1. Couples, families and children* (3rd ed.). New York: Free Press.

Corcoran, K., & Fischer, J. (2000b). *Measures for clinical practice: A sourcebook: Vol. 2. Adults* (3rd ed.). New York: Free Press.

Crowder, C., & Lowe, P. (2000, May 19). 4 accused in rebirthing death. *Rocky Mountain News,* 5A.

Davidson, K. C. H., & Parker, P. R. (2001). Eye movement desensitization and reprocessing (EMDR): A meta-analysis. *Journal of Consulting and Clinical Psychology, 69*(2), 305–316.

Dulcan, M. K. (2005). Practitioner perspectives on evidence-based practice. *Child Adolescent Psychiatric Clinics of North America, 14,* 225–240.

Epstein, W. M. (2004). Confirmational response bias and the quality of the editorial processes among American social work journals. *Research on Social Work Practice, 14,* 450–458.

Eysenck, H. J. (1952). The effects of psychotherapy: An evaluation. *Journal of Consulting Psychology, 16,* 319–324.

Fischer, J. (1973). Is social work effective: A review. *Social Work, 18*(1), 5–20.

Foa, E. B., & Rothbaum, B. O. (1998). *Treating the trauma of rape: Cognitive-behavioral therapy for PTSD.* New York: Guilford Press.

Franklin, C., & Hopson, L. (2007). Facilitating the use of evidence-based practices in community organizations. *Journal of Social Work Education, 43*(3), 1–28.

Gambrill, E. (1999). Evidence-based practice: An alternative to authority-based practice. *Families in Society, 80,* 341–350.

Gambrill, E. (2006). *Social work practice: A critical thinker's guide* (2nd ed.). New York: Oxford University Press.

Haynes, R., Devereaux, P., & Guyatt, G. (2002). Physicians' and patients' choice in evidence-based practice. *British Medical Journal, 324,* 1350.

Herman, D. B., Susser, E. S., Struening, E. L., & Link, B. L. (1997). Adverse childhood experiences: Are they risk factors for adult homelessness? *American Journal of Public Health, 87,* 249–255.

Hogarty, G. (1989). Metaanalysis of the effects of practice with the chronically mentally ill: A critique and reappraisal of the literature. *Social Work, 34*(4), 363–373.

Johansson, I. M., Skärsäter, I., & Danielson, E. (2006). The health-care environment on a locked psychiatric ward: An ethnographic study. *International Journal of Mental Health Nursing, 15*(4), 242–250.

Lipsey, M. W., & Wilson, D. B. (2000). *Practical meta-analysis.* Thousand Oaks, CA: Sage.

Martin, R. P. (1988). *Assessment of personality and behavior problems: Infancy through adolescence.* New York: Guilford Press.

Maruish, M. E. (2000). *Handbook of psychological assessment in primary care settings.* Mahwah, NJ: Erlbaum.

Maruish, M. E. (Ed.). (2002). *Psychological testing in the age of managed behavioral health care.* Mahwah, NJ: Erlbaum.

Maxfield, L., Lake, K., & Hyer, L. (2004). Some answers to unanswered questions about the empirical support for EMDR in the treatment of PTSD. *Traumatology, 10*(2), 73–89.

Mullen, E. J., & Dumpson, J. R. (Eds.). (1972). *Evaluation of social intervention.* San Francisco: Jossey-Bass.

Mullen, E. J., & Magnabosco, J. L. (Eds.). (1997). *Outcomes measurement in the human services.* Washington, DC: National Association of Social Workers Press.

Mullen, E. J., & Shlonsky, A. (2004, September). *From concept to implementation: Challenges facing evidence-based social work.* Presented at Faculty Research and Insights: A Series Featuring CUSSW Faculty Research, New York. Retrieved December 15, 2006, from www.columbia.edu/cu/musher/EBP%20Resources.htm.

Mullen, E. J., Shlonsky, A., Bledsoe, S. E., & Bellamy, J. L. (2005). From concept to implementation: Challenges facing evidence-based social work. *Evidence and Policy, 1,* 61–84.

Mullen, E. J., & Streiner, D. L. (2004). The evidence for and against evidence-based practice. *Brief Treatment and Crisis Intervention, 4,* 111–121.

Nathan, P. E. (2004). The clinical utility of therapy research: Bridging the gap between the present and future. In A. R. Roberts & K. R. Yeager (Eds.), *Evidence-based practice manual: Research and outcome measures in health and human services.* Oxford: Oxford University Press.

National Association of Social Workers. (1999). *Code of ethics.* Silver Spring, MD: Author.

Padgett, D. K. (1998). *Qualitative methods in social work research.* Thousand Oaks, CA: Sage.

Petrosino, A., & Soydan, H. (2005). The impact of program developers as evaluators on criminal recidivism: Results from meta-analyses of experimental and quasi-experimental research. *Journal of Experimental Criminology, 1,* 435–450.

Richmond, M. (1917). *Social diagnosis.* Philadelphia: Russell Sage Foundation.

Robinson, R. A. (1994). Private pain and public behaviors: Sexual abuse and delinquent girls. In C. Reissman (Ed.), *Qualitative studies in social work research* (pp. 73–94).Thousand Oaks, CA: Sage.

Rosenthal, R. N. (2006). Overview of evidence-based practices. In A. R. Roberts & K.R. Yeager (Eds.), *Foundations of evidence-based social work practice* (pp. 67–80). New York: Oxford University Press.

Rubin, A. (1992). Is case management effective for people with serious mental illness? *Health and Social Work, 17,* 138–150.

Rubin, A. (2003). Unanswered questions about the empirical support for EMDR in the treatment of PTSD. *Traumatology, 9,* 4–30.

Rubin, A. (2004). Fallacies and deflections in debating the empirical support for EMDR in the treatment of PTSD: A reply to Maxfield, Lake, and Hyer. *Traumatology, 10,* 89–102.

Rubin, A. (2007). *Statistics for evidence-based practice and evaluation.* Belmont, CA: Thomson Brooks/Cole.

Rubin, A., & Babbie, E. (2007). *Essential research methods for social work.* Belmont, CA: Thomson Brooks/Cole.

Rubin, A., & Babbie, E. (2008). *Research methods for social work* (6th ed.). Belmont, CA: Brooks/Cole.

Rubin, A., Bischofshausen, K., Dennis, B., Hastie, M., Melnick, L., Reeves, D., et al. (2001). The effectiveness of EMDR in a child guidance center. *Research on Social Work Practice, 11,* 435–457.

Rubin, A., & Parrish, D. (2007). Views of evidence-based practice among faculty in MSW programs: A national survey. *Research on Social Work Practice, 17,* 110–122.

Sackett, D. L., Straus, S. E., Richardson, W. S., Rosenberg, W., & Haynes, R. B. (2000). *Evidence-based medicine: How to practice and teach EBM* (2nd ed.). New York: Churchill-Livingstone.

Sanderson, W. C. (2002). Are evidence-based psychological interventions practiced by clinicians in the field? Retrieved January, 11, 2002, from www.medscape.com.

Schoenwald, S. K., Ward, D. M., Henggeler, S. W., Pickrel, S. G., & Patel, H. (1996). MST treatment of substance abusing or dependent adolescent offenders: Costs of reducing incarceration, inpatient, and residential placement. *Journal of Child and Family Studies, 5,* 431–444.

Shadish, W. R. (1995). Authors' judgments about works they cite: Three studies from psychological journals. *Social Studies of Science, 25,* 477–498.

Shadish, W. R., Cook, T. D., & Campbell, D. T. (2001). *Experimental and quasi-experimental designs for generalized causal inference.* New York: Houghton Mifflin Company.

Shapiro, F. (1989). Efficacy of the eye movement desensitization procedure in the treatment of traumatic memories. *Journal of Traumatic Stress, 2,* 199–223.

Shlonsky, A., & Gibbs, L. (2004). Will the real evidence-based practice please stand up? Teaching the process of evidence-based practice to the helping professions. *Brief Treatment and Crisis Intervention, 4*(2), 137–153.

Shlonsky, A., & Wagner, D. (2005). The next step: Integrating actuarial risk assessment and clinical judgment into an evidence-based practice framework in CPS case management. *Children and Youth Services Review, 27,* 409–427.

Simon, C. E., McNeil, J. S., Franklin, C., & Cooperman, A. (1991). The family and schizophrenia: Toward a psychoeducational approach. *Families in Society, 72*(6), 323–333.

Sokal, A., & Bricmont, J. (1998). *Fashionable nonsense: Postmodern intellectuals' abuse of science.* New York: Picador USA.

Thyer, B. (2004). What is evidence-based practice? *Brief Treatment and Crisis Intervention, 4*(2), 167–176.

Tolson, E. R. (1977). Alleviating marital communication problems. In W. R. Reid & L. Epstein (Eds.), *Task-centered practice* (pp. 100–112). New York: Columbia University Press.

Trujillo, A. J. (2004). Do for-profit health plans restrict access to high-cost procedures? *Evidence-Based Healthcare, 8*(3), 116–118.

Vergano, D. (2001). Filed under F (for forgotten). *USA Today.* Retrieved May 16, 2001, from www.usatoday.com/news/health/2001-05-17-drug-companies.htm.

Videka-Sherman, L. (1988). Metaanalysis of research on social work practice in mental health. *Social Work, 33*(4), 325–338.

Index